CHANGING
CONCEPTIONS
OF ORIGINAL SIN

CHANGING CONCEPTIONS OF ORIGINAL SIN

A STUDY IN AMERICAN THEOLOGY SINCE 1750

BY H. SHELTON SMITH

CHARLES SCRIBNER'S SONS   NEW YORK   1955

TO
RICHARD AND ALICE
IN
FAITH, HOPE, AND LOVE

CONTENTS

PREFACE

A T the forefront of recent theological thinking in America has been the concern to achieve a more realistic conception of human nature. All versions of Christian thought which elicit serious interest today recognize the fact of radical human sinfulness. Even the doctrine of original sin, which an earlier liberal era complacently regarded as permanently outmoded, is once more receiving respectful attention.

In view of the present endeavor to revive the idea of original sin, it seems worth while to try to understand the historical changes through which the doctrine of original sin has passed in the course of the development of American theology. The present essay undertakes to make a limited contribution to this understanding.

The original stimulus to enter upon this investigation grew out of an invitation to deliver a series of lectures on the Levi Stone Foundation at Princeton Theological Seminary in the Spring of 1951. These chapters embody the substance of those lectures, although I have expanded the original text at many points, and have even added entirely new sections here and there in order to do greater justice to the theme.

It is to be hoped that the reader will hold in view the nature and limits of this study. In no sense whatever does it presume to present a history of the doctrine of original sin in American theological thought. It undertakes merely to give an interpretative account of the basic changes which were made in that doctrine in certain major movements of American Protestant thought since the middle of the eighteenth century.

The earlier chapters of this essay are occupied with the revisions which were introduced into the doctrine of original sin by New England Calvinist theologians. This results from the fact that they were more concerned with the problem of original sin than any other group of theologians in their period. Indeed, that was their chief theme of controversy for almost a century. The new interpretations which they zealously hammered out in heated controversies had a far-reaching impact upon Protestant theology in general.

While the central theme of this book is the doctrine of original sin, our discussion often includes other closely related theological questions. This broader approach is quite deliberate, and is intended to show how the changing conceptions of man's native predicament are involved in other aspects of religious thought.

In order to reveal the peculiar flavor of the intense discussions that were precipitated by arguments over the question of original sin, I have frequently reproduced the colorful phraseology of the eighteenth and nineteenth century disputants. I have also left entirely intact their peculiar spellings, capitalizations, and italicizations. The reader may assume, therefore, that these characteristics belong in every case to the original productions.

Since the present work had to be grounded in the primary sources, it was necessary to depend heavily upon the great library centers in New England and the Middle Atlantic States, especially for literary materials produced in the colonial period. I have to thank in particular the library staffs at Yale, Columbia, New York Public Library, Union Theological Seminary (New York), and Princeton Theological Seminary. They graciously opened to me their rich collections in the field of American religious life and thought. They also saved me much time and expense by having many of their rare pamphlets microfilmed for my use in Durham. Without their cooperation the research involved in the preparation of this volume could not have been completed.

I should like to express my hearty thanks to President John A. Mackay and the faculty of Princeton Theological Seminary for extending me the invitation to lecture on the historic Stone Foundation. I still recall with thanksgiving the hospitality that was lavished upon me by the Seminary community during a most enjoyable week. Mrs. Mackay deserves a special word for her second-mile effort to keep me physically and mentally fit for the daily lectures.

My indebtedness to my colleagues in Duke Divinity School can never be repaid. Almost every one of them has contributed to this study in some significant respect. I owe special mention, however, to Professor Waldo Beach for his valuable criticisms of my final chapter, and to Professors McMurry S. Richey and Thomas A. Schafer for giving the whole text a painstaking scrutiny and for pointing out numerous faulty phrases and countless infelicitous expressions. In addition, Professor Schafer prepared the useful index. My secretary, Mrs. Helen Hodges, rendered yeoman service in typing several untidy versions of the manuscript. I am deeply obligated to Mrs. McMurry S. Richey who typed an immaculate final copy for the publisher. I am grateful to Duke University Research Council for a generous grant with which to undertake the research involved in the preparation of this work. Finally, I am glad to pay tribute to the unusual skill of Mr. William L. Savage in guiding the manuscript through the press.

H. Shelton Smith

2721 Dogwood Road
Durham, North Carolina
July 16, 1955

CHANGING
CONCEPTIONS
OF ORIGINAL SIN

CHAPTER ONE

THE FEDERAL DOCTRINE
OF ORIGINAL SIN

P RIOR to 1750 New England Puritans maintained their doctrine of original sin with practical unanimity. Within the next decade, however, dissenting notions began to attract attention; and by the end of the century the original doctrine had been considerably modified by some of the more liberal thinkers. Our study begins with this new tendency of thought. But before giving attention to this tendency, we must describe in broad outline the Puritan doctrine of original sin as it was taught by all New Englanders until the latter half of the eighteenth century.

The original Puritans came into the "howling wilderness," not to advocate a new version of Christian theology, but to establish a pattern of church government (Congregationalism) which had been tabooed in their homeland. The celebrated Cambridge Platform, which was adopted by the first Synod of the New England churches in 1648, may be cited as evidence of this fact. According to the Platform's preface (written by John Cotton), the Synod had been requested *"by our godly Magistrates"* to draw up a public confession of faith, but this particular request was not honored. Instead, the Synod, "with much gladness of heart," approved "for the substance thereof" the Confession of Faith as "published of late by the Reverend Assembly in England." [1]

[1] Williston Walker, *Creeds and Platforms of Congregationalism* (New York, 1893), p. 195.

In order to determine the nature of early New England theology one must therefore resort to the Westminster Confession of Faith and its constituent Larger and Shorter Catechisms. That Confession explicitly teaches what we shall call the "federal" or "covenant" doctrine of the fall and original sin. It is a fundamental presupposition of Puritan federalism that, although God is absolutely sovereign, his concern for his creatures prompted him to offer them the benefit of a divinely devised covenant. "The distance between God and the creature is so great that although reasonable creatures do owe obedience unto him as their Creator, yet they could never have any fruition of him as their blessedness and reward but by some voluntary condescension on God's part, which he hath been pleased to express by way of covenant." [2] Hence the first covenant which God made with man was "a covenant of works"—specified as "a covenant of life" in the Larger and Shorter Catechisms—wherein "life was promised to Adam, and in him to his posterity, upon condition of perfect and personal obedience." [3]

Because "our first parents" violated their covenant obligations, they "fell from their original righteousness and communion with God, and so became dead in sin, and wholly defiled in all the faculties and parts of soul and body." [4] Since the covenant was made with Adam, not only for himself but also for his posterity, "all mankind descending from him by ordinary generation, sinned in him, and fell with him, in his first transgression." [5] The sinful estate into which man fell "consists in the guilt of Adam's first sin, the want of original righteousness, and the corruption of his whole nature, which is commonly called original sin; together with all actual transgressions which proceed from it." [6]

[2] *The Westminster Confession of Faith,* VII:1.
[3] *Ibid.,* VII:2.   [4] *Ibid.,* VI:2.
[5] *The Shorter Catechism,* A. to Q. 16.   [6] *Ibid.,* A. to Q. 18.

It is well to pause at this point and note the unique character of the federal doctrine of original sin. It will be observed that it unites the Augustinian idea that Adam's descendants are guilty and depraved because they participated in his first sin, with the idea that they are guilty and depraved because their appointed representative (Adam) failed his covenant obligations. The first idea predicates a direct participation, and the second a representative participation in Adam's first sin. The Puritans thus sought to fix a double grip upon the doctrine of original sin. If the Augustinian idea should prove to be groundless—and it was already on the defensive—they still could defend orthodoxy on the federalist claim that Adam was "a public person," or "a Parliament man," for whose conduct all men are responsible. In the course of time the Augustinian element did lose its force, but in earlier colonial thought it was preserved in varying degrees.[7]

An able historian of New England thought, Professor Perry Miller of Harvard University, seems to believe that the federal doctrine of original sin meant to minimize the aspect of inherited pollution. "In the covenant theology," he writes, "man has been expelled for non-payment, he is not spiritually polluted. Original sin is such disability as a criminal suffers under sentence for embezzlement, not the stench of a corpse."[8] To be sure, federalism did stress the contractual principle; but, even so, the early New England theologians never intended to soften the basic tenet of inherited corruption. Since they believed Adam to be the root of mankind, they considered it impossible for him, in his corrupted state, to generate anything other than a corrupt branch. As truly as Calvin they assumed that "putrid

[7] An illuminating account of the changes that took place in the Augustino-Federal scheme may be found in George P. Fisher's "The Augustinian and the Federal Theories of Original Sin Compared," *The New Englander,* XVII (July, 1868), 468–516.

[8] *The New England Mind* (New York, 1939), p. 400.

branches" must necessarily stem from "a putrefied root." [9] The Larger Catechism expressed their real conviction: "Original sin is conveyed from our first parents unto their posterity by natural generation, so as all that proceed from them in that way, are conceived and born in sin." [10]

As already observed, by action of the Cambridge Synod (1646–1648) the federal doctrine of original sin became an integral part of the common faith of early New England Puritans. That doctrine was officially reaffirmed toward the close of the century by the so-called Reforming Synod of Massachusetts (1679–1680). Because of the general decline in spiritual fervor, the religious leaders of Massachusetts undertook corrective measures through collective action. At its first session in 1679 the Synod appointed a distinguished committee, including Increase Mather, Samuel Willard, Urian Oakes, and Solomon Stoddard, to draw up a confession of faith and submit the same at a second session to be held the following year. Upon deliberation the committee decided not to prepare a new symbol, but instead to recommend the adoption of the Savoy Declaration, a confession of faith which had been ratified by a Synod of English Congregationalists, meeting at Savoy Palace in London, in 1658. When the Reforming Synod reconvened on May 12, 1680, with Increase Mather serving as Moderator, it readily adopted the Savoy Confession without significant modification, except with respect to the role of the civil magistrate.[11] Chapter VI, which deals with the fall and its effects, was left entirely intact, and only such supplementary phrases were added as would clarify and reinforce the original text.[12]

For our present purpose, the most significant thing about the

[9] Calvin, *Institutes of the Christian Religion* (7th American edition: Philadelphia, 1936), Book II, Chapter 2, Section vii.
[10] *The Larger Catechism*, A. to Q. 26.
[11] Cf. Walker, *op. cit.*, p. 393.   [12] *Ibid.*, pp. 373–374.

Savoy Declaration is that it reiterates the theology of the Westminster Confession. So far as the conception of original sin is concerned, it fully duplicates that of the Westminster Symbol. The Reforming Synod therefore reaffirmed its historic federal view of the human predicament.

In 1708 Connecticut Congregationalists held an important Synod at Saybrook, in which they also endorsed the Savoy Declaration in precisely the form in which it had been approved by their Puritan neighbors in Massachusetts. Since these were the two leading colonies in New England, we may reasonably assume that the federal doctrine of original sin prevailed throughout New England Congregationalism.

We have an explicit testimony to the theological unity of New England Puritans in this period in a statement made by Cotton Mather. In his *Ratio Disciplinae* (1726), he commented: "There is no need of Reporting what is the *Faith* professed by the Churches in *New England;* For every one knows, That they perfectly adhere to the CONFESSION OF FAITH, published by the *Assembly* of Divines at *Westminster,* and afterwards renewed by the *Synod* at the *Savoy.*" [13] The word "perfectly" may be an overstatement with respect to some doctrinal points in the Confession, but Mather is unquestionably right so far as the covenant view of original sin is concerned. Since the Savoy Declaration was often republished [14] during the next several decades, it may be fairly surmised that federalism continued to be favorably regarded by the vast majority of New England Puritans throughout at least the eighteenth century.

It is worth emphasizing that the federal doctrine of original sin was no mere lifeless theory perpetuated in colonial theology only because it happened to be enshrined in the historic con-

[13] *Ratio Disciplinae Fratrum Nov-Anglorum* (Boston, 1726), p. 5.
[14] For dates of the several printings of the Savoy Declaration in Massachusetts and Connecticut, see Walker, *op. cit.*, p. 409.

fessions of Westminster and Savoy. It was a vital element in Christian preaching, not only in the seventeenth but also in the eighteenth century. This is clearly revealed, for example, in the dynamic preaching which elicited that far-reaching series of mid-century revivals known as "The Great Awakening." It was the Awakening that impregnated Calvinism with new life and that kept its influence in the ascendancy in American Protestant theology for the next century and a half. The published writings (mostly sermons) of the leaders of the Awakening reveal their firm commitment to the federal conception of the fall and its consequences. Let us take a quick glance at their typical views on this particular point.[15]

One of the greatest leaders of the Awakening in the Middle Colonies was Jonathan Dickinson (1688–1747). A graduate of Yale, he was for many years pastor of the Presbyterian Church at Elizabethtown, New Jersey. In the year 1741 he published an important treatise in which he set forth the central doctrines of the Awakening.[16] Issued at Boston, it bore a commendatory preface by a warm friend of the revival movement, Thomas Foxcroft (1696–1769), senior minister at First Church in that city. One of the five discourses was devoted to a defense of the doctrine of original sin. Dickinson's view is clearly federalist. Moreover, like earlier Puritan federal theologians, he preserved the Augustinian element in his theory of imputation. "We are guilty," said he, "not merely as *Descendants* from *Adam;* but as being naturally, as well as legally, *in him* when he violated the first Covenant." [17]

About ten years later Joseph Bellamy (1719–1790), a pupil of Jonathan Edwards and one of the powerful leaders in the

[15] Jonathan Edwards is here omitted from consideration because his views will occupy our attention in a later context.
[16] *The True Scripture-Doctrine Concerning Important Points of Christian Faith* (Boston, 1741).
[17] *Ibid.*, p. 107.

Connecticut phase of the Great Awakening, published an influential theological work, *True Religion Delineated,* in which he explicitly enunciated the federal view of original sin.[18] Bellamy rarely used the term "covenant" in defining God's relation to Adam. He preferred the term "constitution." Why he employed this term is not entirely clear, but it was probably because he wanted to avoid the notion that Adam became the public head of mankind as the result of a mutual agreement. The term constitution accents God's initiative, rather than man's. In contrast to Dickinson, Bellamy minimized the Augustinian idea of direct participation in Adam's fall. The representative principle occupies the foreground in his theology. "Now it is true," said he, "we did not Personally rise in Rebellion against God in that first Transgression, but he who did do it was *our* Representative. We are Members of the Community he acted for, and God considers us as such; and therefore looks upon us as being legally guilty, and liable to be dealt with accordingly." [19]

A rugged force in the Great Awakening was Gilbert Tennent (1703–1764), whose preaching deeply stirred both New England and the Middle Colonies. A basic premise in his evangelism was the reality of original sin. In an important discourse on this theme, he developed his view in federalist terms.[20] When "our first Parents" fell, he affirmed, there was a "perfidious BREACH OF COVENANT." [21] Because of that fateful breach, every person comes into the world both personally guilty and in a state of total corruption. In a sermon entitled "The wretched State of the Unconverted," he argued "that the natural [man] is not sick and weak, as the *Arminians* tell us, but *dead.*" There

18 *True Religion Delineated* (Boston, 1750), pp. 253–270. Edwards gave his support to this treatise by writing the preface to it.
19 *Ibid.,* p. 256.
20 *Sermons on Important Subjects* (Philadelphia, 1758), pp. 1–33.
21 *Ibid.,* p. 20.

7

"is not the least Spark of Life." An unconverted man "can no more do *spiritual Good,* than a *dead Man* can break open his *Coffin and Walk.*" [22]

Another striking evangelist of this period, Samuel Davies (1723–1761), carried the gospel into Virginia, where he laid secure foundations for Presbyterianism in the South. He succeeded Jonathan Edwards as President of the College of New Jersey (now Princeton University). Though Davies had only a meager formal education, his published sermons are as excellent in form and content as can be found in the colonies at this time. His doctrine of original sin follows faithfully the federal tradition. Expressly teaching that God constituted Adam the federal head and public representative of mankind, he urged that the fall involved mankind in both guilt and corruption.[23] Interestingly, he did not limit the effects of the fall to human beings. "His [Adam's] first sin," he observed, "was an universal mischief to all the inhabitants of the world, . . . both animate and inanimate, rational and irrational; and is the source of all the disorders and miseries that any part of this lower creation groans under." [24] Davies could depict the human situation under original sin as poignantly as any colonial evangelical. Reminiscent of Edwards' famous sermon, "Sinners in the Hands of an Angry God," he warned: "You hang over the pit of destruction by the slender thread of life, held up only by the hand of an angry God, as we hold a spider, or some poisonous insect, over a fire, ready to throw it in. You are ripe for destruction, and therefore in danger every day, every hour, every moment, of falling into it." [25]

These representative assertions of the leading preachers in the Great Awakening demonstrate that the federal idea of the

---

[22] *Ibid.,* pp. 144–145, 147.
[23] *Sermons on Important Subjects* (3 volumes: Boston, 1811), I, 271–290.
[24] *Ibid.,* p. 289. [25] *Ibid.,* II, 262.

human predicament was a living element in the faith of the Congregational and Presbyterian churches at the middle of the eighteenth century. Since these two bodies contained the vast majority of the Protestants of this period, one may confidently affirm that Puritan Calvinism dominated the theology of colonial Protestantism.

CHAPTER TWO

THE IMPACT OF
JOHN TAYLOR

UNDERLYING the propulsive force of the Great Awakening was the firm conviction that all men in a natural state were radically depraved. There was not a single leader in that movement who did not preach the desperate plight of the unregenerate. And according to all of them, the ultimate source of that wretched state could be found in a single colossal catastrophe: the fall of Adam. In consequence of Adam's "first sin," they reasoned, all men begin their existence in guilt and in a state of total corruption, and unless divine grace be interposed they can do nothing that is truly good and acceptable to God.

In light of that chilling premise, it is no wonder that these evangelicals strenuously preached the absolute necessity of radical regeneration. They believed that if that basic assumption was ever surrendered, the gospel would be undermined. To tamper with the doctrine of original sin therefore seemed to them to imperil the foundation of evangelical religion.

Nevertheless, even while the Great Awakening was still stirring New England, alien ideas were already infiltrating that Calvinist stronghold and were destined to undermine the Puritan doctrine of original sin. No one knew this better than Jonathan Edwards. When the revival first manifested itself in his Northampton Church (1734), there was a rumor in that region of the prevalence of "corrupt principles." By mid-century those principles appeared to him to be spreading as a flood. In June of the year 1750 Edwards was rudely expelled from his pastoral charge by a congregational vote of more than 200 to 20. He accused a prominent leader in that revolt, Joseph Hawley, of being tinctured with Arminian sentiments.[1]

Shortly after his dismissal, Edwards described New England's "sorrowful time" in a most pessimistic letter, written to a friend in Scotland. Not only, he lamented, had multitudes of recent converts actually backslidden, but "the doctrines of grace" were "far more than ever discarded." Both Arminianism and Pelagianism, he added, had "made a strange progress within a few years." [2]

I

What was the source of these alien sentiments? In so far as they came from without, they were transmitted from England. Within England elements of the Enlightenment had been penetrating both nonconformist and Anglican thought throughout much of the seventeenth century. By the opening of the eighteenth century, Arian, Socinian, and Pelagian tendencies had all gained a considerable rootage.[3] Because of the growing commercial and cultural contact between Boston and London, eastern Massachusetts was directly exposed to these modes of liberal thought. The two English liberals who became especially influential in that region were Daniel Whitby (1638–1726) and John Taylor (1694–1761). Though we are chiefly concerned

[1] *Works* (Dwight edition: New York, 1830), I, 410. Ten years later Hawley confessed that he "sinned and erred exceedingly" in "persecuting and vexing that just man" (*Ibid.*, pp. 422, 426).
[2] *Ibid.*, p. 413.
[3] Cf. H. J. McLachlan, *Socinianism in Seventeenth Century England* (Oxford, 1951); J. H. Colligan, *The Arian Movement in England* (Manchester, 1913).

with Taylor, Whitby's opposition to the doctrine of original sin must be considered briefly.

An Anglican clergyman, Whitby served for some fifty years as rector of the Cathedral Church at Salisbury. At first a Calvinist, he later became extremely antagonistic toward Calvinism. In 1690 he wrote a tract in Latin (which he never published), severely criticizing the traditional doctrine of original sin. His work of principal influence in America was entitled *A Discourse*, and was published in London in the year 1710.[4] Therein he sharply denounced the Five Points of Calvinism as enunciated at Dort.

Since he believed Calvinism's predestinarianism to be derived from its doctrine of original sin, he sharply condemned the latter. Neither the federal nor the Augustinian theory of imputed sin was acceptable to him. He contended that there was nothing in the Bible which sanctioned "this dismal Compact with *Adam*." Why, then, did the idea of compact arise? It was "forged betwixt God and *Adam*" in order to justify the theory of imputed sin.[5] Whitby considered the Augustinian theory equally groundless. Besides being unbiblical, it is a "Self-Contradiction, that *Adam's* Personal Sin was every Man's Personal Sin, when he only was a Person." But if, on the other hand, "*Adam's* Sin was *every man's personal sin*, . . . then it was not *by the disobedience* of one, but of *all that many were made sinners*." [6]

As those remarks plainly show, Whitby was extremely intolerant of the traditional view of original sin. Though he knew that English Calvinists revered the federal scheme, he unhesitatingly charged that it was "exceeding cruel, and plainly inconsistent with the Justice, Wisdom and Goodness of our

---

[4] An American edition was printed in 1801 (Worcester, Mass.) under the title of *Six Discourses*.

[5] *A Discourse* (London, 1710), pp. 79, 83.   [6] *Ibid.*, p. 79.

gracious God." [7] Naturally, his *Discourse* provoked some caustic rejoinders, including one from John Edwards of Cambridge University and another from Jonathan Edwards, Principal of Jesus College, Oxford University.[8] To the Principal of Jesus College Whitby retorted in a blistering tract.[9] Far from retracting his opinions, he reasserted them even more vehemently.

It was John Taylor, not Whitby, who proved the greatest foreign foe of federalist anthropology in New England. Of nonconformist background, he was prepared for the Presbyterian ministry by Thomas Dixon at Whitehaven Academy; subsequently he also studied under Thomas Hill. He is reputed to have become especially proficient in Hebrew. Following his ordination to the ministry in 1716, he served minor pastorates until 1733 when he became the junior colleague of the Reverend Peter Finch (1661–1754) at Norwich, remaining there until 1757. After Finch's death, he was instrumental in securing the erection of the elegant Octagon Chapel. From 1757 to 1761 he served as tutor of divinity at Warrington Academy.

Taylor, it is said, was still orthodox when he began his labors at Norwich; but if so, his orthodoxy was wearing thin. For by February 5, 1736, he had already composed a notably heretical treatise on original sin, which he published in 1740.[10]

[7] *Ibid.*, p. 84.

[8] John Edwards, *The Arminian Doctrines condemned by the Holy Scriptures, by many of the Ancient Fathers, and by the Church of England, and even by the Suffrage of Right Reason* (London, 1710); Jonathan Edwards, *The Doctrine of Original Sin . . . Asserted and Vindicated from the Exceptions and Cavils of the Reverend Dr. Daniel Whitby* (Oxford, 1711).

[9] *A Full Answer to the Arguments of the Reverend Dr. Jonathan Edwards* (London, 1712).

[10] *The Scripture-Doctrine of Original Sin Proposed to Free and Candid Examination* (London, 1740). The date of the first edition is sometimes given as "1738," but that is incorrect. Through the generous assistance of the President of the Presbyterian Historical Society of England, Dr. S. W. Carruthers, I have established the date as 1740.

Thereafter he wrote many other books, but none of them received as much attention as was given to his *Scripture-Doctrine of Original Sin*. Since it inveighed chiefly against the federal version of original sin, it especially irked English evangelicals. Among others, Isaac Watts and David Jennings strongly condemned it.[11]

The controversy was by no means unwelcome to Taylor, because it served to keep his liberal opinions before the public. Thus a second edition of *Original Sin* was printed in 1741, to which was appended a large *Supplement*, replying to some extent to Jennings, but mainly to Watts. In 1746 a third edition was issued at Belfast, Ireland. It is therefore evident that Taylor's unconventional views attracted considerable attention. As late as 1757 John Wesley encountered these ideas so frequently in English circles that he deemed it necessary to publish a long treatise against Taylor.[12]

Taylor's views were not confined to the Old World; indeed, they became very influential in New England. Hence it is necessary at this point in our study to indicate the main lines of his argument against the federal doctrine of original sin. Broadly speaking, he opposed federalism on both biblical and philosophical grounds. According to him, there are only five places in the Scriptures in which the consequences of Adam's first sin "are certainly spoken of": Genesis 2:17, 3:7–24, Romans 5:12–19, I Corinthians 15:21–22, and I Timothy 2:14.[13]

[11] Watts, *The Ruin and Recovery of Mankind* (London, 1740); Jennings, *A Vindication of the Scripture-Doctrine of Original Sin, from Mr. Taylor's free and candid Examination of it* (London, 1740).
[12] "The Doctrine of Original Sin according to Scripture, Reason, and Experience," *Works* (Jackson edition: London, 1829–1831), IX, 192–464.
[13] *The Scripture-Doctrine of Original Sin Proposed to Free and Candid Examination* (Third edition: Belfast, 1746), p. 5. The third edition is being used not only because it includes the *Supplement*, but because the pages of this edition are numbered consecutively and can be more easily cited.

Dismissing the Timothy passage as insignificant, Taylor confined his attention to the other four.

The first Genesis passage, said he, had nothing to say about Adam's posterity; even the threat of death contained in it referred merely to Adam himself. Besides, the only kind of death with which he was threatened was physical, not moral; if he disobeyed, he would be reduced to dust.[14] As to the longer Genesis account, it shows that Adam and Eve were, in consequence of their transgression, "judicially appointed" to labor, pain, sorrow, and death. Also, it shows that their posterity "are, in fact, subjected to the same Afflictions and Mortality." These disabilities must not, however, be regarded as punishments, because punishment assumes guilt; and Adam's descendants are in no sense guilty of his sin. "We may *suffer* by their Sin, and actually do *suffer* by it; but we are not *punished* for their Sin, because we are not *guilty* of it." [15] Furthermore, these afflictions, far from being punishments, are really a spiritual benefit, for they cause one to curb lust, suppress pride, hate evil, and fear God. Not even death is punishment, since by it God has opened the door to the spiritual riches of the restored life in Jesus Christ.[16]

The Corinthian verses do undeniably teach that all mankind "lose their [physical] Life in *Adam*." But they also unquestionably declare that all who lose their physical life in Adam are, through Christ's righteousness and obedience, restored to life in the resurrection.[17]

The toughest passage for Taylor was Romans 5:12–19. Even had he wanted to sidestep it, he dared not do so, because it was the chief biblical text on which the federalists based their doctrine of original sin. After a lengthy exegetical analysis of words and phrases, he reached the foregone conclusion, that by

[14] *Ibid.*, pp. 6–8.
[16] *Ibid.*, p. 21. Cf. pp. 65–70.
[15] *Ibid.*, p. 21.
[17] *Ibid.*, pp. 23–24.

the term "death" Paul *"evidently, clearly,* and *infallibly"* denoted merely the loss of mortal life.[18] Yet he urged that man did not lose his mortality because of any sin which he had committed, but only because of God's judicial action in consequence of Adam's transgression.[19]

Gathering up his several analyses in a single perspective, Taylor came to a sweeping conclusion. "The Sum of all that we have found," he said, "is this: *That upon the Sin of Adam God subjected him and his Posterity to Sorrow, Labour and Death; from which Death we are delivered, and are restored to Life at the Resurrection, by the Grace of God, having Respect to the Righteousness and Obedience of Christ."* [20]

Taylor next pointed out the philosophical objections to the federal scheme of original sin. First of all, he found wholly untenable the idea that Adam began his life in a state of original righteousness. He agreed, with Genesis 1:27, that Adam was created in the image of God; but he denied that that fact made it necessary to believe that Adam began his existence in a state of moral perfection. The *Imago Dei* merely signified that Adam was endowed with such natural capacities as would, when applied, result in the achievement of moral character. In any case, said Taylor, righteousness cannot be conferred; it must be personally acquired. Hence to affirm that "Righteousness and True Holiness were *created* with him [Adam], or *wrought* into his Nature at the same Time he was made, is to affirm a Contradiction." [21]

The conviction that moral character must be achieved had a direct bearing on Taylor's conception of the fall. The Garden of Eden, he explained, was adapted to the needs and capacities of moral beginners. The tree in the midst of the Garden was a simple concrete device by which God taught Adam and

18 *Ibid.,* p. 27.　　　　　　19 *Ibid.,* pp. 30, 35, 40, 51.
20 *Ibid.,* p. 63.　　　　　　21 *Ibid.,* p. 437.

Eve how to distinguish between good and evil. By means of it he disciplined them in habits of obedience. The whole situation, said Taylor, indicated that Adam and Eve began their existence on a primitive moral plane. Thus the fall "was not surely, as it hath been commonly represented, a *falling from* a State of perfect Holiness, but indeed a *falling short* of such a State." [22]

Taylor was no less critical of the traditional doctrine of original sin. In particular, he repudiated the federal version of it. For him federalism was not only unbiblical, but absurd. "A Representative the Guilt of whose Conduct shall be imputed to us, and whose Sins shall corrupt and debauch our Nature, is one of the greatest Absurdities in all the System of *corrupt Religion*." [23] Imputation of guilt, Taylor argued, is impossible because guilt is always personal and non-transferable. Thus "Imputed Guilt is imaginary Guilt." [24] The doctrine of imputation becomes all the more absurd when, as in the federal scheme, a person is reputed to be guilty of a sin which was committed by his legal representative long before he was born.

Taylor was even more outraged by the supposition that moral corruption could be transmitted from parent to child through natural reproduction. One might, he acknowledged, reasonably believe congenital disorders to be inheritable. He also admitted that these disorders might well expose one to temptation and thus become the occasion of sin. On the other hand, he passionately denied that one generation could hereditarily contaminate the moral character of the next. "Nature cannot be morally corrupted, but by the Will, the depraved Choice of a moral Agent." [25] Taylor was extremely critical of the allegedly orthodox supposition that mankind inherit from Adam a taint or infection whereby they are given a natural propensity to sin. Ac-

[22] *Ibid.*, p. 252.   [23] *Ibid.*, pp. 384–385.   [24] *Ibid.*, p. 244.
[25] *Ibid.*, p. 188.

cording to him, it was a common fallacy "to suppose that something is infused into the human Nature, some Quality or other, not from the Choice of our Minds, but like a Taint, Tincture, or Infection, altering the natural Constitution, Faculties and Dispositions of our Souls, absolutely independent of ourselves, and not from the Will of God." [26] But on that supposition man is no longer a morally accountable being. "If we come into the World infected and *depraved* with sinful Dispositions, then Sin must be *natural* to us; and if *natural,* then *necessary;* and if *necessary,* then no Sin." [27]

Nor can this problem be solved by the attempt to draw a distinction between natural inability and moral inability. "For 'tis plain what Divines here call a *moral,* is a *natural* Impotency; for the supposed sinful Propensities are, according to them, implanted *originally* in our *Nature,* and they tell us expressly our *Nature* is *originally* sinful. The Impotency therefore is *natural;* and consequently with respect to us *necessary.*" [28]

Above everything else, the supposition that man inherits a taint or tincture casts a reproach on the character of God; for whatever our prenatal moral state may be, God must be regarded as its author. If, therefore, infants are already corrupt and under a curse when they are born, this fact blackens the nature of their Creator. "And pray, consider seriously what a God he must be, who can be displeased with, and curse his innocent Creatures, even before they have a Being. *Is this thy God, O Christian?*" [29]

Taylor's treatise thus rejected the federal doctrine of original sin on both biblical and philosophical grounds. He was not content, however, merely to demonstrate the errors of traditional opinion; he came forward with a positive view which he sought to establish. "We are born," he affirmed, "neither righteous nor

[26] *Ibid.,* p. 187. [27] *Ibid.,* p. 200. Cf. pp. 124–125, 129.
[28] *Ibid.,* p. 419. [29] *Ibid.,* p. 151.

sinful; but capable of being either, as we improve or neglect the Goodness of God." [30] But if the child is neither sinful nor righteous at birth, how does he become sinful? Taylor answered that he becomes sinful only by making evil choices in response to the natural appetites and passions. "The original Cause of Sin is a Man's choosing to follow the Appetites of the Flesh." [31] Within themselves the appetites are, he explained, good and necessary; nevertheless, they must be brought under the control of reason. Unless this is done, a sinful life will be the outcome.

In John Taylor's notions of human nature we have a striking preview of a trend that was destined to gather strength in later American religious thought. Though he was often caustic in his criticisms of the Westminster Confession of Faith, he made a considerable case against the federal scheme of original sin. "Of all the books which have ever been written against the doctrine of native depravity," wrote Leonard Woods in 1835, "that of Dr. John Taylor exhibits the greatest adroitness, and the most painstaking plausibility." [32] That opinion was by no means peculiar to Woods; indeed, it is probable that most of the New England theologians of his generation agreed with him.

II

Taylor's *Scripture-Doctrine of Original Sin* made its way into New England soon after its publication. Since Samuel Hopkins, who was born in the fall of 1721, is known to have read it at the age of twenty-three, it must have been in colonial circulation by the early 1740's. "I cannot fall in with him [Taylor]," Hopkins recorded in his Journal. "If I give up this doctrine [of original sin], I must give up Christianity." [33]

[30] *Ibid.*, p. 422. [31] *Ibid.*, p. 127.
[32] *An Essay on Native Depravity* (Boston, 1835), pp. 187–188.
[33] *Works* (Boston, 1852), I, 216.

New Englanders in general doubtless would have agreed with Hopkins in this respect; nevertheless, Taylor's liberal conception of man's native state soon enlisted a measure of sympathy in Boston and other adjacent urban communities. Despite the popular appeal of the Great Awakening, many of the more moderate federalist Calvinists in this region never viewed its strenuous evangelicalism with enthusiasm, while a small party of semi-Calvinist "liberals," led by Charles Chauncy, openly opposed it.[34] The emotional extravagances aroused by the more fanatical revivalists gave the moderate federalists and the liberals a first-rate opportunity to spread skepticism with respect to the value of the Awakening and generate sympathy for their own rationalistic and moralistic mode of thought. No one knew better than Chauncy how to take full advantage of the collapse of the Awakening and cautiously nurture anti-Calvinist views.

The timid and piecemeal fashion in which the federal version of original sin was at first modified is well illustrated in the later religious thought of Experience Mayhew (1673–1758), minister to the Indians on Martha's Vineyard. In 1744 he published *Grace Defended,* a work intended to correct what he considered to be a wrong trend in evangelical religion. Some of the more extreme evangelicals were purveying the idea that man in his natural state could not comply with the terms of the gospel. They commonly advised the unconverted to refrain from using "means," lest they substitute a gospel of works for a gospel of grace. Some were even so bold as to claim that the best actions of the unregenerate were sinful.

It was this unhealthy situation that aroused Mayhew. At the outset he made it clear that he had no intention of abandoning

[34] Cf. Chauncy, *Enthusiasm described and caution'd against* (Boston, 1741); *Seasonable Thoughts on the State of Religion in New England* (Boston, 1743).

the federal conception of original sin. The Assembly's doctrine seemed sound and worthy of unflinching support.[35] Replying directly to Taylor (though never mentioning his name), he insisted that the "death" which Adam's disobedience brought upon himself and his children was both physical and moral. He also argued that death was inflicted as a real punishment, not as a blessing.[36] He further contended that all mankind in a state of nature are spiritually dead: indeed, they are "as uncapable of performing any Actions that are truly spiritual and holy, as Men naturally dead are of performing the Actions to which natural Life is required." [37]

Nevertheless, he strenuously opposed the idea that the best actions of the unregenerate are sinful. "When an unregenerate person feeds the Hungry, and clothes the Naked, out of natural Compassion which he has towards them, it must be acknowledged that this is a good principle. . . . It is really from Grace, *i. e.* the Grace of Nature, or some Remainder of the natural Image of God, left in Man after his Fall, which is good, tho' it is not Goodness of the best Kind." [38] When, for example, the unregenerate sincerely read the Word of God or attend divine service, or when they earnestly beseech the Lord to save their souls, their actions are both good and very necessary to their salvation.[39] Thus it is absurd for "enthusiasts" to charge that the best actions which flow from the operation of the grace of nature are *"Sin and Lust."* [40]

A study of Mayhew's treatise as a whole reveals clearly that, even though he formally acknowledged the truth of the federalist view of man's native predicament, he recognized a considerable element of truth in the Arminian criticism of the ex-

[35] *Grace Defended* (Boston, 1744), p. 12. [36] *Ibid.,* pp. 5–12.
[37] *Ibid.,* p. 6. Cf. Mayhew, *A Letter to a Gentleman, On that Question, Whether Saving Grace be different in Species from Common Grace, or in degree only?* (Boston, 1747), pp. 6–7.
[38] *Grace Defended,* p. 150. [39] *Ibid.,* p. 150. [40] *Ibid.,* p. 148.

treme Calvinist emphasis upon human impotency. Since he had found "Persons of great Seriousness" among Arminians, he wanted to reduce the tension between them and Calvinists if it could be done without sacrificing essential doctrines.[41]

Experience Mayhew's brilliant son, Jonathan (1720–1766), soon went far beyond the theological views of his father. Indeed, when, in 1747, he began his ministry at West Church in Boston, his opinions were already so theologically advanced that his fellow ministers in that city shunned him. None of them would dine with the Council that ordained him.[42] Yet despite their uncharitable attitude, Mayhew soon achieved great esteem among Bostonians, and added to the membership of West Church some of the leading laymen of the city. He was never asked to deliver the historic Thursday Lecture, given regularly at First Church. This was a deliberate snub, since the ministers of Boston normally took turns at giving it. Not to be outdone, he inaugurated a Thursday lectureship in his own Church; and between June and August, 1748, he preached seven sermons that fervently echoed the spirit of the Enlightenment. Issued at Boston in 1749, and republished in England the next year, these discourses were widely acclaimed as the fruit of an exceptionally brilliant mind. This book was largely instrumental in winning for him the prized degree of Doctor of Divinity from the University of Aberdeen, even though he was still under thirty years of age.

Mayhew made no effort to conceal the fact that he held no sympathy for the federal doctrine of native depravity. One reason why he did not like that doctrine was that it supposedly underestimated man's natural abilities, one of which was the ability to discern truth by means of natural reason without the

---

[41] *Ibid.*, p. 194.
[42] Alden Bradford, *Memoir of the Life and Writings of Rev. Jonathan Mayhew* (Boston, 1836), p. 26n.

benefit of special revelation. In his opinion, right and wrong belonged to the basic structure of the universe, and men in a state of nature could perceive the difference between the two.[43] Thus he declared that "The doctrine of a total ignorance, and incapacity to judge of moral and religious truths, brought upon mankind by the apostacy of our *First Parents,* is without foundation." Referring sarcastically to the Augustinian tradition, he commented: "How much brighter and more vigorous our intellectual faculties were in *Adam,* six thousand years before we had any existence, I leave others to determine." [44]

Mayhew unsparingly lashed the *"vain Enthusiasts"* for charging their critics with being "in a *carnal state, blind,* and unable to judge." According to "these enlightened Ideots," whatever is reasonable is perforce carnal. "They impute all their ravings and follies and wild imaginations to the spirit of God; and usually think themselves *converted,* when the poor, unhappy creatures are only *out of their wits."* As against these fanatical fulminations, Mayhew argued that reason was the badge of human dignity and the mark that man was created in the image of God. The fall did not obliterate reason. This *"candle of the Lord* which was lighted up in man at first . . . was not extinguished by the original apostacy, but has been kept burning ever since." [45]

In his second book of sermons, published in 1755, Mayhew revealed even stronger attachment to John Taylor's notions. His omissions were quite as significant as his expressed views. For instance, he had nothing whatever to say on the question of original righteousness. To be sure, he predicated the fall of Adam, but he was a Taylorite in his conception of its consequences. Men were originally designed for immortality, but

[43] *Seven Sermons* (Boston, 1749), pp. 5–13, 22–29.
[44] *Ibid.,* p. 38.   [45] *Ibid.,* p. 39.

the apostasy of "our first parents" entailed upon them temporal death and its related infirmities, including "our turbulent, disorderly, and uneasy passions." [46] These infirmities and passions, even though not sinful *per se*, become the indirect cause of sin since they expose man to temptation. Mayhew insisted, however, that the newborn child has no sinful nature. "No passion or affection, with which we are born, can be in itself sinful; it becomes so, only by wilful or careless indulgence." [47]

In later years Mayhew became especially severe in his criticism of the idea of imputed sin. For example, in a sermon delivered at West Church on December 9, 1762, he declared:

To suppose that they [children] either properly committed any sin, long before they were conceived in the womb; or that the sin of Adam and Eve, is or can be so imputed to them, as to render them justly liable to eternal misery, is one of the grossest of all absurdities.[48]

Sometimes Mayhew spoke as though he believed in the doctrine of native depravity. For example, he addressed the youth of West Church in these words: "Consider yourselves at all times as the degenerate off-spring of Adam. . . . Consider the moral depravation of your minds; your proneness to vice; the

[46] *Sermons* (Boston, 1755), pp. 428–431. Since Mayhew was a student of Locke, he could have derived his ideas of imputation from him as well as from Taylor. In his commentary on Romans 5:12–19, Locke wrote: "Adam, transgressing the law, . . . forfeited immortality, and becoming thereby mortal, all his posterity, descending from the loins of a mortal man, were mortal too, and all died, though none of them broke that law, but Adam" (*The Works of John Locke* [10th edition: London, 1801], VIII, 292). Cf. Locke, "The Reasonableness of Christianity, as Delivered in the Scriptures," *Works,* VII, 4–6.

[47] *Sermons,* p. 434.

[48] *Two Sermons on the Nature, Extent and Perfection of the Divine Goodness* (Boston, 1763), pp. 62–63. Cf. Mayhew, *Christian Sobriety* (Boston, 1763), p. 75.

24

many sins and follies which you have been guilty of, from your early childhood." [49] Nevertheless, he immediately softened the blow by assuring the "degenerate" youth that they were not depraved before they were capable of distinguishing between good and evil.[50] Their predicament stemmed not from Adam's fall but "from ignorance, or weakness of understanding on the one hand, and from strong passions on the other." [51]

Mayhew occasionally called attention to the sinful state of human nature, but he more often spoke of the essential goodness of man. In particular he emphasized man's natural ability to comply with the terms of the gospel. Thus he was extremely critical of those evangelicals who stressed the grace note of the gospel. Though acknowledging in words that salvation was by faith, he usually emphasized the importance of "good works." He argued, indeed, that a work element was necessarily involved in both faith and repentance. Consequently, he insisted that it was both unbiblical and contrary to reason to draw a sharp line between faith and "evangelical obedience." [52]

In the year 1761 Mayhew accentuated his moralistic gospel in two notable discourses. He admonished the unregenerate to put forth their utmost endeavors in quest of their salvation. The promises of the gospel were such, he affirmed, as to lend men confidence that their "evangelical obedience" would be effectual toward accomplishing their redemption.[53]

This open challenge to the Calvinists deeply aroused the rising young theologian, Samuel Hopkins. In a spirited tract, published in 1765, he summed up his protest by affirming "that there are no promises [in the Scripture] of regenerating grace

[49] *Christian Sobriety* (Boston, 1763), pp. 79–80. Cf. pp. 72–78.
[50] *Ibid.*, p. 75. [51] *Ibid.*, p. 74.
[52] Cf. *Sermons*, especially discourses 4–10.
[53] *Striving to Enter in at the Strait Gate Explained and Inculcated* (Boston, 1761).

or salvation made to these exercises and doings of the unregenerate." [54] In elaborating his position, he not only affirmed that men "are perfectly passive in the work of regeneration," but he even recklessly declared that until God gives the regenerate a "new heart," all their exercises on behalf of salvation are necessarily sinful.[55]

It is thus no surprise that Hopkins should have been astonished by Mayhew's bold effort to stimulate the unregenerate to strive to enter "the Strait Gate." Yet undoubtedly the new cultural and moral climate supported Mayhew, not Hopkins. Affluent Bostonians might continue to repeat the federal doctrine of original sin on Sunday, but they felt more at home with Mayhew's conception of man on Monday.

III

One indication that Taylor's *Original Sin* was winning converts in New England is that, by the later 1750's, books began to appear directly attacking his anti-federalist views. For example, in 1757 the venerable Samuel Niles (1674–1762), pastor of the Second Church at Braintree in Massachusetts, published *The True Scripture-Doctrine of Original Sin Stated and Defended*, challenging Taylor's opinions point by point and reaffirming federalism. Since a second edition was soon printed, it evidently received more than passing notice. The book need not be examined in detail because it merely repeated the traditional federalist apologetic. He labored zealously to destroy Taylor's claim that Adam's fall cost him and his posterity merely physical life. Niles contended that Adam's first sin immediately plunged him into a moral death so radical that he was "as im-

[54] "An Inquiry Concerning the Promises of the Gospel," *Works* (Boston, 1852), III, 237.
[55] *Ibid.*, pp. 233–236.

potent to perform any spiritual Duty, as the literally Dead are to do any vital Action." His children, moreover, derive from him a "like State of spiritual *Death*." [56]

When it came to explaining exactly how Adam had imparted a corrupt nature to his offspring, Niles frankly admitted that he had no solution. "The particular *Manner* of the Cause's Operation to produce such an Effect, I confess, is a *Mystery*, which I never expect in this World to be able to unfold." [57] Nevertheless, he firmly maintained that, in consequence of Adam's federal headship and fall, all men are inherently sinful when they draw their first breath. Indeed, their sin is actually coincident with their coming into existence. "The very Moment they [Adam's seed] begin to have personal Existence, they commence *Sinners*." [58]

The one orthodox treatise of this period that must be given extensive analysis is that which was produced by Jonathan Edwards (1703–1758). Entitled *The Great Christian Doctrine of Original Sin Defended,* it was going through the press at the time of his death. The main purpose of this unusually penetrating polemic was to overthrow Taylor's arguments and firmly re-establish the Calvinist doctrine of original sin. Thanks to a gift from his Scottish friend, John Erskine, he had owned Taylor's *Scripture-Doctrine* since the summer of 1748.[59] The minuteness with which Edwards dissected Taylor's treatise "in all its parts" shows that he recognized its great danger to the orthodox view of original sin. It was all the more menacing, he thought, because of its superficially impressive arguments.

Unlike Niles, Edwards did not initiate his critique of Taylor's anti-federalist views with an immediate appeal to the

[56] *The True Scripture-Doctrine of Original Sin Stated and Defended* (2nd edition: Boston, 1757), p. 113.
[57] *Ibid.*, p. 299.　　　　[58] *Ibid.*, p. 114.
[59] *Works*, I, 251. Erskine's gift also included a copy of Taylor's *Key to the Apostolic Writings* (1745).

witness of the Scriptures, although he later made lavish use of biblical texts as unanswerable proof of his contentions.[60] First of all he appealed to "evidences of original sin from facts and events, as founded by observation and experience." This empirical approach may have been prompted by the fact that Taylor had exposed himself to a most effective attack from this standpoint, since he had acknowledged that all men do actually commit sin to a greater or less degree. In any case, Edwards began with a basic proposition upon which he and Taylor were supposed to agree: "that they [men] *universally are the subjects of that guilt and sinfulness, which is, in effect, their utter and eternal ruin.*" [61] If, then, said Edwards, mankind does universally commit sin, does not this uniform result or effect imply the operation of a steady tendency which is inherent in the nature of things? "A common and steady effect shews that there is somewhere a preponderation, a prevailing exposedness or liableness in the state of things, to what comes so steadily to pass." [62] Reasoning in this fashion, Edwards confidently concluded that the "steady effect," the universal commission of sin, must have its permanently productive root within original human nature itself. He ruled out environmental stimuli as the possible source of the steady effect on the ground that mankind has universally sinned under all sorts of external changes and circumstances.

Having thus established (to his own satisfaction) the certain existence of a *"very evil, depraved, and pernicious"* pro-

---

[60] Professor Perry Miller, in his recent brilliant study of Edwards' thought, remarks that the *Original Sin* "is a strictly empirical investigation, an induction, in the manner of Boyle and Newton, of a law for phenomena" (*Jonathan Edwards* [New York, 1949], p. 267). Although Edwards always presupposed the supremacy of biblical authority over that of human experience, there is no doubt that in Part One of *Original Sin* he made telling use of empirical data.

[61] *Works,* II, 320.   [62] *Ibid.,* p. 321.

pensity as the fixed cause of sin, Edwards then trained his heavy artillery on what he called Taylor's "evasions." Two of these evasions deserve specific consideration. The first relates to the weight of example. Though Taylor conceded that all men do sin more or less, he argued that the cause lay, not in an inherently sinful propensity, but in the influence of bad example.

Edwards immediately perceived the weak spot in that mode of reasoning, although he granted that evil example was a force in spreading and perpetuating wickedness. Taylor's argument falls down because he "is accounting for the thing by the thing itself"; the real problem is to explain why evil examples got started in the first place. Furthermore, if, as Taylor has said, mankind is no more inclined to evil than to good, then "how come there to be so many more bad examples than good ones, in all ages?" [63] Again, why is it that men so generally forsake good examples and destroy high civilizations? New England, for example, "was planted with a *noble vine*. But how is the gold become dim! How greatly have we forsaken the pious examples of our fathers!" [64] Beyond all of that is the fact that children universally commit sin "as soon as capable of it," even in families in which the highest moral examples prevail. Surely, then, it is only an evasion to maintain that wickedness is caused merely by the influence of bad examples.

The other alleged evasion was Taylor's contention that sin was caused, not by a sinful propensity, but by the misuse of freedom. According to him, men begin their existence "neither righteous nor sinful" and are equally free to choose either right or wrong. But if they enjoy any such freedom, replied Edwards, why do they agree to exercise their freedom in favor of evil? "If the *cause* be indifferent, why is not the effect in some measure indifferent? If the balance be no heavier at

[63] *Ibid.*, p. 384.　　　　[64] *Ibid.*, p. 386.

one end than the other, why does it perpetually preponderate one way?" [65] Obviously Edwards put no faith in Taylor's theory of freedom; it did not account for the steady bias toward evil. "A steady effect requires a steady cause; but free-will, without any previous propensity to influence its determinations, is no *permanent* cause." [66]

Edwards was no less perceptive in his reply to Taylor's argument that death was wholly beneficial to mankind since it served to mortify pride, quench the passions, and increase a sense of the vanity of earthly things. Why, then, asked Edwards, have we not seen more success in those respects? In truth, if this be the test, one must confess that the remedy has largely failed, because mankind, despite the certainty and imminence of death, still is vain, sensual, and worldly. All recorded history reveals the same dismal story: the medicine of death has never purged mankind of pride, ambition, and lust.[67]

In this connection Edwards struck his adversary a body-blow, based on his observation of the high mortality of infants. If suffering and death be brought upon mankind solely as a benefit, why should these great afflictions fall so heavily on infants who do not live long enough to profit spiritually from them? [68]

Edwards was at his best in meeting Taylor's arguments against the Assembly's doctrine of original sin. The first of these concerns Adam's state prior to the fall and therefore is preliminary to the question of original sin. According to Taylor, Adam could not begin his existence in a state of original righteousness because that state presupposes a previous choice to be righteous. In other words, there can be no virtuous or holy principle in man until he has first exercised virtuous choices. But this notion, said Edwards, violates the common understand-

---

[65] *Ibid.*, p. 382.　　　　　　　[66] *Ibid.*, p. 383.
[67] *Ibid.*, pp. 361–374.　　　　　[68] *Ibid.*, p. 398.

ing of all mankind; indeed, it is as absurd as to argue that fruit must be before the tree or the stream before the fountain.[69] As a matter of fact, he continued, Taylor himself did not always stick to this absurdity; for he sometimes acknowledged that the essence of virtue lay in benevolence or love.[70]

Though Edwards insisted that Adam came into the world already righteous, he was careful to explain what he meant. To be perfectly righteous, according to him, is equivalent to being perfectly innocent. Thus Adam was under the rule of right action the moment he was created. "He was obliged as soon as he existed to *act aright*. And if he was obliged to act aright as soon as he existed, he was obliged even then to be *inclined* to act aright." [71] In saying that Adam's perfection consisted only in an inclination or tendency to act aright, and not in a personally achieved positive quality, Edwards was pointing toward a modern solution to the problem of original righteousness. Thus Adam's innocent state amounted only to potential perfection, not actual perfection.

Having thus disposed of the objection to original righteousness, Edwards next vigorously assailed Taylor's crucial threefold attack upon native depravity. The first was Taylor's charge that total depravity involves a scheme of natural necessity which annuls sin. As he often put it, a necessary sin is no sin.

In his effort to meet that charge Edwards drew a distinction between two kinds of necessity, a distinction which he had already perfected in his celebrated *Freedom of Will* (1754) and employed skillfully against Daniel Whitby.[72] Since he drew upon the reasoning of that treatise in answering Taylor, we may properly make use of it in the present discussion. There is, said Edwards, one kind of necessity which is involved in natural

---

[69] *Ibid.*, p. 407. [70] *Ibid.*, p. 408. [71] *Ibid.*, p. 411.
[72] "A Careful and Strict Inquiry into the Modern Prevailing Notions of that Freedom of Will," etc., *Works*, II, 32–35, 148–153.

causation. A lump of lead, for example, necessarily moves downward unless supported. There is another kind of necessity which is connected with the operation of moral causes, such as habits and dispositions of the heart. A firmly habituated alcoholic, for instance, necessarily yields to strong drink. (To state the same thing negatively, the alcoholic is unable to resist the bottle.) The first kind may be called natural necessity, the second moral necessity. The first annuls accountability, the second does not.[73]

The novel aspect of Edwards' thought at this point is his contention that moral necessity "may be as *absolute,* as natural Necessity. That is, the effect may be as perfectly connected with its moral cause, as a natural necessary effect is with its natural cause." [74] Yet even though moral necessity may be as absolute as natural necessity, the former kind of necessity, unlike the latter, is not inconsistent with sin. In this sense, therefore, a necessary sin still is sin.

The second aspect of Taylor's argument was that to suppose men come into existence in a state of native corruption, is, in effect, to make God the author of that corruption. But Taylor drew this false conclusion, replied Edwards, by assuming what his opponents never have assumed: that nature must be corrupted by infusing into it from without some positive influence in the form of a taint, tincture, or infection. In other words, sinful dispositions are supposed to be implanted in the foetus of the womb, in consequence of which the child is born with a quantum of evil in his heart. One need not, urged Edwards, agree to any such false notion in order to maintain the doctrine of native depravity. His alternative solution is highly imaginative. When God created Adam he implanted in him two kinds of principles, inferior and superior. The first are principles of "mere human nature," and manifest themselves in terms of self-love and the natural appetites and passions.[75] The second

[73] *Ibid.,* pp. 32–33.   [74] *Ibid.,* p. 33.   [75] *Ibid.,* pp. 534–536.

are "spiritual, holy, and divine, summarily comprehended in divine love," and are "immediately dependent on man's union and communion with God." They "were given to possess the throne, and maintain an absolute dominion in the heart; the other [inferior principles] to be wholly subordinate and subservient." [76]

As long as both kinds of principles operated within Adam's nature, he was one integrated whole and enjoyed a happy existence in communion with God. But, alas, when he sinned and broke God's covenant, the "superior principles left his heart," the Holy Spirit forsook him, and communion with God "entirely ceased." As a room is left in darkness when the candle is withdrawn, so Adam "was left in a state of darkness, woeful corruption and ruin; nothing but *flesh* without *spirit*." [77] This moral catastrophe was in no way the result of a bad principle or corrupt taint having been infused into Adam's natural constitution; it all came about through his willful violation of a divinely established covenant or constitution. To be sure, God withdrew his presence from rebel Adam, but that was only just since Adam set up his own natural affections and appetites in the place of God. [78]

The third aspect of Taylor's argument was that the imputation of Adam's sin to his posterity is unreasonable and unjust because Adam and his posterity are not one and the same. In order to turn the tide of this increasingly popular contention, Edwards evolved his most spectacular theory. In his opinion, God never at any time dealt with Adam as independent of the race. Instead, in all God's covenant dealings with Adam he "looked on his posterity as being *one with him*." "And though he dealt more immediately with Adam, it yet was as the *head* of the whole body, and the *root* of the whole tree; and in his proceedings with him, he dealt with all the branches, as if they

[76] *Ibid.*, pp. 536–537.   [77] *Ibid.*, p. 537.   [78] *Ibid.*, p. 538.

33

had been then existing in their root." [79] Consequently, "both guilt, or exposedness to punishment, and also depravity of heart, came upon Adam's posterity just as they came upon him, as much as if he and they had all coexisted, like a tree with many branches." [80] In fact, "The *guilt* a man has upon his soul at first existence, is one and simple, *viz.* the guilt of the original apostacy, the guilt by which the species first rebelled against God." [81] Likewise, "The *first existing* of a corrupt disposition, is not to be looked upon as sin *distinct* from their participation in Adam's first sin. It is as it were the *extended pollution* through the whole tree, by virtue of the constituted *union* of the branches with the root; or the *inherence* of the sin of that head of the species in the members, in their consent and concurrence with the head in that first act." [82] The first depravity of heart and the imputation of Adam's sin "are both the consequences of that established union; but yet in such order, that the evil disposition is *first,* and the charge of guilt *consequent,* as it was in the case of Adam himself." [83]

But how is all this possible? Is it not truly absurd? Edwards answered in terms of a daring metaphysical speculation. Mankind's concurrence in and consent to Adam's first sin, he declared, is the consequence of a divinely constituted personal identity between Adam and his posterity. "All oneness, by virtue whereof *pollution* and *guilt* from *past* wickedness are derived, depends entirely on a *divine establishment.*" [84] If any should object to treating Adam and his posterity as one and the same on the ground that his personal identity is inconsistent with truth, let him consider what really makes truth in matters of this kind. In reality, "a *divine constitution* is what *makes truth,* in affairs of this nature." [85]

[79] *Ibid.,* pp. 542–543. [80] *Ibid.,* p. 543. [81] *Ibid.,* p. 543.
[82] *Ibid.,* p. 544. [83] *Ibid.,* p. 544. [84] *Ibid.,* p. 557.
[85] *Ibid.,* p. 556.

Thus Edwards met Taylor's objection that Adam and his posterity are not one with the emphatic affirmation that they were constituted one by him whose wisdom is unquestionable. Upon the principle of personal identity, therefore, "the sin of the apostacy is not theirs [Adam's offspring] merely because God imputes it to them; but it is truly and properly theirs, and on that *ground* God imputes it to them." [86]

Edwards' venturesome metaphysical argument for the idea that mankind constitutes one moral whole, or one complex person, shows how important he thought it was to maintain the position that Adam's posterity really participated in his first sin. He gave little attention to the federal theory, a fact which probably indicates that he doubted that it sufficiently safeguarded the principle of direct participation. He was perceptive enough to realize that when once the principle of direct participation is surrendered, the ground is cut from beneath the doctrine of imputation. Our later study will show that when Edwards' followers ceased to believe mankind sinned in Adam, they abandoned altogether the notion of imputed sin.

In point of dialectical skill, *Original Sin* must be ranked with the *Freedom of Will*. Sereno Dwight, in his life of Edwards, declared that it "admitted of no reply" and "was death to the controversy." [87] On the other hand, Williston Walker remarked that although *Original Sin* was as intellectually acute as any book Edwards ever wrote, "none has met so little acceptance." [88] Both comments must be qualified. It is true that Edwards' theory of personal identity fell flat so far as his theo-

---

[86] *Ibid.*, p. 559.
[87] *Works*, I, p. 613. Dwight also stated that Taylor, "in his larger work," had "indiscreetly boasted" that "it never would be answered." I find no evidence to support Dwight's charge. On the contrary, Taylor explicitly acknowledged that he "may have said several weak and imperfect Things" (Taylor, *Original Sin*, p. 266).
[88] *Ten New England Leaders* (New York, 1901), p. 257.

logical successors were concerned; still, many other elements of his doctrine of original sin were conserved in the teaching of his followers for at least a century. But it is a mistake to assume that Edwards' treatise was "death to the controversy" over original sin; on the contrary, it was a potent force in keeping the controversy alive for many decades.

CHAPTER THREE

THE SPREAD OF TAYLORISM:
SAMUEL WEBSTER AND
CHARLES CHAUNCY

I

ALTHOUGH John Taylor's anti-federalist opinions were strenuously fought by New England Calvinists, they eventually met with sympathy among some of the more independent clergymen. Besides Jonathan Mayhew, an early example of this development was Samuel Webster (1718–1796). A graduate of Harvard College (1737), he served as pastor of the Congregational Church at Salisbury in Massachusetts from 1741 to 1796. Webster is of particular interest to our study, because his attack upon the federal doctrine of original sin provoked a controversy that disturbed the theological climate for about three years.

Webster's first tract came from the press in the year 1757.[1] Issued anonymously, it was cast in the pattern of a conversation between Webster and three of his neighbors. Only one of the neighbors was a firm Calvinist; the other two were little more than "yes" men to Webster. When the Calvinist (who opened the conversation) deplored the fact that ministers were confusing the laymen by their disagreements over the "fundamental" doctrine of original sin, Webster pooh-poohed the no-

[1] *A Winter Evening's Conversation Upon the Doctrine of Original Sin* (Reprint edition: New Haven, 1757).

tion that that doctrine was really fundamental. After all, it is "a very little thing." Christians should be concerned with more fundamental doctrines. Nevertheless, he agreed to examine the question briefly. There was no disagreement, he explained, as to whether there was such a thing as a first sin of Adam; the only question was, "*Whether we, and all* of Adam's *posterity, are charged by God with this first sin of his,* so as *that men, women and children, are exposed, by this alone, to the eternal damnation of hell?*" When the Calvinist bravely acknowledged, "That's my opinion," Webster exclaimed: "What! and do you think that in consequence of this there are many *infants* now weltering in that lake of fire?" "I don't doubt it at all," the neighbor persisted. "I tremble to think of it," snapped Webster. "How can you reconcile it to the *goodness, holiness* or *justice* of God?" [2]

From this point onward, Webster argued in the spirit of Taylor, contending that the federal doctrine of imputed sin was unreasonable, unbiblical, and evil in its practical consequences. To begin with, he insisted that even if Adam could be regarded as in some sense our federal head and representative, this fact would not make men guilty of his sin. Why not? Because the act of our representative is not our personal act. Should our chosen representative murder a family, or commit adultery, would we thereupon become a murderer or an adulterer? "By no means. We may *suffer* the ill consequences of their sin and folly; but we are not guilty of their *sins.*" [3] If this be true in ordinary human relations, it is even more true in the case of our relation to Adam since we certainly had no voice in choosing him as our representative.

The Calvinist sought to retrieve himself by observing that "we were all in *Adam,* and so sinned in him." But in that case, rejoined Webster, few would be so absurd as to "venture to

[2] *Ibid.,* p. 5. [3] *Ibid.,* p. 7.

say we were *moral agents* at that time." Moreover, if we did truly sin in Adam and fall with him, the doctrine of imputation is invalidated. "There is nothing left to be done by any decree of imputation. For it was all done by ourselves in the beginning." [4]

Since, then, the theory of imputation is grossly absurd, it cannot be biblical. "If it be *plainly impossible* to be *true,* tis in vain to pretend to prove it by scripture. For if the scripture be the word of God, impossibilities can't be found there. And if you should find them there, it must shake the credit of the revelation." [5] Suffice it to say, Webster's faith in revelation remained unshaken; for, having speedily examined the usual Genesis passages, he rendered a typically Taylorian verdict. There is "not one word about any such *covenant* made with *Adam* as is pretended! nor one about *his* being such a *representative* for his *posterity,* as that we should be charged with his sin!" [6] Besides, Adam himself was never threatened with anything more serious than being reduced to dust.

A member of the group then asked Webster a hard question: "What can you say to Rom. v. 12?" Webster admitted that there were "some things in *Paul's* epistles hard to be understood." [7] Nevertheless, he argued that "at the utmost, this 12th *verse* only represents us as having sinned *in* or *by* Adam, in some sense or other, so as to *suffer death,* or to *return to the dust* on that Account. But still there is not a word either of *Adam* or *his posterity's suffering eternal damnation* on account of this one transgression." [8]

At this point another neighbor raised a crucial question. If men are not really guilty of Adam's sin, why should they suffer even physical death? In reply Webster simply echoed John Taylor: the afflictions of life, including physical death, are "of

[4] *Ibid.,* p. 9.   [5] *Ibid.,* pp. 9–10.   [6] *Ibid.,* p. 12.
[7] *Ibid.,* p. 11.   [8] *Ibid.,* p. 12.

vast use in the *moral* world to *check sinners, increase* the *virtue* of the *saints* and brighten their crown of glory hereafter." [9]

In the closing stage of the conversation, Webster argued (as did Daniel Whitby) that the doctrine of original sin was never heard of until four centuries after Christ, and that it was Augustine "who first hatch'd" it. It arose, he thought, only because the church became ignorant and corrupt.[10] In any case, many evils had been connected with the spread of the erroneous doctrine. It had not only made numerous infidels, but it had always encouraged men to dodge responsibility by charging their own sins to Adam.[11]

Being enamored of the Enlightenment, Webster finished the dialogue with an admonition to his neighbors "to examine all doctrines by *reason* and *scripture,* embrace all *truth* whenever you find it, and *reject* all *error* how old soever, and never *make void* the *truths* of God by the *traditions* of men." [12] Obviously, here was a Taylorite who was confident that he had found the truth. Nor did he consider himself a poor teacher, for he finally persuaded even the rigid Calvinist to restudy the evidence for the doctrine of original sin.

Webster's spirited attack upon federalism aroused the venerable Peter Clark (1693–1768), Congregational minister at Danvers (Salem Village) in Massachusetts from 1717 to 1768. His disapproval of liberalism is revealed by the fact that he declined to participate in the Council which settled Jonathan Mayhew over West Church in Boston. Now that liberalism had emerged in even bolder form in Webster, he determined to do his best to suppress it. His tediously reasoned *Scripture-Doctrine of Original Sin* came from the press in 1758.[13] This tract

[9] *Ibid.,* p. 14.   [10] *Ibid.,* p. 20.   [11] *Ibid.,* pp. 22–25.
[12] *Ibid.,* p. 26.
[13] *The Scripture-Doctrine of Original Sin, stated and defended. In a Summer Morning's conversation, between a Minister and a Neighbor* (Boston, 1758).

carried special weight, because it bore the hearty endorsement of five influential Calvinists, all Harvard-bred: Joseph Sewall, Thomas Prince, Samuel Phillips, Thomas Foxcroft, and Ebenezer Pemberton.

Clark's reply assumed the form of a conversation between himself and the "Neighbor" who participated in the *Winter Evening's Conversation,* and who had been most opposed to Webster's views on original sin. At the outset of the conversation the Neighbor frankly admitted to Clark that he might well have been too extreme when he told Webster that because of Adam's first sin alone there were infants in hell. In any case, he would like to be told what Calvinists believed on this particular point. Do Calvinists, then, really teach that any of those who die in infancy are liable to suffer the torments of hell? That doctrine, replied Clark, "few or none maintain"; although "some may suppose them liable to eternal *Death,* that is, an eternal Privation of Life." To be sure, he added, this is a matter which belongs to the secret counsel of God; still, "we have great Reason to hope the best of their State, and no reason to conclude they suffer the eternal Torments of Hell." [14]

Clark was well aware that his opinion did not represent the usual interpretation given to an important passage in the Shorter Catechism. According to the answer to question nineteen in that Catechism, "All mankind by their fall lost communion with God, are under his wrath and curse, and so made liable to all miseries in this life, to death itself, and to the pains of hell forever." All he could say in reply was that he wished this passage "might be explained, so as not to include those who die in Infancy." [15] But regardless of whether Clark's views could be read into the Shorter Catechism, his Neighbor was delighted with a "softer Scheme" than he had maintained in his encounter with Webster.

[14] *Ibid.,* p. 8.   [15] *Ibid.,* p. 8n. Cf. pp. 51–52, 96–98, 115.

But although Clark was fully in favor of this softer scheme, he insisted that "we don't (with this Gentleman [Webster]) hold Infants to be *perfectly innocent*, but the contrary." [16] Why are infants not innocent? In his effort to answer this question Clark repeated the old federalist argument: "If Adam was constituted by the Law of his Creation the natural Head and Representative of Mankind, they [infants] must be included in God's Covenant-Transaction with him." [17] Perceiving the legalistic implication of that explanation, he supplemented it with the remark that mankind "were all in" Adam in precisely the same sense in which the trunk and the branches of a tree are in the root. He even added that "All mankind, as many as they be, are but Adam multiplied." [18] Yet he guarded himself by observing that although Adam's offspring were in him, they did not participate directly in his sinful act. "No Man in his right Wits ever held, that the actual Sin of *Adam* was the *personal* Sin of all, or any of his posterity." [19]

But if infants did not commit Adam's first sin, why then are they not innocent? They are not innocent, replied Clark, "by virtue of a righteous constitution." [20] When pressed to say why the alleged constitution was righteous, he took refuge in biblical passages which were familiar to all federalists. In self-defense he sharply reprimanded Webster and other "rational Gentlemen" for twisting the Scripture to comport with their rationalist predilections. Instead of "going nakedly to the Word of God," they "scan the Doctrines of supernatural Revelation, by their own weak, fallible, and *depraved* Reason." [21] Claiming that he himself had examined the Word "nakedly," Clark assured his Neighbor that the federal doctrine of imputed sin was thoroughly biblical. [22] As the conversation drew to a close,

[16] *Ibid.*, p. 116.   [17] *Ibid.*, p. 17.   [18] *Ibid.*, p. 17.
[19] *Ibid.*, p. 42.   [20] *Ibid.*, pp. 30–37.   [21] *Ibid.*, p. 53.
[22] *Ibid.*, pp. 54–97.

the patient Neighbor replied, "These are agreeable Tidings indeed!"

Clark's polemic brought glad tidings also to Webster, for it contained a damaging admission which he could turn against his adversary. Casting away the clumsy conversational scheme of his former pamphlet, he now spoke directly in his own name. The main issue, said he, had been removed, because Clark explicitly declared that those dying in infancy were really in no danger of eternal torment on account of Adam's first transgression. "It is manifest beyond all doubt, that we are agreed in the main Point I oppos'd in my former Piece: Mr. *Clark* opposes it too." The friendly signers of his tract also have "given it up." [23]

Webster might have allowed the matter to drop at this point, but he pressed his advantage. He pointed out that when Clark said that "few or none" of the New England Calvinists held to infant damnation in consequence of Adam's fall, he asserted what was very far from the truth. "Would to God" he were right! But a clergyman of Clark's experience should know better. "Is Mr. Clark a Stranger in the Land?" [24]

Webster deeply resented Clark's charge that he was a "Champion of the *Pelagian* cause." That, said Webster, is pure slander. Whereas Pelagius believed Adam's offspring to have suffered no ill effects from the fall, he himself believed that Adam's first transgression entailed upon mankind many afflictions, including even death itself. What is more, he had urged that all the offspring of Adam needed a Redeemer. "Neither the most *innocent Children,* nor the *holiest Parents* can *merit,* or *procure* for themselves, that salvation which is by Jesus Christ." Thus for Clark to stigmatize his view as Pelagianism "*new vamp'd*," was a cheap device "to make me odious." [25]

As a parting word, Webster showed wherein he and Clark

[23] *The Winter Evening Conversation Vindicated* (Boston, 1758), p. 16.
[24] *Ibid.*, p. 9.   [25] *Ibid.*, pp. 13–14.

43

still were in basic disagreement. His adversary, said he, continued to believe that in consequence of Adam's fall, all men are born in a state of moral depravity. On the other hand, he himself believed that men come into life in a state of pure innocency. Thus they disagreed fundamentally on the question of imputed sin.[26]

Clark delayed more than a year before making any written response to Webster. Meanwhile, partisan tempers flared; Websterites even jeered the aged minister in the public press. In the year 1760 he finally came forward with a long and labored tract.[27] At the outset he revealed marked sensitivity to the charge that he had given up the main point for which Webster had originally contended. In an effort to clear himself, he restated his view in great detail. Like all federalists, he said that he was certain that all believers' children dying in infancy were not liable to suffer the fires of hell. But what will become of unbelievers' children who die in infancy? That is a question, replied Clark, which one should be content to leave entirely with God and not try to answer either positively or negatively.[28] He pointed out that the Synod of Dort had wisely remained silent on this matter, and that this was the true Calvinist attitude.

Clark was historically correct when he pointed out that the Synod of Dort (1619) said nothing with respect to the ultimate destiny of the children of unbelievers who die in infancy.[29] But the point is, he himself did not follow Dort and remain silent. Although he warned that it was "a criminal Boldness in Men" to speculate on this question, he himself freely speculated. He offered the opinion—which was commendably humane—that unbelievers' children dying in infancy were in no

[26] *Ibid.*, pp. 21–24.
[27] *A Defence of the Principles of the "Summer-Morning's Conversation"* (Boston, 1760).
[28] *Ibid.*, p. 20.
[29] *The Canons of the Synod of Dort,* Chap. I, Art. 17; Chap. II, Rejection of Errors, Sec. 5.

danger of eternal damnation on account of Adam's sin. "I think it unreasonable," said he, "to maintain, (nor do I know of any that do maintain it) that they [the infant dead of unbelievers] either suffer, or are liable to suffer those extreme torments of Hell-Fire, that are threatened in the Gospel against those who are guilty of actual Disobedience, Unbelief and Impenitency." [30] At the very worst, he added, such infants will only be deprived of "the blessed presence of God." Unquestionably, therefore, Clark here only repeated his "softer Scheme."

Let us remember, however, that while he expected all those dying in infancy to escape eternal torment, he did not, as did Webster, base his expectation upon the assumption that men come into the world pure and undefiled. He repeatedly urged that there is "something sinful and vicious in the Nature of Man, which he brings with him into the World." [31] Thus his hope for the future peace of the infant dead rested upon the faith that their original sin would be purged through the atoning work of Christ.

Clark stubbornly refused to withdraw his charge that Webster was a Pelagian. He saw no reason why the label should be resented, because "the grand leading Error of *Pelagius* . . . was his Denial of Original Sin in Infants." [32] Now, Webster unquestionably was Pelagian to some extent. Yet he was not so radical as Pelagius because he did not limit the effects of the fall exclusively to Adam. As already indicated, he held that in consequence of Adam's fall, every man not only bears the mark of mortality, but is afflicted with passions and appetites which prompt him to sin.

But because Webster was not a full-fledged Pelagian, his doctrine of the human predicament involved an inconsistency which he never overcame. He contended that infants were in-

[30] *A Defence of the Principles of the "Summer-Morning's Conversation,"* p. 19.
[31] *Ibid.,* pp. 46–50.   [32] *Ibid.,* p. 29.

nocent, but at the same time he insisted that they needed a Redeemer. Clark naturally exposed this vulnerable spot in Webster's thought.[33]

On the other hand, Clark placed himself in a dilemma when he halfway agreed with Webster's contention that all sin is voluntary. He argued, on the one hand, that original sin is involuntary in the sense that it is "the Sin of Nature" and is prior to all acts of the will.[34] On the other hand, he affirmed "that original Sin is not altogether involuntary." Elaborating this point, he explained that "It was the voluntary Act of the human Nature, in our common Projenitor, in the Commission of the first Sin. And he being the principle [sic] and common Head of our Nature, his Will was reputatively the Will of all Mankind." [35] Clark's predicament lies in the fact that he wanted to save his cake and eat it too. He argued ambiguously that sin is somehow both voluntary and involuntary. Implicitly admitting his quandary, he remarked that "there are some Things difficult to be accounted for in all this." But "since the Word of God represents . . . that we are defiled with Sin from our Original, Is it not equitable and meet, that our poor imperfect and fallible Reasonings should submit to the authoritative Determination of divine Revelation?" [36]

Webster made no further response. It was just as well, for the debate had reached dead end.

II

But there is another phase of the controversy which must be considered in order to round out the picture. Shortly after Clark's first tract came from the press, he asked his respected

[33] *Ibid.*, pp. 27–28, 148–149. [34] *Ibid.*, pp. 54–55, 60.
[35] *Ibid.*, p. 61. [36] *Ibid.*, p. 51.

friend, Charles Chauncy (1705–1787), pastor of First Church in Boston, to give him his opinion of it. Although generally outspoken, Chauncy was reluctant to comply with the request; after repeated invitations, however, he decided to give his views on it. His provocative tract was issued anonymously and took the form of an open letter.[37]

Clark must have regretted that he ever solicited Chauncy's reaction to the *Conversation*. For it would be most difficult, even in this tongue-lashing period, to find anything as ruthless as the *Opinion*. Chauncy started out by criticising the spirit of self-pride and bitterness in which the author had answered Webster's "plausibly wrote" pamphlet. "I see not, that he discovers a more modest sense of his own fallibility, than his antagonist; or that he writes with a less embittered spirit." [38] Aside from the fact that the *Conversation* smacks of pride and bitterness, it is marked by "ambiguity, darkness, and perplexity." Indeed, it is downright "unintelligible" in some parts.

Having cited these "comparatively small things," Chauncy then proceeded to what he mainly wanted to say. His indictment is summarized in these stinging words:

The *first* is, that this Gentleman . . . has unhappily said that, which renders it impossible the doctrine of the *imputation of* Adam's *guilt to his posterity* should be true . . . in the full sense in which it is maintained by *Calvinists*. The *second* is, that tho' he wears the appearance of a friend to the doctrine of imputed guilt, as held by Calvinists, yet he has deserted this doctrine, nay, given it up, as it maintains that mankind *universally*, infants as well as others, are liable to the damnation of hell-fire, on account of *Adam's* first Sin.[39]

---

[37] *The Opinion of one that has perused the Summer Morning's Conversation, concerning Original Sin, wrote by the Rev. Peter Clark* (Boston, 1758).

[38] *Ibid.*, p. 4.   [39] *Ibid.*, p. 5.

Having cited many Calvinist authorities, Chauncy declared: "I don't know of one thoro' Calvinist, besides this Gentleman, that says in the peremptory manner he does, 'we have no reason to conclude they [those dying in infancy] will suffer the torments of hell.' The contrary is rather their opinion, that is, that some of them, at least, will in fact suffer *eternal damnation*." [40] Furthermore, when "this Gentleman" said that "eternal privation of life" was the most that any Calvinist supposed infants liable to, he was badly mistaken. What Calvinist would, in the first place, understand eternal death to mean merely the privation of life? Not one, unless he had already departed from classical Calvinism. In reality, the author has "substituted the private opinion of such men as Mr. *Lock,* and *Taylor,* in the room of the universally known tenet of Calvinism." [41]

Chauncy hastened to add that he had no desire to blame "this Gentleman" for excluding infants from eternal damnation; on the contrary, he applauded him. But why should a man of Clark's notions write against the *Winter Evening's Conversation,* when its main point of contention was that infants were not liable to suffer the fires of hell on account of Adam's first transgression? [42]

The "five venerable attestators," continued Chauncy, are no less mistaken than Clark when they say that "the Patrons" of original sin "are wont to leave the future State" of those dying in infancy "among the secret Things which belong to God alone." [43] In proof that they were mistaken, Chauncy quoted from Calvin and the leading early New England Calvinists, and especially from Michael Wigglesworth's celebrated *The Day of Doom.* This poetical description of the Last Judgment, which was first published in 1662, had passed through numerous editions and was still widely respected in Chauncy's generation. It

[40] *Ibid.,* p. 16.   [41] *Ibid.,* p. 14.   [42] *Ibid.,* pp. 16–17.
[43] *Ibid.,* p. 19.

was especially relevant to his argument, because it described in
detail the future state of non-elect infants who passed straight-
way "from the womb unto the tomb." These infants plead:

> O Great Creator, why was our nature
> depraved and forlorn?
> Why so defil'd, and made so vile
> while we were yet unborn?

"Not we but he [Adam] ate of the tree," they protested. Nevertheless, the "judge most dread" replied:

> But what you call old *Adam's* fall,
> and only his trespass
> You call amiss to call it his;
> both his and your's it was.
>
> You sinners are, and such a share
> as sinners may expect,
> Such you shall have; for I do save
> none but my own *Elect*.[44]

Upon playing this theological ace, Chauncy (doubtless chuck-
ling to himself) challenged "the Reverend Clergymen" to say
that the author of *The Day of Doom* was not a respectable pa-
tron of the doctrine of original sin. Needless to say, they had
no real comeback.

Clark replied to this blistering letter in the summer of 1758.[45]
His *Remarks* consisted of a confusing mixture of denials and
concessions. He now denied, against all the evidence, that he
had ever passed judgment on the future state of children dying
in infancy. All he had ever attempted, he argued, was to de-

---

[44] *Ibid.*, pp. 24–25. The Judge was willing, however, to let infants off with
"the easiest room in Hell."
[45] *Remarks on a Late Pamphlet, Intitled, "The Opinion of One that has
Perused the Summer-Morning's Conversation, concerning the Doctrine of
Original Sin"* (Boston, 1758).

scribe the immediate effects that Adam's fall had upon his descendants.[46] Yet squarely in the face of that disclaimer, he wrote: "I still say, whether any *Calvinist* has said it, or not, we have *no Reason* to conclude, that they [infants] suffer the eternal *Torments of Hell.*" [47]

Clark now acknowledged that "divers good and pious Men" in the past had "too boldly" taught infant damnation; and he implicitly admitted that Wigglesworth was among that number. But this false teaching, said he, had been given up; "there are few or none that do now maintain" it.[48] But in this case, Chauncy's question was highly pertinent: Why did Clark and his "five venerable attestators" blame Webster for a doctrine which they themselves had come to entertain? Whatever their answer may have been, the over-all effect of the Webster-Clark-Chauncy controversy was a boost for Taylorism.

III

Peter Clark's lame and compromising defense of the federal doctrine of original sin was not the main reason for Chauncy's sharp and satirical tract. A more important reason was that he himself had come to doubt the validity of federalism. This becomes quite evident when one examines his able work, entitled *Twelve Sermons,* published in 1765. A lengthy footnote in it shows that Chauncy was favorably disposed toward Taylorism.[49] However, for conclusive evidence of this fact, one must turn to his *Five Dissertations.*[50] Although this significant study was not published until 1785, a letter which Chauncy wrote to President Stiles of Yale University revealed that he had "mostly"

---

[46] *Ibid.,* pp. 5, 8, 18–21, 35–37.   [47] *Ibid.,* p. 33.
[48] *Ibid.,* p. 26.   [49] *Twelve Sermons* (Boston, 1765), pp. 18–25n.
[50] *Five Dissertations on the Scripture Account of the Fall; and its Consequences* (London, 1785).

finished it as early as 1768.[51] It shows the positive influence of
John Taylor, although it does not follow him or any other
writer slavishly; on the contrary, it reflects many original views.
As is true of most of Chauncy's works, it has never received the
attention which it deserves.

At the outset Chauncy gave serious thought to the question
of Adam's original state. He concluded that Adam, although
created in the image of God, was not formed in a state of moral
perfection. Instead, Adam is assumed to have been created
"with nothing more than those capacities which are proper to a
being of that order in which he was created." [52] As in the case
of his posterity, he had to develop his intellectual and moral
capacities through a process of growth and experience. Thus
Adam was created perfect only in the sense that he was endowed with basic abilities which enabled him progressively to
attain such perfection as was possible for a human being.[53] On
the supposition that Adam was subject to the law of moral
growth, Chauncy argued that his trial in the Garden of Eden
was adapted to that of a moral beginner. Therefore he considered it "the fruit of fancy" to assume that Adam was placed
under a covenant of works which demanded perfect obedience
to the moral law as a condition of God's favor. As a matter of
fact, God not only made demands which were adapted to
Adam's primitive moral capacities, but he specially revealed the
particular tree to be avoided. Even before his "lapse," Adam
enjoyed a considerable measure of special grace.[54]

Yet despite all of God's gracious provision, Adam broke the
divine commandment. Consequently, two types of evil came
upon him. The first type was natural evil, consisting of fear,

[51] Ezra Stiles, "A Sketch of Eminent Men in New England," *Collections of
the Massachusetts Historical Society* (Boston, 1809), X, 163.
[52] *Five Dissertations*, p. 23.   [53] *Ibid.*, pp. 61–63.
[54] *Ibid.*, pp. 50–54.

shame, and the sense of guilt. The second was "judicial" evil. Through a judicial act God so changed the structure of the earth as to subject Adam to labor, sorrow, and suffering, ending in the loss of life. Chauncy agreed with Edwards, as against Taylor, that God cursed the ground as a means of cursing man.[55]

The larger part of Chauncy's book is concerned with the effects of Adam's fall upon his descendants. This is to be expected, since the anthropological controversies of that time centered in the question of the imputation of Adam's first sin. His stimulating doctrine is neither that of Taylor nor that of federalism, but draws ideas from both. Thus according to Chauncy, the fall brought upon Adam's posterity two types of evil, both types being "unavoidable": (1) physical death, and (2) a more imperfect nature than Adam had before he fell.

Although Chauncy argued that physical death was the unavoidable consequence of Adam's original transgression, he rejected the doctrine of imputed sin. He taught that "The sin of one man cannot be the sin of another, unless he has been in some way or other accessary to it"; [56] and he contended that federalism had failed to show how Adam's posterity could be accessory to his original transgression. The notion that God constituted a relation between Adam and his offspring whereby they sinned in his first sin was regarded as "the invention of man." "There is no hint given in the Mosaic history of the fall, of Adam's being so constituted the head of his posterity, as that they SINNED when he eat of the forbidden tree." [57] Federalists appeal confidently to Paul's epistle to the Romans (5:12, 19), but "it is one of the grossest mistakes to suppose, that the apostle intended to convey this idea, that Adam's posterity *sinned* when he sinned." [58]

[55] *Ibid.*, pp. 108–112.   [56] *Ibid.*, p. 151.   [57] *Ibid.*, p. 150.
[58] *Loc. cit.*

Edwards' speculation to prove that Adam's posterity participated in his first sin because God constituted mankind "one
complex person," evoked a caustic outburst from Chauncy. It
reminds one of the bitter Edwards-Chauncy controversy in the
period of the Great Awakening.[59] "No man is more certain," he
retorted, "that he is not *one person* with his next father, or with
the rest of the human race, than that he is not *one person*
with the original progenitor." Edwards' scheme "is as wild a
conceit of a vain imagination as was ever published to the
world. It cannot be paralleled with anything, unless the doctrine of *transubstantiation*." [60]

If, then, Adam's posterity did not participate in his first sin,
why were they subjected to physical death on account of that
sin? Chauncy replied: "As Adam was the NATURAL HEAD, root,
or stock, from whence the human species were to come into
being, their subjection to suffering and death became unavoidable, upon the judicial act of God, which condemned him
thereto. For as the stock, so must the branches be; and as is the
fountain, so must the waters be that flow from it." [61] Apparently
Chauncy believed that because Adam had been sentenced to
death, nothing but mortal beings could be begotten by him.
Thus, even though Adam's children are not guilty of his transgression, they nevertheless unavoidably inherit mortality in consequence of it.

The second type of evil which derived from the fall is a nature less perfect than Adam originally possessed. In what does
this imperfection consist? Chauncy first eliminated two explanations that seemed to him unsound. The first was the federal idea
that man comes into existence, as a result of the fall, with
a nature which is morally depraved. For Chauncy, this notion

---

[59] Cf. Williston Walker, *Ten New England Leaders* (New York, 1901),
pp. 275–287.
[60] *Five Dissertations,* pp. 267, 271–272.   [61] *Ibid.,* p. 155.

was absurd because it assumed that character, as distinguished from natural capacities, could be propagated from parent to child. Fundamental with him, as with Taylor, was the conviction that moral character is the result alone of one's personal choice and action. Therefore he repeatedly argued that, whatever weaknesses a person may manifest at birth, moral depravity is not one of them.[62]

There were two arguments used in this connection which he considered utterly false. One of these was the argument that inasmuch as sin has been universal in the human race, only the doctrine of native depravity can adequately account for it. Even though wickedness be universal, said Chauncy, this "is no argument that we are born with *morally* depraved or sinful nature." Consider, for example, Adam and Eve; their first sin did not presuppose a previously sinful nature. If, therefore, they could sin without a previously corrupted nature, may not their posterity do the same?[63] The other argument was that since children begin to sin at an extremely early age, they must come into existence with a morally corrupt nature. Chauncy declared that this was pure conjecture. According to him, it is more reasonable to suppose that sin arises out of the temptations which are prompted by the unregulated appetites and passions of early childhood. Although these appetites and passions, considered within themselves, are neither good nor bad, they will issue in a morally corrupt character unless they are carefully disciplined.[64]

Hence Chauncy found it impossible to accept the federal claim that man's imperfection at birth consisted in an inherited corrupt nature.

The other explanation of native imperfection rejected by Chauncy was that which Edwards had given in his argument

[62] *Ibid.*, pp. 151, 168–169. [63] *Ibid.*, p. 173.
[64] *Ibid.*, pp. 174–176, 186.

against John Taylor. In consequence of Adam's fall, said Edwards, God withholds the "superior principles" from Adam's descendants as they come into existence, with the result that they all become wholly corrupt and expose themselves to eternal misery. Chauncy remarked that this notion was both irrational and immoral.[65] It seemed to him no less absurd than depriving a person of all color capacity and yet expecting him to distinguish black from white. But far more seriously, it mocks divine justice. A God who would bring his child into life destitute of those principles which are necessary to becoming virtuous and at the same time condemn him to torment because of his moral failure, would be unspeakably cruel. "The plain truth is, it is always taken for granted, in the gospel scheme of grace, that the posterity of Adam come into existence with implanted capacities, or principles, in the due use of which they may attain a moral likeness to God." [66]

The conclusion of Chauncy's study was that the imperfection with which men are born in consequence of Adam's fall had been misinterpreted by federal theology, including the Edwardean version of it. Men do indeed come into life with an imperfect nature, but that imperfection does not consist either in native depravity or in a want of superior principles.

In what, then, does man's native imperfection consist? Chauncy was unable to give a positive answer to that question; he could say what the imperfection was not, but he could not say what it was. But although he was unable to specify the exact nature of man's natural imperfection, he unwaveringly affirmed it as an undeniable fact. At this point he sharply disagreed with John Taylor, saying: "It would be greatly beside the truth to say, that it [human nature] is as *perfect* as our first father received it from the creating hand of God, and that we are as able, notwithstanding any disadvantage that has hap-

---

[65] *Ibid.*, pp. 199–203.   [66] *Ibid.*, p. 203.

pened to us, by reason of his lapse, to obey our Maker as he was in paradise." [67]

Chauncy was a very close student of the epistles of Paul, and he found it inconceivable for anyone to be conversant with them and fail (as did Taylor) to see that men, in consequence of the fall, are born "under a *disadvantageous* state of nature." He himself believed in native imperfection mainly because of Paul's epistle to the Romans. "The apostle Paul, in his Epistle to the Romans, has distinctly and largely proved, . . . that, when they [men] are capable of moral action, they will so far transgress the rule, as to be incapable of claiming justification upon the foot of naked law." [68] But what brought about this human predicament? The answer, replied Chauncy, is to be found chiefly in Romans 5:12-19. He considered the most crucial passage to be verse twelve: "Wherefore, as by one man sin entered into the world, and death by sin; and so death passed upon all men, for that all have sinned." The Greek in the last cause—ἐφ᾽ ᾧ πάντες ἥμαρτον—should, he contended, be translated "UPON WHICH, IN CONSEQUENCE OF WHICH, all have sinned." [69]

Modern biblical scholars doubtless would reject Chauncy's rendering of the Greek, but the point here is that his particular version of it reveals his novel doctrine of original sin. According to his interpretation of the clause involved, Paul taught that two kinds of evil result from the fall: physical death and sin. Since the first is a natural and the second a moral evil, they derive differently from Adam's fall. Physical death results involuntarily, but sin involves a choice on the part of the subject. "The sentence of God, taking rise from Adam's lapse, may well enough be considered as *that*, by means of which all men are subjected to death: but they cannot, in virtue of any judicial

[67] *Ibid.*, pp. 207–208. Cf. pp. 216–218.
[68] *Ibid.*, p. 208.   [69] *Ibid.*, p. 298.

56

sentence, either of God, or man, be made sinners, without their own wicked choice." [70] That is to say, God inflicted physical death upon mankind in consequence of Adam's fall, but sin arose only through the exercise of free choice.

Yet death, according to Chauncy, is not unrelated to sin; it is the *"occasional cause"* of sin. It occasions sin in the sense that there are "appendages" of death, such as labor, pain, fear, anxiety, and sorrow, which inevitably expose men to numerous and subtle forms of temptation.[71] In view of these severe trials and temptations, is it supposable that men will not transgress the law of God? No! "It is as certain, in consequence of the lapse, that they [men] will *all* turn out *sinners* in the eye of *strict law*, as that they will fall by the stroke of *death*." [72]

In view of Chauncy's ardent affirmation of the principle of self-determination, that statement is most remarkable. If sin is as certain as death, one may well question whether men, under the fall, are as free as he usually assumed them to be. But however that may be, one must acknowledge that Chauncy did not take a superficial view of human depravity; indeed, he was far more realistic in this respect than John Taylor. It was his awareness of the sinful propensity of mankind that prompted him to contend that man is finally saved, not by works, but by grace.[73]

There is one feature of Chauncy's doctrine of original sin which makes it necessary to point out the nature of his eschatology. Although he did not develop a comprehensive eschatology, he gave much thought to that aspect of it which involves the question of human destiny. As already demonstrated, Chauncy firmly rejected the federal doctrine of imputed sin; nevertheless, he contended that God entailed upon mankind the natural evil of suffering and mortality in consequence of Adam's first sin alone. On the other hand, he was one of the

[70] *Ibid.*, p. 274.   [71] *Ibid.*, p. 275.
[72] *Ibid.*, p. 298.   [73] Cf. *Twelve Sermons*, pp. 1–30.

most ardent champions of God's "infinite benevolence," writing one of his ablest books on this theme.[74] But if God is infinitely benevolent, wherein can he justly consign men to misery and death for an act in which they had no part and for which they are not guilty? God did this, explained Chauncy, as a "judicial" act. But was this judicial act an infinitely benevolent act?

A man of Chauncy's mental acuteness and moral sensitivity could not fail to be aware of the problem at this point. Thus his eschatology was in part at least the result of his effort to meet this difficulty. Weight is lent to this supposition by the fact that his major treatise on eschatology, *Salvation of All men*,[75] and his *Five Dissertations* were written at about the same time, both being practically completed by the year 1768.[76]

How, then, does Chauncy's eschatology solve the problem already indicated? He believed that Paul developed his doctrine of the fall in Romans 5:12–19 in close conjunction with Romans 8:19–24, and that consequently the two passages should be interpreted as a unit. Proceeding on this assumption, he regarded Paul as teaching that all men were subjected to a suffering state "not on the account of *any sin*, or *sins*, they had been guilty of *previous* to this subjection, but by the *will of God*, taking rise from, and grounded on, the *sin* of *the one man Adam;* and that he [God] subjected them to this suffering condition, not as a *final condemnation*, but having first given them reason to *hope*, not only that they should be delivered from their *sufferings*, but with ABOUNDING ADVANTAGE by being *finally* made meet for, and then crowned with, *immortality* and *glory* as the sons of God." [77] Then Chauncy made a most interesting remark: "It is this thought only, so far as I am able to judge, that

---

[74] *The Benevolence of the Deity* (Boston, 1784).

[75] *The Mystery hid from the Ages and Generations, made manifest by the Gospel-Revelation: or, the Salvation of all Men* (London, 1784).

[76] Cf. Ezra Stiles, *op. cit.*, p. 163.

[77] *The Mystery hid from the Ages*, pp. 120–121.

can reconcile the *unavoidable sufferings* of the race of men, as occasioned by, and taking rise from, the *lapse* of their common father *Adam*, with the perfections of God, particularly his infinitely perfect and unbounded benevolence. And this, as I imagine, will effectually do it." [78]

Therefore Chauncy's eschatology is an integral part of his doctrine of original sin, and is intended to show how God could judicially afflict mankind with suffering and mortality in consequence of Adam's first sin and yet be infinitely benevolent.

As already implied, Chauncy believed that all men ultimately would be restored to divine sonship, and this belief reinforced his confidence in the divine benevolence. Although he was sure that "all men will be finally happy," he admitted that those who become deeply steeped in sin might well have to go through several stages of discipline in the world to come. Nevertheless, the divine discipline will eventually purge even the most corrupt son of Adam.[79] Let the Old Adam do his worst; the New Adam will be victorious. "The Son of God, and Saviour of men, will not deliver up his trust into the hands of the Father, who committed it to him, till he has fully discharged his obligations in virtue of it; having finally fixed all men in heaven, where God will be all in all." [80]

[78] *Ibid.*, p. 122. [79] *Ibid.*, pp. 7–12. [80] *Ibid.*, p. 13.

CHAPTER FOUR

THE UNITARIAN CHALLENGE
TO NATIVE DEPRAVITY

BY the time of Chauncy's death (1787) the anti-federalist notions of John Taylor had probably been imbibed by a good many ministers in the eastern part of Massachusetts. At any rate, this was the case at the opening of the next century. Thus it is not surprising that one of the major issues involved in what is known as the Unitarian Controversy related to the character of man in his native state. As we shall see, it was during this heated debate (which finally resulted in Congregational schism) that a full-fledged Taylorite emerged.

I

The Unitarian revolt, it is important to note, was directed not merely against the older federal doctrine of original sin (as enunciated in the Westminster Confession of Faith), but also against that modified version of it which had been developed by the followers of Jonathan Edwards. Hence, before dealing with the Unitarian Controversy as such, it is necessary to set forth the main characteristics of the Edwardean theory as it lay in the minds of its leading exponents at the dawn of the nineteenth century. The Edwardean school of theologians—President Ezra Stiles satirized them as "New Divinity gentlemen"—were remarkably independent thinkers. Although they affirmed their allegiance to Edwards, they evolved a scheme of

so-called New Divinity which was by no means a mere reproduction of his own views. What is no less important, they
differed greatly among themselves; in fact, almost every leading Edwardean stamped the New Divinity with some peculiarity of his own mind. Consequently, Edwardean theology consisted of many different shades of Calvinistic thought.[1] In order,
therefore, to form a substantially representative conception of
the Edwardean theory of original sin as it prevailed at the beginning of the Unitarian Controversy, we must examine the
views of three New England theologians: Samuel Hopkins
(1721–1803), Nathanael Emmons (1745–1840), and Timothy
Dwight (1752–1817).

Shortly after receiving his A. B. degree from Yale (1741),
Hopkins entered the household of Edwards for special theological study. Thus began a relationship which ripened into an intimate friendship. Upon the death of Edwards, Hopkins became the custodian of all his unpublished manuscripts. As
a preacher, he was undistinguished, but as the author of a
strenuous type of Edwardean theology generally known as
"Hopkinsianism" or "Consistent Calvinism," he achieved great
renown. Into its final formulation went the best part of ten
years of exhaustive labor. The celebrated *System of Doctrines*,
filling two large volumes, came from the press in 1793.[2]

On first acquaintance, Hopkins' conception of original sin
appears to be in accord with that of Edwards; however, a careful study of his teaching as a whole dispels this impression. As
already observed, fundamental with Edwards was the idea that
in consequence of a divinely established connection, mankind

[1] For a full-length study of the growth and development of Edwardean-
ism, see Frank H. Foster, *A Genetic History of the New England Theology*
(Chicago, 1907). A brief account may be found in Williston Walker's *A
History of the Congregational Churches in the United States* (6th edition:
Chicago, 1894), pp. 279–305.

[2] *System of Doctrines* (Boston, 1793).

is one complex whole, and therefore Adam's posterity sinned in his sinful act and fell with him. In some of his comments Hopkins seems to agree with Edwards' theory of our identity with Adam. For example, he wrote: "By the constitution and covenant with Adam, his first disobedience was the disobedience of all mankind." [3] Yet in the very next sentence he qualified the implication of that assertion by saying, "That is, the sin, and consequent ruin of all the human race, was by this constitution infallibly connected with the first sin of the head and father of the race." [4] What did Hopkins mean by the phrase "infallibly connected"? He meant only that the connection was such as to render it infallibly certain that, if Adam sinned, his offspring would begin their existence as sinners. "The disobedience of Adam," said he, "rendered it certain, according to a divine, revealed constitution, that they should be born, and rise into existence as moral agents, in disobedience and rebellion." [5] Thus Hopkins taught that "as soon as children are capable of the least motion and exercise of the heart, which is contrary to the law of God, such motions and exercises are sin in them, though they are ignorant of it." [6] How early may children engage in these sinful exercises? They may do so, according to Hopkins, "as soon as they exist the children of Adam."

One feature of Hopkins' thought deserves special notice. According to him, Adam's offspring did not really participate in his first transgression. As we saw, he held that Adam's sin merely rendered it certain that all men would begin their existence as sinners. Nevertheless, Hopkins argued that they are answerable for Adam's apostasy.[7] According to him, Adam's sin "is as much *their own sin,* and they are consequently

---

[3] *System of Doctrines,* I, 309.　　[4] *Loc. cit.*
[5] *Ibid.,* p. 310. Cf. pp. 319–320.　　[6] *Ibid.,* p. 339.
[7] *Ibid.,* pp. 310–318.

as answerable and blameable for it, as if this their sinfulness had taken place in any other or different way that is conceivable or possible." [8] Yet by not taking Edwards' position that mankind directly participated in Adam's apostasy, Hopkins unintentionally loosened the foundation of the doctrine of imputation. Other Edwardeans were to abandon that doctrine altogether.

The most influential disciple of Samuel Hopkins was Nathanael Emmons. Following his graduation from Yale (1767), he was privately instructed in theology by the able Edwardean John Smalley (1734–1820). From 1773 to 1827 Emmons served as Congregational minister at Franklin, Massachusetts. He is said to have personally tutored between eighty and ninety men for the Christian ministry. Meanwhile he developed, upon the foundation of Hopkins, a scheme of "Consistent Calvinism" which disturbed the more moderate Edwardeans. Unlike Hopkins, he did not write a systematic theological treatise; yet his published sermons demonstrate that he was one of the most acute thinkers within the Edwardean school.

His doctrine of original sin reflects a mind that was remarkably unwedded to traditional modes of thought, whether federalist or Edwardean. He opposed the old federal notion that God entered into a covenant or contract with Adam. Instead, said he, God established a "law of Paradise." "There was no form of a contract between God and Adam, which was absolutely necessary to constitute a covenant. But there was the simple and precise form of a proper law: Thou shalt not eat; and if thou eatest, thou shalt surely die." [9] The law of Paradise, said Emmons, applied exclusively to Adam and had nothing to

---

[8] *Ibid.*, p. 334.
[9] Jacob Ide (editor), *The Works of Nathanael Emmons, D. D.* (Boston, 1842), IV, 465.

do with his posterity. But in addition, God is supposed to have "formed a constitution" by which he determined that mankind would become sinful if Adam fell.[10]

This novel speculation, which postulated both a law and a constitution, had a vital bearing on Emmons' theory of original sin. He attached great importance to the text, "By one man's disobedience many were made sinners" (Romans 5:19), and therefore he firmly believed that in some manner Adam had made—he preferred the term "constituted"—all men sinners. But how did Adam make men sinners? Emmons could not agree with the traditional answers. Adam did not, said he, make men sinners by causing them to commit his sin. Therefore original sin was Adam's sin alone.[11] Nor did Adam make men sinners by transferring to them the guilt of his own offense. "Guilt is a personal thing, which belongs to him alone who does a sinful action." [12] Shades of John Taylor! Finally, Adam did not make men sinners by conveying to them a morally corrupt nature. "There is no morally corrupt nature distinct from free, voluntary, sinful exercises." [13] Again, shades of Taylor!

How, then, did Adam make his posterity sinners? "God placed Adam as the public head of his posterity," replied Emmons, "and determined to treat them according to his conduct." [14] But why should God determine to treat Adam's children as sinners when he alone committed the first sin? It "was an act of mere sovereignty" on God's part. God's actions, said Emmons, transcend human norms of justice and injustice. "The constitution which connected Adam's sin with the sin of his posterity was such a constitution as God had an original and sovereign right to make." [15] Yet this divinely established constitution involved drastic consequences for the offspring of fallen Adam. It determined the fact that as soon as men become moral

[10] *Ibid.*, p. 468. [11] *Ibid.*, p. 487. [12] *Ibid.*, p. 488.
[13] *Ibid.*, p. 490. [14] *Loc. cit.* [15] *Ibid.*, p. 496.

agents, they will "always choose evil, before they choose good."
But why must men always choose evil first? Emmons admitted
that the best answer he could give was as follows: "God appointed Adam to be the public head of his posterity; and determined, in case of his disobedience, that they should begin to
sin before they should begin to be holy. This determination God
has executed, by directly operating on the hearts of children
when they first become moral agents." [16]

In order to appreciate the full implication of that statement,
one must remember that Emmons accounted for the "first sin"
in the same manner. He held that since Adam was created in a
state of moral perfection, it was not possible for him to be
tempted until God had first directly produced within his heart
an inclination to evil. "It is in vain," said Emmons, "to attempt
to account for the first sin of the first man, by the instrumen-
tality of second causes. And until we are willing to admit the
interposition of the supreme first Cause, we must be content
to consider the fall of Adam as an unfathomable mystery." [17]
Emmons even claimed that both the fall of Adam and the apostasy of the human race were actually "designed" by God.[18] He
could not be intimidated by the protest that his scheme of
divine causality would logically make God the author of sin.
He explicitly asserted that God could as consistently produce
sinful exercises as holy exercises. "It is . . . as consistent with
the moral rectitude of the Deity to produce sinful, as holy exercises in the minds of men." [19]

In Timothy Dwight we meet an Edwardean who was much
less rigid than Hopkins and Emmons. Like them, he was educated at Yale, graduating in 1769. From 1771 to 1777 he served
his Alma Mater as tutor. After completing a twelve-year ministry at Greenfield, Connecticut, he became President of Yale,

[16] *Ibid.*, p. 508.   [17] *Ibid.*, p. 456.   [18] *Ibid.*, pp. 492–493.
[19] *Ibid.*, p. 351.

rendering conspicuous service in that capacity from 1795 to 1817. In addition to giving general direction to the College, Dwight preached to the students every Sunday and taught theology during the week. He led Yale through many evangelistic campaigns and turned his ablest converts into the Christian ministry, among them Lyman Beecher, Moses Stuart, and Nathaniel Taylor.

Although Dwight wrote no formal treatise in systematic theology, he produced a well-rounded scheme of moderate Edwardean thought in the form of a carefully prepared series of doctrinal sermons, first published in the year 1818.[20] These sermons were not the result of a mind that was isolated from the world of events; rather, they grew out of the experience of seriously grappling with the theological and ethical problems of the day. In published form they circulated widely on both sides of the Atlantic.

In his doctrine of the fall Dwight took Emmons sharply to task for teaching that Adam could not be tempted until God had first produced sinful volitions within his heart. He could find neither biblical nor rational proof for this speculative notion. *"That God by an immediate agency of his own, creates the sinful volitions of mankind, is a doctrine, not warranted, in my view, either by Reason, or Revelation."* [21] On the other hand, he believed Emmons' scheme to have the monstrous effect of abrogating free moral agency in man and of making God the efficient cause of sinful affections and exercises. Dwight saw no reason to assume that finite holiness was necessarily invulnerable to temptation. In fact, he considered it "not within the limits of created perfection to resist temptation in all possible cases." [22] Adam as first created, said Dwight, was the efficient cause of his own volitions, and could be influenced by motives,

---

[20] *Theology Explained and Defended* (12th edition: New York, 1857).
[21] *Ibid.*, I, 254.   [22] *Ibid.*, p. 412.

either sinful or holy. Thus, although God permitted Adam to sin, he was not the efficient cause of that sin.

Dwight assumed that there was a causal connection between Adam's first sin and that of his posterity, but he frankly acknowledged that the nature of that connection was "very mysterious, and very perplexing." While he believed all men to be sinners "*in consequence of the Apostacy of Adam*," he refused to charge them with guilt on account of that apostasy. He based his refusal on the assumption that guilt was strictly personal and nontransferable. "Moral actions are not, so far as I can see, transferable from one being to another. The personal act of any agent is, in its very nature, the act of that agent solely; and incapable of being participated by any other agent. Of course, the guilt of such a personal act is equally incapable of being transferred, or participated." [23] Nevertheless, Dwight maintained that man is born in a depraved state on account of Adam's fall. Why this should be the predicament of a being who is entirely innocent of Adam's transgression he was unable to fathom. He could only suggest that native depravity results from "that state of things, which was constituted in consequence of the transgression of *Adam*." [24] Nor did he attempt to show how it was possible for Adam to transmit a corrupt nature to his offspring. "I am unable to explain this part of the subject," he said. Noting that all the schemes which he had seen had failed to remove the difficulties, he declared that he would "not add to these difficulties by any imperfect explanations" of his own. [25]

Yet despite these difficulties Dwight not only regarded natural depravity as a reality, but he defended it on the basis of human experience. He argued that native depravity "*is strongly evinced by the conduct of Children*." They universally sin "as soon as they become capable of moral action."

[23] *Ibid.*, p. 478.   [24] *Ibid.*, p. 480.   [25] *Loc. cit.*

They "neither love, fear, nor obey" God. He climaxed his arraignment with a significant personal testimony. "I have been employed in the education of children and youth more than thirty years, and have watched their conduct with no small attention and anxiety. Yet among the thousands of children, committed to my care, I cannot say with truth, that I have seen *one*, whose native character I had any reason to believe to be virtuous." [26]

For Dwight, as for his grandfather Edwards, "Uniform sin proves uniform tendency to sin"; and the only way he could account for that universal tendency was to predicate a native corruption derived from Adam.[27]

Our study of these representatives of the New Divinity—Hopkins, Emmons, Dwight—shows that all three of them modified Edwards' doctrine of original sin. None of them retained his basic metaphysical theory of the personal identity between Adam and his posterity. Only so much of his theory was kept as asserted some sort of unalterable connection between Adam's first sin and the existence of a depraved nature or sinful affection in his descendants. On the other hand, all three resolutely asserted that, in consequence of a divinely established constitution, all men come into the world with a sinful and corrupt nature.

II

Although the fundamental causes of the Unitarian Controversy were operative in New England thought long before the nineteenth century, there were three events in the early part of that century which served to precipitate it. The first was a vigorous contest over who should control the Hollis Professorship of Divinity at Harvard. That important post had fallen

[26] *Ibid.*, p. 432. [27] *Ibid.*, p. 484.

vacant in 1803 through the death of David Tappan, an Old Calvinist.[28] The Old Calvinists, led by Jedidiah Morse, minister at Charlestown, Massachusetts, labored strenuously to place in the Hollis Chair a man of the Tappan point of view; but they were finally defeated. Henry Ware (1764–1845), the choice of the liberals, was elected to that position in 1805.[29]

This shock to orthodox Calvinism resulted in a second event of importance in the growth of doctrinal partisanship. The Old Calvinists and radical Edwardeans or Hopkinsians had been slowly drifting apart in Massachusetts, but the threat of liberalism caused them to close ranks and organize a new theological school as the bulwark of orthodoxy.[30] The leaders in this coalition were chiefly Morse and the moderately Hopkinsian Leonard Woods (1774–1854). Their labors, after prolonged negotiations, resulted in the establishment of Andover Theological Seminary (1808).[31] In the early stages of the negotiations, Woods had warned that "Hopkinsians must come down, and moderate men [Old Calvinists] must come up, till they meet." [32] The two groups finally did "meet," but it was largely on the terms of the Hopkinsians.

The merger enabled the zealous Hopkinsians to wage effective war on the Unitarians, and they fully employed their new

[28] The term "Old Calvinist" refers to those Calvinists who did not follow the Edwardeans and who adhered to the doctrinal tenets of the Westminster Confession of Faith.

[29] Cf. James K. Morse, *Jedidiah Morse: A Champion of New England Orthodoxy* (New York, 1939), pp. 82–98. The action of the Corporation prevailed by only one vote.

[30] By 1800 Edwardeanism (including both moderate and radical versions) was numerically dominant over Old Calvinism in Connecticut and western Massachusetts, and was also penetrating the eastern section of the latter (cf. Walker, *Ten New England Leaders*, p. 362).

[31] For a full account of the negotiations leading to this remarkable achievement, see Leonard Woods, *History of the Andover Theological Seminary* (Boston, 1884), pp. 72–114. See also Morse, *op. cit.*, Chapter VIII.

[32] Quoted in Morse, *op. cit.*, p. 104.

power. One of their tactics was to establish in the Boston area new churches of a Hopkinsian cast, and to settle in them only those ministers who would refuse to exchange pulpits with the liberal clergymen. Joseph Buckminster, the liberal minister at Brattle Street Church, viewed the aggressive methods of the conservatives with no little concern. Writing to the English Unitarian Thomas Belsham on December 5, 1809, he remarked that "The most exclusive spirit of Calvinism seems now reviving, and perhaps gaining ground, in Boston." [33]

In the year 1815 there was a third episode which served to create animosities. The redoubtable Morse again played a significant role. Through the help of his oldest son, who was then studying in England, Morse discovered that Thomas Belsham had recently published the *Memoirs of the Life of Theophilus Lindsey*, founder of Essex Unitarian Chapel in London, in which he described the progress of Unitarianism in America. Morse perceived his golden opportunity to convict the Boston liberals out of the mouth of a liberal. After some effort he managed to obtain a copy of the *Memoirs*, and found in chapter nine just the evidence which he needed. He secured the separate republication of that chapter in Boston in 1815, and for it he wrote a preface in which he enlarged upon its heretical nature.[34] The Old Calvinist magazine *Panoplist* promptly reviewed the pamphlet in the most scathing terms.[35]

The publication of this pamphlet, and particularly the harsh manner in which the *Panoplist* reviewed it, produced a stormy

---

[33] Eliza B. Lee, *Memoirs of Rev. Joseph Buckminster, D. D., and of his son, Rev. Joseph Stevens Buckminster* (2nd edition: Boston, 1851), p. 335.
[34] In the second edition of *Memoirs* Belsham said, "I have republished this chapter without material alterations" (*Memoirs*, p. 209). This can be accepted as true and still not rule out the claim that Morse was the primary agent in securing its republication (cf. Morse, *op. cit.*, p. 145).
[35] "Review of American Unitarianism," *Panoplist*, XI (June, 1815), 241–272.

reaction in the Unitarian camp. Hitherto the liberals had endeavored to placate, or at least not to irritate, the Hopkinsians; but now they became militant. William E. Channing fired the first shot in an open letter (1815) to his friend Samuel C. Thacher of Boston. The reviewer, he charged, had a threefold evil design: (1) To prove that the "liberal christians" of Boston believe, with Belsham, that Jesus "is a mere man"; (2) to accuse the liberals of "hypocritical concealment of their sentiments"; and (3) to induce the orthodox to refuse Christian fellowship with the liberals.[36] Channing admitted that "a small proportion" were of the mind of Belsham, but he insisted "that a majority of our brethren believe, that Jesus Christ is more than a man." The second charge, said Channing, was "infinitely more serious than the first." "To believe with Mr. Belsham is no crime. But artifice, plotting, hypocrisy *are* crimes." But he called the charge an "aspersion." In regard to point three, he wrote: "For myself, the universe would not tempt me to bear a part in this work of dividing Christ's church, and of denouncing his followers." [37]

As a result of the cumulative impact of these three closely related developments, the Calvinist-Unitarian debate became intense and often bitter. As is well known, it ultimately issued in denominational rupture.[38] Our concern here is not with the issue of institutional separation, but with that of original sin. Unquestionably, this was a major point of conflict in the so-called Unitarian Controversy. As Williston Walker pointed out many years ago, the "loudest strife" in the debate "was over the doctrine of the Trinity; but its most vital point was after all the

[36] Channing, *Letter to the Rev. Samuel C. Thacher, on the Aspersions Contained in a Late Number of the Panoplist, on the Ministers of Boston and the Vicinity* (Third edition: Boston, 1819), pp. 4–5.
[37] *Ibid.*, p. 21.
[38] For a brief account of this development, see Walker, *A History of the Congregational Churches in the United States,* pp. 329–346.

practical question of the nature of man and the way of salvation." [39]

Channing's famous discourse on "Unitarian Christianity," preached at Baltimore in 1819, contains much that bears out Walker's observation.[40] Calvinism was most repulsive to him because he considered it to be in effect a denial of the moral perfection of God. "Other errors we can pass over with comparative indifference, but we ask our opponents to leave us a God, worthy of our love and trust." [41] In Channing's opinion, the Calvinist doctrine of original sin was supremely objectionable because it was assumed to cast dishonor on the Creator. His caustic critique is worth quoting at length.

According to its old and genuine form, it [Calvinism] teaches, that God brings us into life wholly depraved, so that under the innocent features of our childhood is hidden a nature averse to all good and propense to all evil, a nature which exposes us to God's displeasure and wrath, even before we have acquired power to understand our duties, or to reflect upon our actions. According to a more modern exposition, it teaches, that we came from the hands of our Maker with such a constitution, and are placed under such influences and circumstances as to render certain and infallible the total depravity of every human being, from the first moment of his moral agency; and it also teaches, that the offence of the child, who brings into life this ceaseless tendency to unmingled crime, exposes him to the sentence of everlasting damnation. Now, according to the plainest principles of morality, we maintain, that a natural constitution of the mind, unfailingly disposing it to evil and to evil alone, would absolve it from guilt; that to give existence under this condition would argue unspeakable cruelty; and that to punish the sin of this unhappily constituted child with endless

---

[39] *Ibid.*, p. 345.
[40] "Unitarian Christianity," *Works* (11th edition: Boston, 1849), III, 59–103.
[41] *Ibid.*, p. 87.

ruin, would be a wrong unparalleled by the most merciless depotism.[42]

By the phrase "old and genuine form" Channing referred to the federal doctrine of original sin as set forth in the Westminster Confession of Faith; and by the words "a more modern exposition" he signified the Edwardean or New Divinity version of original sin. Thus he intended to be all-inclusive in his indictment of the Calvinist doctrine of human depravity.

It was immediately clear to the faculty of Andover Seminary that Channing's whole Baltimore discourse had to be refuted. Moses Stuart, Professor of Sacred Literature, opened Andover's reply, directing his attention to Channing's views of the Bible, the Trinity, and the Person of Christ. Not long thereafter Woods came forward with a pamphlet dealing with the other theological aspects of the discourse, including the doctrine of original sin.[43] Our interest here is in Woods' defense of the Calvinist view of original sin.

Channing's discourse required Woods to show wherein the doctrine of total depravity was not inconsistent with the paternal character of God, but he was reluctant to undertake this task. He even asserted that it was unsound to try to reason with respect to God's character in terms of human analogy. Why? Because, said he, God had not always acted on as high a moral plane as would be expected of a human parent. "What human father . . . would ever treat his children, as God treated his rational offspring, when he destroyed the world by a deluge, or Sodom by fire, or when he caused the earth to open and swallow up the company of Korah?" [44] Finding him-

---

[42] *Works*, III, 85–86. Cf. Channing, "The Moral Argument Against Calvinism," *Works*, I, 222–223.
[43] *Letters to Unitarians Occasioned by the Sermon of the Reverend William E. Channing at the Ordination of the Rev. J. Sparks* (Andover, 1820).
[44] *Ibid.*, pp. 21–22.

self slipping into difficulty at this point, he next argued that one would be quite justified in believing in the doctrine of total depravity even though it might seem inconsistent with the moral character of God. "I may *really believe* a certain important doctrine, though I believe other things inconsistent with it." [45] In the final analysis, however, Woods completely side-stepped the question of consistency, contending that he was required only to determine whether moral depravity was a fact, not whether it was inconsistent with the moral perfection of God. [46]

Like all New Divinity theologians, Woods firmly believed native depravity to be a basic fact of human existence. Adam's descendants, said he, "are from the first inclined to evil, and . . . while unrenewed, their moral affections and actions are wholly wrong." [47] When it came to furnishing proof that the moral affections of unrenewed men were wholly wrong, he declared that since the Bible was "infinitely better" than all human reasoning, its teaching constituted "proof enough." [48] Nevertheless, he added that observation and experience confirmed the teaching of the Scripture. "This disorder of our nature is indicated by as clear, as various, and as uniform symptoms, as ever indicated the existence of a fever, or a consumption, in an individual." [49]

What, then, is the basic cause of man's native disorder? Appealing to the fifth chapter of Romans, Woods reiterated the New Divinity teaching. Because of a divinely established connection between Adam and humanity, all his descendants "were constituted sinners" and subjected to death and all other afflictions "as penal evils." [50] At the same time, Woods could not accept the Old Calvinist doctrine of imputed sin. Although he

[45] *Ibid.*, p. 25. [46] *Ibid.*, p. 29. [47] *Ibid.*, p. 31.
[48] *Ibid.*, p. 30. Cf. pp. 148–152. [49] *Ibid.*, p. 32.
[50] *Ibid.*, p. 46.

74

expressed warm affection for the Assembly's Shorter Catechism, he said, "Every attempt which has been made, to prove that God ever imputes to man any sinful disposition or act, which is not strictly *his own*, has, in my judgment, failed of success." [51]

III

Channing was content to let his Baltimore discourse speak for itself, and therefore took no further part in the controversy. But Henry Ware of Harvard entered the controversy with a lively tract in defense of the liberal cause.[52] He charged that Woods had not met Channing's contention that the doctrine of total depravity was inconsistent with the moral perfection of God. It was not enough, he argued, for Woods merely to ask whether the idea of depravity was biblical, because that was not the issue raised in the Baltimore sermon. Then he threw down the gauntlet to the Andover theologian: "If the doctrine of depravity, as it is maintained by the Orthodox, cannot be perceived by us to be consistent with the moral perfection of God, the presumption is very strong, that it is not true; since, if it actually be inconsistent, it certainly cannot be true." [53]

Ware agreed that the question of man's native state lay "at the very foundation of the controversy" between the Calvinists and the Unitarians, and therefore he critically examined Woods' notion of original sin. The Unitarians, said he, were "glad to witness" that recent New England Calvinists had given up the

[51] *Ibid.*, p. 45. Some years later Woods ceased to protest the doctrine of imputed sin, because he came to believe that the word "imputed" signified only that God gave Adam a posterity like himself (cf. Woods, *Works* [Andover, 1850], IV, 34n.).
[52] *Letters Addressed to Trinitarians and Calvinists, Occasioned by Dr. Woods' Letters to Unitarians* (Cambridge, 1820).
[53] *Ibid.*, p. 14.

erroneous idea of imputed sin.[54] The same correct mode of reasoning, he added, would lead to the rejection of the idea of total depravity, since the two ideas *are* inseparably connected." "If the imputation of Adam's guilt is a solecism, and inconsistent with the moral character of God, it is equally so, that, in consequence of it, all his posterity should come into being with a nature so totally corrupt and inclined to sin, as to be incapable of any good." [55]

Ware was not content merely to pick flaws in the views of the Calvinists; he laid down his own sharply contrasting doctrine of original human nature:

Man is by nature . . . innocent and pure; free from all moral corruption, as well as destitute of all positive holiness; and, until he has, by the exercise of his faculties, actually formed a character either good or bad, an object of the divine complacency and favour. . . . He is by nature no more inclined or disposed to vice than to virtue, and is equally capable, in the ordinary use of his faculties, and with the common assistance afforded him, of either. . . . He has natural affections, all of them originally good, but liable by a wrong direction to be the occasion of error and sin.[56]

John Taylor of Norwich had never expressed a more romantic view of human nature than that. It is no wonder the Old Calvinists and Hopkinsians opposed the movement to place Ware in the Hollis Chair of Divinity.

No less confidently than Taylor, Ware argued that his conception of original nature was biblical and in accord with human experience. Speaking first from the standpoint of experience, he urged that Calvinists, laboring under a false doc-

[54] In this connection Ware correctly pointed out that the doctrine of imputed sin "is wholly given up in the [special] Creed adopted by the Theological Institution in Andover" (*ibid.*, p. 18). He failed to state, however, that the doctrine of imputation was part of the Westminster Shorter Catechism, which also was adopted by Andover.
[55] *Ibid.*, p. 19.   [56] *Ibid.*, pp. 20–21.

trine of total depravity, had greatly exaggerated man's sinfulness. "I insist that if we take a fair and full view, we shall find that wickedness, far from being the prevailing part of the human character, makes but an inconsiderable part of it, . . . and that even in the worst men good feelings and principles are predominant." [57] Ware observed that in order to form a true view of original nature one had to take account of the characteristics of infants. If original nature were morally depraved, its unequivocal marks would be manifest in the behavior of children. But do we see evidences of native depravity in little children? "Far from it. Innocence, and simplicity, and purity are the characteristics of early life. Truth is natural; falsehood is artificial. Veracity, kindness, goodwill flow from the natural feelings. Duplicity, and all the cold, and selfish, and calculating manners of society are the fruit of education, and intercourse with the world." [58] There are, to be sure, marks of a feeble and helpless nature in infants, requiring sympathy and assistance; still "we see no proofs of depravity, of malignity, of inclination to evil in preference to good."

Nor does the Scripture countenance, except to a prejudiced mind, the doctrine of total depravity. Had Jesus regarded human beings as natively corrupt, he never could have said, "Suffer little children to come unto me" (Matthew 19:14). Neither could he have warned, "Unless ye be converted, and become as little children, ye cannot enter into the kingdom of heaven" (Matthew 18:3). Until turned from their obvious meaning, these and similar remarks of the Master clearly imply not only that young children exhibit commendable affections and dispositions, but also "that they are, what men are to become by conversion or regeneration." [59] In other words, the moral life of little children, far from being sinful, is the very model of the redeemed life!

[57] *Ibid.*, pp. 24–25.   [58] *Ibid.*, p. 26.   [59] *Ibid.*, pp. 30–31.

In his survey of biblical teaching, Ware naturally gave special attention to Romans 5:12, the classical text of his opponents. This verse did not seem to him to deserve the weight commonly attached to it, since biblical scholars could not agree on its real meaning. Nevertheless, he affirmed that it gave Woods no ground for holding that Adam's posterity were constituted sinners in consequence of the first sin. "Understood literally, the only assertion it contains with certainty is that of a fact, which none will deny, the universality of sin, that *all* have sinned." [60] It says nothing as to the circumstances under which all have sinned. Thus it is not incompatible with the view that all have sinned "as soon as they are *moral agents.*"

On the other hand, said Ware, if one assumes with Woods that men do come into the world with a corrupt and sinful nature, then the Calvinist must reckon with Channing's charge that the theory of total depravity is in radical conflict with the doctrine of the divine perfection. For whatever the character of original nature may be, it is chargeable to one's Creator. If therefore the child be wholly wrong in his original moral affections he cannot justly be blamed. "If God be a just being, he cannot be displeased with him for being what he made him. If he be a good being, he cannot punish him." [61]

Considered in historical perspective, Ware's tract has a threefold importance: (1) It demonstrated that the question of original human nature lay at the bottom of the Unitarian Controversy; (2) it presented a distinctly modern theory of original nature which was destined to triumph in later American religious thought; and (3) it made the Calvinists henceforth argue their case in terms of the moral nature of children, and consequently raised issues which prepared the way for the historic role of Horace Bushnell.

[60] *Ibid.*, p. 44.　　　　　[61] *Ibid.*, p. 48.

IV

The movement which Channing spearheaded in 1815, and for which he enunciated a theological creed in 1819, was now to be guided (at least with respect to the doctrine of original nature) by Henry Ware. The remainder of the controversy therefore centered in a pamphlet warfare between Harvard and Andover, Ware and Woods serving as the respective spokesmen.

In the fall of 1821 Woods published a lengthy rejoinder to Ware's *Letters*.[62] The basic question, as he correctly perceived, concerned the native state of children. He acknowledged that little children manifested many charming natural qualities. But what did these prove as to moral character? Nothing! "They neither prove the existence of holiness, nor freedom from sin." [63] Indeed, children may exhibit all these amiable affections and yet be morally corrupt. In order to determine whether or not such affections constitute a truly holy nature, we must evaluate them in terms of the moral law, the law of absolute love to God. If children are by nature good, they will as soon as they are capable manifest their love to God. But do they? On the contrary, "they have not the love of God in them"; their hearts reveal a "relish for the pleasure of sin." "Now as soon as children have ability and occasion to show their dispositions, they generally exhibit as clear evidence of initial depravity, as of intelligence." [64]

Seeing, then, that young children are unquestionably opposed to the law of love, must not their nature be inherently depraved? Woods not only answered this question in the affirmative, but he argued in favor of his answer in terms of five considerations. Moral depravity (1) is as universal as reason,

[62] *A Reply to Ware's Letters to Trinitarians and Calvinists* (Andover, 1821).
[63] *Ibid.*, p. 20.　　　　　　[64] *Ibid.*, pp. 46–47.

memory, and the bodily senses; (2) it shows itself as soon as children can reveal their feelings to others; (3) it cannot be traced to any change wrought in the nature of children after they are born; (4) it manifests itself spontaneously and is hard to eradicate; (5) it enables one to predict that the child will certainly be a sinner.[65]

By this time Woods had been forced to recognize that he must attempt to show wherein the doctrine of native depravity was not inconsistent with the moral perfection of God. He observed that in ordinary cases he would only have to show that the Bible taught both in order to prove their consistency with each other. But Unitarians would not accept this mode of reasoning; besides, they would actually twist the Bible to suit their own predilections. "See how clearly and strongly the Scriptures assert the natural corruption of man. If with half the clearness and strength they asserted his native purity, how would Unitarians glory in the firm foundation of their faith." [66] He also accused the Unitarians of depending upon human reason, not divine revelation. Finally, after various circumlocutions, he got around to the question of consistency. "Now the native depravity of man is plainly consistent with the divine benevolence," he explained, "if it is, on the whole, consistent with the greatest good of the intelligent system. Do you ask how it can possibly be made consistent? My answer is, it may, in one way or another, be the means of making a brighter and more diversified display of the divine perfections, and thus of giving the intelligent creation, as a whole, a higher knowledge and enjoyment of God." [67]

That statement amounts only to "if" and "may"; it proves nothing. Yet when considered in context, it shows that Woods took the position, held by many New Divinity men, that since

[65] *Ibid.*, pp. 51–61.   [66] *Ibid.*, p. 75.   [67] *Ibid.*, p. 80.

God could bring good out of evil, a world in which evil existed was, on the whole, better than a world not having evil in it. But this was only a supposition for which he offered no proof. Nevertheless, he went on to argue that because God can bring good out of moral evil in general, he can also bring good out of the evil of native depravity. "May not God so overrule the corruption of our nature, that, in the final result of his administration, it shall be the occasion of a brighter display of his holiness, and an augmentation of happiness in his universal empire? Cannot Omnipotence bring good out of evil in this case, as well as in others?" [68] Woods merely asked questions; he did not give positive proof of the point at issue.

He then endeavored to show that native depravity was not inconsistent with human agency; but again his mode of reasoning was far from persuasive, and, indeed, at points surprising. For example, Woods argued that even though the native moral affections of children be wholly wrong, they are nevertheless answerable for those affections. "Suppose the first moral feelings and actions of such a being to be sinful; are they not still his own feelings and actions, for which he is justly accountable?" [69] He even declared that "in whatever way, man has what the divine law forbids, or is destitute of what it requires, he is culpable." [70]

In his effort to refute Ware's charge that children are not sinful by nature, Woods took the position that unless a sinful nature be presupposed, one could not account for the origin of sin in the individual. He asserted that a sinful effect must presuppose a prior sin as its cause. He further asserted that human volition could not generate a sinful nature unless that nature was already sinful. "The first sinfulness or depravity of the heart is no more *produced* by a sinful volition or action," said

[68] *Ibid.*, pp. 82–83.   [69] *Ibid.*, p. 84.   [70] *Ibid.*, p. 101.

he, "than the principle of gravitation is produced by the falling of a stone, or the descent of a river." [71] But in that case, how was it possible for Adam to become a sinner? This was the difficult question which Taylor had posed for Calvinists, and it was brought forward by Ware and other New England liberals. Woods held that Adam began in a state of holiness; still he maintained that Adam's first sinful act presupposed a prior sinful disposition. "It is as true of Adam, as of any other man, that every sinful volition and act of his presupposed a sinful disposition, and must have arisen from it." [72]

When Woods advanced this theory, he raised the difficult question of the ultimate cause of evil. He declined to follow the path of Emmons and attribute its beginning to divine causality. Finding himself in a dilemma, he acknowledged that he could not solve the problem. The commencement of sin, said he, "is to be regarded as an ultimate fact in God's empire." [73]

In the spring of 1822 the Hollis Professor replied in a penetrating pamphlet. [74] First of all, he categorically denied the validity of his opponent's five arguments for native depravity. Those arguments would, he contended, as readily establish natural holiness as natural depravity. (1) If it be true that children exhibit sinful affections, it also is true that they manifest good affections. (2) If depraved affections exhibit themselves very early, so do good affections. (3) If sinful affections cannot be traced to any radical change produced in the child's natural constitution subsequent to birth, neither can virtuous affections. (4) If sinful reactions are spontaneous and not easily eradicable, so are virtuous reactions. (5) If it is predictable that all children will certainly sin, it is no less predictable that

---

[71] *Ibid.*, p. 99.   [72] *Ibid.*, p. 112.   [73] *Loc. cit.*
[74] *Answer to Dr. Woods' Reply, in a Second Series of Letters Addressed to Trinitarians and Calvinists* (Cambridge, 1822).

they will also certainly manifest some good traits.[75] Thus these arguments could as well prove the child to be natively good as natively depraved. But as a matter of fact, said Ware, they prove neither; they only show that the child is endowed with native capacities which will enable him to achieve either a sinful or a virtuous character.

Ware scored heavily against Woods by demonstrating that he had failed to deal forthrightly with the question of the consistency of the doctrine of native depravity with the moral perfection of God. He showed that Woods had either evaded the main point at issue, or else had merely raised questions and offered hypotheses.[76]

Turning then to the question of the relation of moral agency to the commencement of sin in Adam and his posterity, Ware reminded Woods that if he had unwaveringly followed his logic through to the end, he would have landed precisely where Emmons did. That is to say, he would have made God the efficient cause of sin. But being less intrepid than Emmons, he had let the matter drop with the defeatist remark that sin must be accepted as an ultimate fact in the divine empire.[77]

By this time the major differences between the two contestants had been fully disclosed, and the debate might well have ended. Nevertheless, there was another round of pamphlet warfare. Since both Woods and Ware largely repeated themselves, the two final contributions call for no extended treatment.

In September of 1822 Woods issued his final pamphlet in the controversy.[78] He once more denied that the natural affections of children contained any quality of moral holiness, however amiable they might appear to be from a social and domestic standpoint. But he had no new light to shed on why

[75] *Ibid.*, pp. 26–36.   [76] *Ibid.*, pp. 40–42.   [77] *Ibid.*, pp. 61–63.
[78] *Remarks on Ware's Answer* (Andover, 1822).

83

this was the case. Woods was annoyed by Ware's charge that only timidity had kept him from joining Emmons in attributing Adam's first sin to the divine efficiency. "Some may wish me to go further," he said. "But how is this possible? When I come to ultimate facts I must stop." [79]

To the *Remarks* Ware replied in a short *Postscript*, published in 1823.[80] By now he was weary of being repeatedly told that the lovable natural affections of children could be no evidence of holiness, and he presented a final challenge to his adversary: "If those amiable qualities and actions are no evidence of *holiness* or *a good moral state,* I see not how the opposite qualities, dispositions and actions can be evidences of *sinfulness,* or *a bad moral state.*" [81] This left with Woods the puzzling problem of trying to determine just why one set of characteristics should carry moral significance and the other not.

Ware shrewdly took full advantage of Woods' late admission that Adam, although created in a state of original righteousness, yielded to temptation and committed the first transgression. If that be so, commented Ware, then Adam's offspring may also begin to sin under similar circumstances. "In whatever manner the sin of Adam is accounted for, he being admitted to be previously holy, to have no sinful disposition, nothing but temptation operating on a heart inclined only to love and obey God; in the same manner may the first sin of each individual of his posterity be accounted for, without the supposition of any natural disposition or propensity to sin, or deriving from him a corrupt nature." [82] Ware here advanced the same argument which John Taylor had used against the Puritan federalists in the eighteenth century.

[79] *Ibid.,* p. 30.
[80] *A Postscript to the Second Series of Letters Addressed to Trinitarians and Calvinists, in Reply to the Remarks of Dr. Woods on Those Letters* (Cambridge, 1823).
[81] *Ibid.,* p. 7.   [82] *Ibid.,* pp. 33–34.

When the Woods-Ware controversy finally came to a close, the two contestants were still as far from agreement as they were in the beginning. Each held tenaciously to his original position. Nevertheless, one thing seems clear: Woods had defended the doctrine of original sin so clumsily that he had unwittingly given aid and comfort to Ware's romantic anthropology. If the New England Calvinists were to stem the rising tide against the doctrine of native depravity, a more perceptive thinker than Woods had to emerge.

CHAPTER FIVE

THE NEW HAVEN CONCEPTION
OF ORIGINAL SIN

B Y the time the Woods-Ware controversy reached its climax, it should have been clear to the Edwardeans that their doctrine of original sin could not be successfully maintained against the Unitarian challenge on the basis of the arguments which had been employed by Leonard Woods. The new situation demanded a type of creative thinking and vigorous leadership for which he was not equipped.

I

It was at this crucial juncture that there emerged within New England Calvinism an unusually gifted theologian: Nathaniel William Taylor (1786–1858).[1] During his junior year in Yale College he was converted under the evangelistic preaching of President Dwight. Upon graduation, he engaged in special theological study under Dwight. For a period of two years he also acted as Dwight's private secretary. In February of 1812 he accepted a call to New Haven's prominent First Church (popularly known as Center Church), remaining there about ten years. Like Dwight, Taylor was a forceful evangelist, and dur-

[1] For an illuminating study of his background and life-work, see Sidney E. Mead's *Nathaniel William Taylor: Connecticut Liberal* (Chicago, 1942).

ing his ministry First Church witnessed four notable seasons of revival.[2]

In the year 1822 Taylor was appointed Dwight Professor of Didactic Theology in the newly organized Yale Divinity School.[3] Here he labored zealously for the next thirty-five years, retiring in 1857. Although a great preacher, he excelled as metaphysician and theologian. One who knew him well said that "he was a philosopher, who has had no equal in this department, on our side of the ocean, since President Edwards."[4] Frank H. Foster pronounced him "the most original, powerful, and widely influential mind which New England theology ever possessed."[5]

Taylor considered himself a disciple of Jonathan Edwards, but he did not agree with the father of the New Divinity in all respects. As early as 1819, he pointed out in a letter to his friend Lyman Beecher that Edwards was defective in "his definition of moral agency and free will."[6] "For example, he [Edwards] thought it to be enough to show that certainty of conduct and moral agency did coexist in fact, without venturing any hypothesis concerning the *quo modo*. Leaving this untouched, he left the loophole for Emmonism."[7] Much of Taylor's thought was to be devoted to remedying this defect in Edwards' theology. In 1818 he took an important step in this direction by writing a prophetic tract, entitled *Man, a Free Agent without the Aids of Divine Grace*, in which he main-

---

[2] *Ibid.*, p. 68.

[3] This School was also known as "the Theological Department in Yale College."

[4] George P. Fisher, "The 'Princeton Review' on the Theology of Dr. N. W. Taylor," *The New Englander*, XXVII (April, 1868), 285.

[5] *A Genetic History of the New England Theology*, p. 246.

[6] Charles Beecher (ed.), *Autobiography, Correspondence, etc., of Lyman Beecher* (New York, 1865), I, 385–386.

[7] *Ibid.*, p. 385.

tained that free agency is inherent in man as a being who possesses understanding, conscience, and will, and that man did not lose his free agency in the fall of Adam.[8] Thus he regarded man, despite the effects of the fall, as a completely free agent without the aid of supernatural grace through Jesus Christ. He also insisted that sin can be sin only if man is free to choose either good or evil. "There can be no sin in choosing evil unless there be power to choose good." [9] Hence if it be true that man will certainly sin, as a result of Adam's fall, that certainty must not rest upon any scheme which is inconsistent with free agency.

In view of this pronounced emphasis upon human freedom, it was natural for Taylor to follow with keen interest the progress of the Woods-Ware controversy over the question of native depravity. He is reported to have expressed dissatisfaction with Woods' mode of arguing the case for the Calvinists.[10] This may partly explain why he went out of his way in 1821 to provoke an argument with Andrews Norton of Harvard University. On August 10, 1819, Norton had delivered his inaugural address as Dexter Professor of Sacred Literature. Long after this discourse had been quietly gathering dust, Taylor brought it before the public in a sharply critical review, published in *The Christian Spectator*.[11] "Our author's system of religion, so far

[8] *Man, a Free Agent without the Aids of Divine Grace* (Doctrinal Tract No. 2, New Haven, 1818), pp. 5–6.
[9] *Ibid.*, p. 6.
[10] Cf. Bennet Tyler, *Letters on the Origin and Progress of the New Haven Theology* (New York, 1837), p. 6. According to Tyler, "He [Taylor] was heard to say . . . that Ware had the better of the argument, and that Dr. Woods had put back the controversy with the Unitarians fifty years" (*loc. cit.*). It must be borne in mind, however, that Tyler was strongly prejudiced against Taylor and may have represented him as more favorably disposed to Ware than was actually the case.
[11] "Review of Norton's Inaugural Discourse," *The Christian Spectator*, III (February, 1821), 74–83.

as he discloses any," said Taylor, "is too meager for creatures that need all the riches of divine mercy in their forgiveness and salvation." [12] He considered the inaugural basically defective in its perception of human nature, because it failed to consider man "as a depraved and ruined being." [13]

Yet the inaugural was not half so disturbing to him as Norton's "Thoughts on True and False Religion," published in *The Christian Disciple* in the fall of 1820. Portraying Unitarianism as true religion and Calvinism as false religion, Norton wrote:

True religion is an inestimable blessing, because it teaches that God is the everlasting Friend and Father of his creatures; a God of infinite goodness. But what shall we say of a religion, which teaches that he has formed men, so that they are by nature wholly inclined to all moral evil; that he has determined in consequence to inflict upon the greater part of our race the most terrible punishments; and that unless he has seen fit to place us among the small number of those whom he has chosen out of the common ruin, he will be our eternal enemy, and infinite tormentor: that having hated us from our birth, he will continue to exercise upon us forever his unrelenting and omnipotent hatred. Whatever may be the worth of true religion, it surely does not follow, that this system of blasphemy must be also of great value, and very beneficial in its effects.[14]

To find the religion of his New England fathers branded as a "system of blasphemy" stirred Taylor's emotions. In particular he resented the insinuation that Calvinism taught that God formed men with a sinful nature. He bluntly accused Norton of presenting a "distorted caricature" which could not be substantiated by fair quotations from standard Calvinist authorities.[15]

Viewing Taylor's charge as character assassination, Norton

[12] *Ibid.*, p. 83.   [13] *Ibid.*, p. 79.
[14] "Thoughts on True and False Religion," *The Christian Disciple*, II (New Series, September-October, 1820), 340.
[15] "Review of Erskine's Evidences, and Norton on True and False Religion," *The Christian Spectator*, IV (June, 1822), 301, 303.

became exceedingly furious. He at once dispatched a peremptory letter to the conductors of *The Christian Spectator*, serving notice that in case they did not publish it in the next issue of the *Spectator* "without alteration or omission," he would "take every other means in my power to give it publicity." Much of the letter consisted of excerpts from Calvinistic writings which were supposed to refute Taylor's claims.

Of course, the next number of the *Spectator* did not publish the letter. "Professor N. himself," the conductors commented, "could not expect us to submit to this haughty dictation, without regarding us as abandoned to a sense of character." [16] They promised to print the letter "whenever it is purged" of "reproachful and menacing expressions." Anticipating that Norton would publish a broadside against them, they determined to soften the blow by answering him in advance. They expected him to undertake to show that Calvinists taught as a doctrine that God creates men with a sinful nature, and therefore they quoted numerous authorities to disprove his charge.[17] Then they calmly awaited "the fearful consequences" of his anger.

Norton speedily obliged them with a wrathful essay, published in *The Christian Disciple*.[18] In order to reach the widest possible constituency, he at once republished it in a pamphlet for general distribution. Norton was most contemptuous of his New Haven critics. Citing a loosely constructed clause in the *Spectator*, "regarding us as abandoned to a sense of character," he haughtily remarked that it was "a humble labor to be engaged in controversy with men, who cannot write our language with common correctness." [19] Then he unwittingly walked into

[16] "Answers to Correspondents—Prof. Norton," *The Christian Spectator*, IV (August, 1822), 446.

[17] *Ibid.*, pp. 446–448.

[18] "Views of Calvinism," *The Christian Disciple*, IV (New Series, July-August, 1822), 244–280.

[19] *Views of Calvinism* (Cambridge, 1822), p. 30.

the trap of his opponents by saying "I now affirm it to be the doctrine of Calvinism, that *God creates men with a sinful nature.*"[20]

This charge pleased Taylor highly, and for two reasons. In the first place, it made the issue of native depravity the sole question under debate, and thus gave Taylor the opportunity to carry on with the Unitarians where Woods left off. In the second place, Norton blundered by using the phrase "the doctrine of Calvinism" in his charge, and thereby made it easy for Taylor to deliver a knock-out blow on a verbal technicality. Had Norton been wary enough to assert that Calvinism's doctrine of original sin logically implied that God is the author of man's sinful nature, he would have given Taylor a more difficult task. Taylor's reply was spirited and pointed, and it was important in two respects. On the one hand, he exposed the fallacy of Norton's accusation; on the other hand, he set forth his own peculiar version of the doctrine of original sin.

As sustaining his indictment of Calvinism, Norton had appealed to Calvin, the Westminster Confession, and Edwards. Taylor's answer was easy: he correctly pointed out that none of these authorities had ever espoused the so-called "doctrine" imputed to them.[21] "We say then that the passages quoted by Professor N. from Calvin, from the Westminster divines and from Edwards, furnish not even the shadow of warrant for ascribing to Calvinists the doctrine, that *God creates men with a sinful nature.*"[22]

Yet although Taylor could easily show that Calvinists had never held the doctrine that God creates men with a sinful nature, he conceded that some Calvinists might possibly have

[20] *Ibid.,* p. 31.
[21] "Review of Norton's Views of Calvinism," *The Christian Spectator,* V (April, 1823), 198–203.
[22] *Ibid.,* p. 203.

91

adopted a mode of accounting for the certainty of sin in Adam's offspring which would logically imply that God is the author of sin. This could be said of any Calvinist if, for example, he were to maintain that native depravity consists "in some physical attribute, some *taste* or *bias* or *propensity* or disposition to sin, which is not from the choice of the mind nor an act of choice, but which as a physical property, has the influence of a physical cause, and yet possesses a moral quality and justly exposes to punishment." [23]

Taylor then pointed out the fact that Calvinists held a "great diversity" of views as to how to account for the certainty of sin in Adam's descendants. Some Calvinists, though not New Englanders, would regard it as the result of the imputation of Adam's sin; others would attribute it to the voluntary exercise of a moral agent, combined with the operation of the divine efficiency; and still others would give different interpretations. Thus while Calvinists would agree that all men will certainly sin in consequence of Adam's fall, they would disagree as to what it was that made the sin a certainty. It was Taylor's reflection upon this situation within the Calvinist household that led him to take an interesting position: "Now not the *mode* of accounting for the fact [of sin], or for the certainty of the fact, but *the fact* itself is the doctrine of Calvinism." [24] He then proposed a version of the doctrine of original sin with which he believed Calvinists "as a class" would agree. "All who take the denomination of Calvinists, will agree that, *Mankind come into the world in such a state, that without the interposition of divine grace, all as soon as they become moral agents, sin in every accountable act.*" [25]

---

[23] *Ibid.*, p. 216. Not many years later Taylor was to argue with Calvinists whom he accused of taking essentially this view of original sin. They held what he called a doctrine of "physical depravity."
[24] *Ibid.*, p. 219.　　　　　　[25] *Ibid.*, p. 217.

Significantly, these words are almost literally those of Jonathan Edwards. In part one of his treatise on *Original Sin*, he had written: "I now assert, that mankind are all naturally in such a state, as is attended, without fail, with this consequence or issue; that THEY UNIVERSALLY RUN THEMSELVES INTO THAT WHICH IS, IN EFFECT, THEIR OWN UTTER ETERNAL PERDITION, as being finally accursed of God and the subject of his remediless wrath through sin." [26] In reproducing the substance of this statement, Taylor evidently meant to connect his own conception of original sin with that of Edwards. He did not, however, explain that Edwards' doctrine of original sin included the idea of the imputation of Adam's sin.

As we shall see, Taylor proved to be wrong in thinking that Calvinists would unite on the statement proposed by him. Nevertheless, his statement is significant in that it enunciates clearly and succinctly his own peculiar doctrine of original sin. By employing this formula he hoped to hold the Calvinists together and refute the Unitarian charge that God creates men with a sinful nature.

Despite Norton's initial belligerency, he suddenly dropped out of the controversy at this point, and therefore Taylor's spirited review might have ended matters had not a Norton sympathizer taken up the cause.[27] The review purported to deal primarily with the pamphlets of the Woods-Ware controversy, but it actually directed most of its attention to the objections which Taylor had raised against Norton's *Views*. It is apparent that Taylor's tactic had frustrated Norton because the reviewer nowhere charged that a part of the Calvinist doctrine was that

---

[26] *Works*, II, 314.
[27] "State of the Calvinistic Controversy," *The Christian Disciple*, V (New Series, May-June, 1823), 212–235. Professor Mead believes that this review was "probably written at least in part by Norton" (*op. cit.*, p. 192). Taylor himself suspected that Norton may have had a hand in the reply, and yet he directed his reply to Norton's "co-adjutor."

God creates men with a sinful nature. After all, he explained, "the question before us is not what Calvinists profess, or what this or that nominal Calvinist believes; but what is Calvinism itself, considered as a system, when properly understood and explained. Now Unitarians have said and still say, that Calvinism itself, properly understood and explained, teaches by necessary implication, that God is the author of sin." [28] Obviously the reviewer has retreated from Norton's original charge. He tried to meet Taylor's onslaught by charging that no reliance could be placed on his analysis of Calvinist writings. Citing as an example Taylor's statement that Edwards did not regard a native propensity as itself sinful, he declared the assertion to be "entirely false." [29] At this point the reviewer undoubtedly had the weight of evidence on his side.

The reviewer skillfully took advantage of Taylor's observation that Calvinists held a variety of views with respect to accounting for native depravity in Adam's offspring. For one thing, he reminded Taylor that the Saybrook Platform was still the official standard for Connecticut Calvinists.[30] Then he asked, "Can there be two systems differing from one another, and yet each one be Calvinism, properly so called?" It might then be true to say, "not that we [Unitarians] have misrepresented Calvinists, but that the modern Orthodox of New England are not Calvinists." [31] Unitarians would not, he added with a smirk, stress these differences between "the nominal Calvinists of New England" and other Calvinists, lest "we expose ourselves to the imputation of attempting, in an unworthy manner, to promote groundless divisions and jealousies among our opponents." [32]

Not until a year later did Taylor take any public notice of this review; doubtless he still hoped for a direct reply from Norton

[28] *Ibid.*, p. 217.   [29] *Ibid.*, p. 234.   [30] *Ibid.*, p. 228.
[31] *Ibid.*, p. 227.   [32] *Ibid.*, p. 229.

himself. When none seemed to be forthcoming, he fiercely assailed Norton's "co-adjutor." [33] At the outset he expressed amazement that Norton "would leave a cause under which he had evidently embarked under so strong an impression of its importance, in the hands of a co-adjutor so comparatively disqualified to undertake the burden of its defence." [34] Since Taylor spent most of his review in convicting the "co-adjutor" of having evaded the main point at issue between himself and Norton, it is not necessary to dwell on his argument. A few points, however, must be considered. The first concerns the correctness of Taylor's analysis of Edwards' conception of original sin. His critic had probed a tender spot, for Taylor reacted emotionally. He promised to deal later with the question as to whether Edwards had actually taught that the propensity to sin is itself sinful.[35] But he remarked that even supposing his critic to be right, still it would not follow that Edwards had taught that God creates men with a sinful nature. "If Edwards has taught the doctrine that 'God creates men with a sinful nature,' adduce the passage in which it be made to appear." [36]

Taylor was greatly incensed by the reviewer's insinuation that modern New England Calvinists were not true Calvinists. "Who then," he demanded, "are Calvinists in the Unitarian vocabulary?" [37] Perceiving the artifice of his adversary, Taylor stormed, "We are not here to be turned over to the etymology

[33] "Review Reviewed," *The Christian Spectator*, VI (June, 1824), 310–327; VI (July, 1924), 360–374. The pagination in the June issue is faulty, and therefore the citations are based upon a corrected version.
[34] *Ibid.*, p. 311.
[35] For the discussion of this question, see Taylor, "Edwards' View of Original Sin," *The Christian Spectator*, VI (November, 1824), 567–575. He insisted that Edwards did not teach that a propensity to sin is itself sinful.
[36] "Review Reviewed," *op. cit.*, p. 362.
[37] *Ibid.*, p. 369.

of the term, and to be gulled into the admission that those only are Calvinists, 'properly so called,' who adopt the exact creed of Calvin. This subterfuge is too palpable. Such a Calvinist is not to be found in this country." [38]

He caustically denounced the Unitarians for attempting to saddle modern New England Calvinists with an outmoded doctrine of original sin. If they were really fair-minded, said he, they would deal with the merits of the doctrine of original sin in the form in which it was currently defended by Calvinists. The modern form, he explained, was that in which President Edwards himself defended it: *"that men come into the world in such a state that without grace, they will sin and only sin in every accountable action when they become moral agents."* [39] If it were thus formulated, "every Calvinist in the country would subscribe" to it. If the Unitarians were not honorable enough to debate the Calvinist doctrine of original sin in this form, they might justly be regarded as guilty of slander.[40]

II

Taylor's new doctrine of original sin undoubtedly helped to thwart the Unitarians, but it became the occasion of long and bitter controversies within both Congregationalism and Presbyterianism. In order to show the far-reaching influence of Taylor's conception of man's native predicament, attention must be given to these controversies.

As already indicated, Taylor first publicly stated his view of original sin in his argument with Andrews Norton in April, 1823. The gist of his conception, however, had already been presented by his Yale colleague, Chauncy Goodrich (1790–1860), in December of 1821. It might be argued that since Taylor and Goodrich were close friends, the former had a leading hand in

[38] *Loc. cit.*   [39] *Ibid.,* p. 373.   [40] *Ibid.,* p. 374.

formulating it. That could well be so; still, it must be said that Goodrich first gave public expression to what we shall call the "New Haven" view of original sin. Lecturing to his students on December 15, 1821, he gave an interpretation of original human nature which was understood to resemble that for which Ware had contended in his controversy with Leonard Woods.[41] By some means the vigilant Lyman Beecher, minister of the Congregational Church in Litchfield, Connecticut, got word that the lecture had created theological unrest on the Yale campus.[42] According to the report, Goodrich "seemed to imply the denial of original sin," since he found "nothing sinful in infants." "The minute I heard of that," said Beecher, "I saw the end. I never felt so bad. I wrote a long letter to him [Goodrich] and Taylor, telling them they must take that back, or they would have the old fight over under new names." [43]

Taylor's reply has not been preserved, but what Goodrich had to say for himself (at least in part) is reported in his letter to Beecher, written on January 6, 1822.[44] Thanking Beecher "for the frankness and warmth" of his letter, he explained what he had advocated in his lecture on original sin. He had maintained "that, previous to the *first* act of moral agency, there is nothing in the mind which can *strictly* and *properly* be called sin— nothing for which the being is accountable to God." [45] But although denying human nature to be sinful previous to the first act of moral agency, he insisted that the cause of universal sinfulness could not be adequately explained in terms of the influence of bad example or of faulty education. The very fact that every individual will certainly sin as soon as he can, proves that sin has its fundamental cause in human nature.[46] Interestingly,

---

[41] Bennet Tyler, *Letters on the Origin and Progress of the New Haven Theology*, p. 7.
[42] *Ibid.*, p. 8. [43] Beecher, *Autobiography*, II, 157.
[44] *Ibid.*, I, 469–471. [45] *Ibid.*, p. 469. [46] *Ibid.*, p. 470.

Goodrich went on to say that the ideas which he had advocated in his lecture were by no means novel; indeed, they were "the exact opinions of Edwards" on original sin. Nor were they unlike Beecher's "unless it be in phraseology." He added, "I expressed them many years ago to Brother Taylor, whom I found to accord with me entirely." [47] This was an effective reminder to Beecher that if his lecture was off theological color, he enjoyed good company.

Beecher probably agreed in the main with what Goodrich had advocated; and if so, then his objection was likely motivated by the fear that the lecture had been badly timed. This was natural, since he was well aware that intra-Calvinist friction was imminent and could be easily incited. Goodrich made it clear that he could not endorse the policy of expediency, contending that truth would "never suffer by discussion." Besides, he considered it imperative to repel the Unitarian charge, that Calvinism makes God the author of man's native corruption. "On my statement of the subject [of total depravity]," he explained, "the complaint is taken away from the enemies of truth that we make God the author of sin in our constitution previous to voluntary agency; and the whole guilt of our total apostasy is brought to press on the conscience of the man himself, who is the sole author of his rebellion." [48]

But Goodrich and Taylor were not alone in their efforts to checkmate "the enemies of truth." They had the hearty support of Eleazar T. Fitch (1791–1871). In 1817, soon after his graduation from Andover Theological Seminary, he was chosen preacher to Yale College and appointed Livingstone Professor of Divinity. He was foremost among those who brought about the establishment of Yale Divinity School in 1822. Next to Nathaniel Taylor, he was the ablest theologian in the Yale

[47] *Ibid.*, p. 469.   [48] *Ibid.*, p. 471.

faculty.[49] On Sunday July 30, 1826, he preached to Yale College two remarkable sermons in which he clearly expounded the New Haven conception of original sin.[50] Taking as a text Romans 5:13 ("Sin is not imputed when there is no law"), Fitch laid down the "unlimited proposition" that "Sin, in every form and instance, is reducible to the act of a moral agent in which he violates a known rule of duty." [51] According to him, the term "act" refers not so much to overt action as to immanent acts of the will, which take the form of preferences and choices. The phrase "known rule of duty" is understood to include "all moral obligations," whether made known by the conscience, by the works of God, or by published statutes.[52]

By so redefining the nature of sin, Fitch hoped to render the Calvinist doctrine of original sin less vulnerable to its critics. This is clearly demonstrated by the five applications which he deduced from his "unlimited proposition." Let us summarize these applications. First, because all sin consists in the act of a moral agent in violation of known duty, sin is not to be confused with the ground of its certainty.[53] This was Fitch's way of criticizing the prevalent notion that the certainty of sin required the postulation of sin as its cause. Second, in view of the fact that sin consists in immanent acts of the will, one cannot properly refer to a sinful heart as distinct from sinful preferences and choices.[54] To do so will result in a theory of "physical depravity." "They who affirm that moral disposition, moral affection, moral quality, in an agent . . . is not, in its nature, an act of will, a choice or preference of the agent, but an essen-

---

[49] George P. Fisher, "The First Half Century of Yale Theological School," in *The Semi-Centennial of the Divinity School of Yale College,* May 15th and 16th, 1872 (New Haven, 1872), p. 18.
[50] *Two Discourses on the Nature of Sin* (New Haven, 1826).
[51] *Ibid.,* p. 4.   [52] *Ibid.,* pp. 4–5.   [53] *Ibid.,* p. 15.
[54] *Ibid.,* pp. 18–22.

tial property or part of his created disposition, maintain the doctrine of physical depravity which is opposed in these discourses." [55] Third, because sin always involves an immanent preference or choice of the agent, the doctrine of imputed sin cannot be maintained.[56] Nevertheless, Fitch believed Adam's sin bore a causal relation to the sin of his posterity; indeed, he thought it was precisely Adam's sin which made the sin of his posterity a certainty. But exactly how this certainty was determined, he acknowledged inability to explain.[57] Fourth, because all sin consists of immanent acts of the will, one must distinguish between Adam's sin and that of his offspring. "Nothing can with truth be called his [man's] original *sin*, but his first moral choice or preference being evil." [58] Fifth, since nothing can be sin except one's own acts in violation of known duty, all guilt is necessarily personal. This view will cause the world to "fall prostrate and plead to all the accusations of its Maker: guilty! guilty!" [59]

As might be supposed, the orthodox Calvinists were not slow to condemn Fitch's provocative *Discourses.* One of the sharpest condemnations came from the Old Calvinist, Ashbel Green, editor of the *Christian Advocate,* a Presbyterian monthly.[60] At three basic points he challenged "the learned Professor." In the first place, he strenuously denied that all sin could be reduced to "acts." This becomes clear, said he, when one remembers that "the root of all sin is the *omission* of loving God." [61] Again, he

---

[55] *Ibid.,* p. 35. It is important to note the precise meaning of the term "physical depravity," because this term will appear frequently in subsequent controversies.

[56] *Ibid.,* pp. 22–23.   [57] *Ibid.,* p. 24.   [58] *Ibid.,* p. 28.

[59] *Ibid.,* p. 32.

[60] *Christian Advocate,* V (March, 1827), 136–141; (April, 1827), 162–167.

[61] *Ibid.,* pp. 138, 163.

criticized the view that the underlying cause of sinful volitions is not itself sinful. "What we assert and what Professor F. denies, is, that the causes of sinful choices, which exist in the disposition, or temper of the soul itself, are sinful." [62] Finally, he accused Fitch of surrendering the doctrine of original sin "in all its parts." Not even Pelagius would want a more complete rejection of that doctrine.[63] In denying original sin, said Green, Fitch has created for himself insuperable problems with respect to infants. Infant baptism becomes meaningless if infants are not sinners. Furthermore, on Fitch's view there is no reason why infants should suffer and die.[64]

The editor of the *Advocate* charged that Yale had repudiated "the sound theology of President Edwards." This "subversive" system, he added, would be shocking to those who have assumed that Edwards' principles took deeper root there than anywhere else.[65]

Green's bitter and sarcastic attack upon the *Discourses* provoked a trenchant rejoinder from Fitch.[66] He candidly acknowledged that his "grand object" had been "to oppose the idea that depravity is a physical thing." Now that his adversary had openly championed that notion, he proposed to show its basic weaknesses. His exposure was ruthless. To Green's assertion that it was absurd to hold that a sinful effect could come from a source not itself sinful, he retorted that it was far more absurd not to do so. For the final logic of "physical depravity" is to postulate the existence of sin from all eternity, despite its shocking metaphysical implications. "This is his [Green's] dilemma. Sin has either existed from all eternity, or else it may come into being from some means, occasion, or cause, whether *ab intra*

[62] *Ibid.*, p. 163.   [63] *Ibid.*, p. 165.   [64] *Ibid.*, p. 166.
[65] *Ibid.*, p. 167.
[66] *Inquiry into the Nature of Sin* (New Haven, 1827).

or *ab extra,* which is not itself sinful. This is mine. Here is the very hinge of the whole subject; how shall it turn? For him? or for me?" [67]

Having shown his adversary's dilemma, Fitch pursued him relentlessly. Green had, said he, espoused the idea that the very first sinful volition in the child presupposes a preëxisting sin in the soul as its necessary cause. In the final analysis, therefore, "he makes sin begin with the conception of the foetus." [68] On this basis original sin necessarily involves "physical depravity." The objections to a theory of physical depravity are serious. In the first place, it cannot be reconciled with moral character. The soul is a dynamic agent, the moral qualities of which depend upon free volitions. Not to predicate the soul's character upon genuine moral choice "is to confound it with material substances and their qualities." [69] Again, the theory of physical depravity reduces man to a mere machine. It therefore not only calms the conscience of the sinner but it compels him to admit that he is helpless to change his tragic situation. "His [Green's] view makes the *sinner wait for God* to move. Truly he can tell the sinner consistently, to do nothing else, than wait and see whether it shall be the good pleasure of God to insert in him a new fountain." [70] Lastly, a theory of physical depravity makes a mockery of the moral government of God.[71]

Fitch was now determined to clear the air on the question of infants, a question which had been bobbing up ever since the time of John Taylor. Why, then, do infants die? Fitch replied: "The explanation which I conceive the Scriptures to give of this event, considered as an event *common to the race,* is this: that they inherit the causes of mortality from sinning Adam." [72] He explicitly denied that an infant dies because of being natively corrupt. He put to Green a searching question: "Will he

[67] *Ibid.,* p. 42.   [68] *Ibid.,* p. 48.   [69] *Ibid.,* p. 72.
[70] *Ibid.,* p. 85.   [71] *Ibid.,* pp. 84–86.   [72] *Ibid.,* p. 78.

call it a crime deserving the pains of dying . . . that the foetus was not conceived and formed as it ought to be?" [73] Why are infants baptized? "I return that question," retorted Fitch. Since Green had admitted that newborn infants are not moral agents, Fitch knew that his critic, as a Calvinist, could not explain why they should be baptized so far as the effect upon original sin was concerned. As for himself, he was content to regard infant baptism as the seal of God's gracious covenant.[74] What is the future state of those dying in infancy? Fitch confessed that he could not give any answer to this question. Challenging his opponent, he asked: "How then is this reviewer [Green] to dispose of infants in a future state himself?" [75]

Fitch deeply resented Green's "ignorant insinuations" with respect to theology at Yale. Many Presbyterians "may have come to the trembling conclusion that the foundations of truth with us are tottering; and that our institution—the hope and joy of many hearts—is about surrendering itself to the power of Unitarianism and Heresy!" [76] But "this uncharitable insinuation of our accuser" is completely groundless. "When I maintain that man is natively a sinner, and totally estranged from God and holiness; and that this universal apostasy is the consequence of the sin of Adam; and that this apostasy renders an entire moral change in man necessary in order to his recovery to the favor and kingdom of God; and that this change is effected only by the Holy Spirit, where is the heresy?" [77]

Without hesitation Fitch acknowledged that he did not agree with Edwards' "strange philosophy by which he attempts to make Adam and his posterity one identical being"; yet he maintained that in all other respects his *Discourses* "exactly concur with the principles of Edwards." [78] Though admitting that Yale no longer taught the doctrine of the imputation of

[73] *Ibid.*, p. 79.   [74] *Ibid.*, pp. 79–80.   [75] *Ibid.*, p. 81.
[76] *Ibid.*, p. 93.   [77] *Ibid.*, pp. 94–95.   [78] *Ibid.*, p. 57.

Adam's sin, he pointed out that this represented no recent innovation. President Dwight, for example, had taken this same position many years earlier. Fitch further remarked that what was true of Yale was true also of New England Calvinists; in general, they had abandoned the idea of imputed sin.

He was remarkably bold in asserting his freedom to depart from theological tradition when it became necessary. Not even the label "Pelagian" could intimidate him in his search for the truth. "If Augustine held that there is a sin in any one before sin begins to be, or that there is sin in any without beginning; or if he affirmed that sin begins in something totally different in kind from all choice or preference of mind; verily, on this specific point, I must look somewhere else for truth and correctness, even if I wander, in search of it, to the door of Pelagius." [79] This declaration demonstrated that the Yale theologians were not to be muzzled.

III

It is from this perspective that one can appreciate the strategic importance of Nathaniel Taylor's famous *Concio ad Clerum.* Preached to the Connecticut clergy in Yale Chapel on September 10, 1828, it forcefully enunciated and confirmed the positions which Fitch had expounded in 1826. Its immediate background, according to a contemporary account, was a recent attack made upon Taylor's views at Fairfield, Connecticut, in connection with an effort to raise funds for Yale Divinity School.[80] Taylor and his colleagues realized that unless the rising adverse criticism could be checked, the School would

[79] *Ibid.,* p. 54.
[80] Zebulon Crocker, *The Catastrophe of the Presbyterian Church, in 1837* (New Haven, 1838), p. 121.

suffer a major setback. Since for Taylor the best defense was always offense, his historic discourse is a superb example of his aggressive strategy.

Taking as his text Ephesians 2:3 ("And were by nature the children of wrath, even as others"), Taylor concentrated his attention upon the most controversial question within Calvinist circles, native depravity. His purpose was twofold: (1) to determine in what moral depravity consists, and (2) to show that moral depravity is "by nature." [81]

Before giving his own view on the first point, Taylor endeavored to show in what moral depravity does not consist. It does not consist in any property or essential attribute of the soul created in man by God. Nor does it consist in a sinful nature which men have brought upon themselves by acting in Adam's act. He thought it absurd to try to support this notion by predicating the identity of mankind with Adam. "To believe that I am one and the same being with another who existed thousands of years before I was born, and that by virtue of this identity I truly acted in his act, and am therefore as truly guilty of his sin as himself,—to believe this, I must renounce the reason which my Maker has given me." [82] Nor does moral depravity consist in any constitutional propensities in men's nature. Nor does it consist in a tendency or disposition which itself presupposes a previous sin as its cause. Challenging Woods and Green, he said "that which is the cause of *all* sin, is not itself sinful. The cause of all sin, itself sin! Whence then came the first sin? Do you say, from a previous sin as its cause? . . . Then you say, there is a sin before the first sin. Our first parents and fallen angels were once holy. Tell us now, whence came

[81] *Concio ad Clerum: A Sermon Delivered in the Chapel of Yale College*, September 10, 1828 (New Haven, 1828), p. 5.
[82] *Ibid.*, pp. 5–6.

their first sin? Do you still repeat, from a previous sin? . . . Do you say there must be *difficulties* in theology?—I ask must there be *nonsense* in theology?" [83]

After thus eliminating all the commonly held notions as false, Taylor affirmed that moral depravity *"is man's own act, consisting in a free choice of some object rather than God, as his chief good;—or a free preference of the world and of worldly good, to the will and glory of God."* [84] Obviously this is a restatement of what Fitch had already elaborated in his *Discourses* of 1826.

Taylor next undertook to show wherein "this depravity is by nature." What did he understand the phrase "by nature" to mean? *"Such is their* [men's] *nature,"* said he, *"that they will sin and only sin in all the appropriate circumstances of their being."* [85] In order to see the full import of this assertion, the meaning of two basic expressions contained in it must be understood. The first is, "in all the appropriate circumstances." According to Taylor, moral depravity is not caused by circumstances of temptation, even though there can be no sin without temptation. An example will reveal his reasoning. If a tree bears good fruit when planted in one kind of soil and bad fruit when planted in another, one would naturally infer that the soil (environment) and not the nature of the tree caused the difference in the fruit. On the other hand, if a tree bears bad fruit regardless of the kind of soil in which it is planted, one would conclude that the cause is in the nature of the tree, not in the soil. So of mankind, urged Taylor. Since all men, regardless of their environmental situation, sin and only sin prior to the intervention of grace, their moral depravity must be ascribed to their nature.

The second expression is, "such is their nature." We have already seen that Taylor first used those words in his debate

[83] *Ibid.*, p. 7.   [84] *Ibid.*, p. 8.   [85] *Ibid.*, p. 13.

with Andrews Norton. He never explained their meaning in positive terms, but he indicated what they do not mean. They do not mean that human nature is itself sinful or morally corrupt, or that human nature is the physical or efficient cause of one's sinful preferences and choices. When, therefore, he declared mankind to be depraved by nature, he only intended to say "that their nature is the occasion, or reason of their sinning." [86] As to precisely how Adam's first sin served to occasion universal sinfulness in his offspring, Taylor never attempted to explain. In his opinion the mode was secondary; the main thing was the certainty of the fact of sin. And as proof of the certainty of sin he appealed to the Bible, human consciousness, and the history of the race.

Before having his discourse published, Taylor appended some fifteen pages of "Remarks" which he hoped would serve to clarify his doctrine of native depravity. The Remarks are subdivided into five sections. In light of later controversies, each of these sections requires a brief analysis. The first section deals with the nature of infants. "The very birth of a human being," said Taylor, "is an event which involves the certainty of entire moral depravity, without the supernatural interposition of God to prevent it." [87] How early then will the human being begin to sin? "I *do not know,* the precise instant," he confessed. Nevertheless, he contended that infants "sin as soon as they become moral agents." They sin so "very early," said he, that the Bible figuratively represents them as sinning "from their birth." [88] What is the destiny of an infant if he dies before becoming a moral agent? "In my belief he is saved through the redemption that is in Christ Jesus," concluded Taylor.[89] If the infant must be redeemed through Christ, does not this fact logically imply that he is sinful prior to the exercise of moral

[86] *Ibid.,* p. 14.   [87] *Ibid.,* p. 23.   [88] *Ibid.,* pp. 23–24.
[89] *Ibid.,* p. 24.

agency? But in that case Taylor's main thesis with respect to the nature of native depravity seems to break down. He left this problem unsolved.

In section two Taylor argued that "the doctrine of physical depravity" was never espoused by the earlier Calvinist theologians. Even though they believed man to be born with a corrupt nature, they held that he corrupted himself by actually participating in Adam's sinful act. This was true, said he, in the case of Edwards. His novel theory of the personal identity of mankind with Adam was designed to prove that man, although corrupt at birth, brought that corruption upon himself by actually sinning with Adam.[90] The main purpose of this section was to show that inasmuch as New Englanders had rejected the doctrine of imputation, they could no longer cling to the idea that men are born with a corrupt and sinful nature.[91] Thus they would be compelled to repudiate the "theological novelty" of physical depravity.

The third section of Remarks insisted that the New Haven doctrine of depravity did not represent any attempt to set up any anti-orthodox "peculiarity." "For, they who adopt this view, as fully believe in the certainty of the universal and entire sinfulness of mankind . . . as any other men. . . . The charge then of adopting this view of sin, for the purpose of opposing any doctrine of orthodoxy, is a slanderous charge." [92]

In section four Taylor argued at great length that "The universal depravity of mankind is not inconsistent with the moral perfection of God." [93] He implied that inconsistency would be inevitable if the novel scheme of physical depravity were adopted. On the other hand, he urged that inconsistency could

---

[90] *Ibid.*, pp. 25–26.
[91] Henry Ware emphasized this same point in his controversy with Leonard Woods (cf. Ware, *Letters Addressed to Trinitarians and Calvinists*, pp. 18–19).
[92] *Concio ad Clerum*, pp. 27, 28.   [93] *Ibid.*, pp. 28–35.

not be true in the case of the New Haven view of original sin, because it assumed all sin to be voluntary in character. According to this view, "God does not compel him [a human being] to sin by the *nature* he gives him. Nor is his sin, although a consequence of Adam's sin, in such a sense its consequence, as not to be a free and voluntary act of his own." [94]

Taylor devoted the final section to emphasizing the special merit of his doctrine of human depravity in relation to preaching the gospel.[95] He said that his theory made man solely responsible for his moral condition. On its terms man may not charge God with the authorship of his moral corruption, nor may he hide behind old Adam. In a vigorous exhortation to his fellow ministers, he wrote: "Let us then go forth with it [the gospel message]; and clearing God, throw all the guilt of sin with its desert of wrath, upon the sinner's single self. Let us make him see and feel that he can go to hell only as a self-destroyer." [96]

Taylor's treatment of the New Haven doctrine of original sin was too explicit to be misunderstood and too bold to be ignored. How would New England Calvinists receive it? That is the theme of our next chapter.

[94] *Ibid.*, p. 28.   [95] *Ibid.*, pp. 35–38.   [96] *Ibid.*, p. 37.

CHAPTER SIX

THE NEW HAVEN CONCEPTION
OF ORIGINAL SIN (CONTINUED)

NATHANIEL TAYLOR'S *Concio ad Clerum* presented a view of original sin which had already been taught at Yale for many years and which he himself had previously defended in his controversy with Andrews Norton. Thus it was significant not for its novelty, but for its polemical dexterity and its uncompromising attitude. Few theologians could state issues as incisively and as provocatively as Taylor. Whenever he spoke, he got attention. His *Concio ad Clerum* was Taylor at his best.

I

It created a theological storm in Calvinist circles, and evoked a series of heated controversies which had far-reaching consequences. The first of these controversies was initiated by Joseph Harvey, pastor of the Congregational Church in Colchester, Connecticut.[1] His attack was directed mainly against two alleged "peculiarities" in Taylor's discourse. The first was the "peculiar" idea that all sin consists in free, voluntary acts. Harvey maintained "that moral depravity does not consist wholly or exclusively in man's own voluntary acts."[2] In addition

[1] *A Review of a Sermon, delivered in the Chapel of Yale College September 10, 1828, by Nathaniel W. Taylor, D. D.* (Hartford, 1829).
[2] *Ibid.,* p. 14.

to voluntary or actual sin, said he, there is "native sin" which consists in a corrupt nature and which is the source or cause of all actual sin. He declared that in taking this position he was only being loyal to historic Calvinism, which Taylor had betrayed. He cited pertinent passages against Taylor from Calvin, the Westminster divines, Joseph Bellamy, and Edwards. Taylor had, he charged, greatly distorted the teaching of Edwards' treatise on *Original Sin* by arbitrarily wrenching words and phrases from their contexts.[3] In his effort to show that men are really sinners prior to voluntary action, Harvey drew special attention to the moral character of infants. Infants are not moral agents at their moment of birth, yet "God has always treated them, both in his moral government, in the plan of salvation, and in the regulations of his church, as sinners." [4] Besides, "God teaches us in his word, in the most explicit forms of which language will admit, that infants are sinners." [5] Thus it is manifest that not all sin can be confined to voluntary acts.

The second "peculiarity" to which Harvey took exception was Taylor's assertion that human nature is not itself sinful but yet is "the occasion" of sin. The word "occasion," he protested, only "means an accidental cause," or a cause that may or may not produce a given effect. In other words, it involves merely probability, not certainty. "If then Dr. Taylor means, as he says he does, that nature is not the *efficient cause* of sin, but the *occasion* or reason of it; he relinquishes the certainty of the effect, and admits that its actual occurrence depends on circumstances. And this, according to his own definition, is Arminianism." [6]

In direct opposition to Taylor, Harvey argued that the only way to account for the certainty of sin is to presuppose a sinful nature as its efficient cause. "To ascribe a certain uniform

[3] *Ibid.*, pp. 7–9.
[4] *Ibid.*, p. 16. Cf. pp. 17–20.
[5] *Ibid.*, p. 20.
[6] *Ibid.*, p. 28.

effect to occasion or contingency, is absurd. . . . Actual sin then, if it be a certain and exclusive effect, must result from a cause which is sinful." [7] Lest anyone should consider his opinion a novelty, he pointed out "that the views of the most eminent divines of New England are in accord with the above conclusion. They have, it is believed without an exception, taught the sinfulness of nature as an efficient cause or source of actual sin." [8] In order to make certain that Taylor knew to whom he especially referred, he identified by name Edwards, Bellamy, and Dwight, all truly "eminent divines."

Henceforth the issue was sharply joined between two factions within Congregationalism, each protesting its fidelity to Jonathan Edwards. Those taking Harvey's position may be identified as conservative Edwardeans, and those agreeing with Taylor may be characterized as liberal Edwardeans. Connecticut became the scene of a protracted debate between these two factions, each seeking to win a victory over the other.

Foreseeing the need for a journal through which to promote and defend the New Haven views, Chauncy Goodrich purchased *The Christian Spectator,* and in 1829 began the publication of *The Quarterly Christian Spectator.* In the June number for that year he analyzed the issues at stake in the Taylor-Harvey controversy, aligning himself firmly with his Yale colleague. [9] "Nothing can be more important to Calvinists at the present day," he began, "than to settle with entire precision the import of their statements respecting the *nature* of sin, and the ground of its *certainty* as a characteristic of our whole race." [10] He acknowledged that the use of "ambiguous language" with

---

[7] *Ibid.,* p. 29. In his debate with Henry Ware, Leonard Woods had taken precisely the same position.
[8] *Ibid.,* p. 30.
[9] "Review of Taylor and Harvey on Human Depravity," *The Quarterly Christian Spectator,* I (June, 1829), 343–384.
[10] *Ibid.,* p. 345.

regard to this subject had been "a prolific source of obloquy and error." In his opinion, Taylor was rendering a distinct service to "evangelical truth" by criticizing the "unguarded statements" which many former Calvinists had made. By seeking to maintain these unguarded interpretations of the doctrine of original sin, Harvey had only further magnified their inadequacies. For example, when he asserted that human nature is itself sinful prior to all voluntary action, he used loose language which logically implied that God is the author of sin. "We are far, indeed, from imagining that his mind ever assented, for a moment, to so dreadful a conclusion. But we are constrained to say, that he must either abandon his fundamental principle, or that he must not shrink from its 'unavoidable consequences.'" [11]

In this connection Goodrich frankly conceded to Harvey that Edwards did regard the human heart as sinful. On the other hand, he pointed out that Edwards also believed that sin consisted wholly in man's own voluntary acts. But how could he hold to both views? He could do so, Goodrich explained, only because he "speculated himself into the notion" that mankind constituted "one moral whole" and thus supposed that Adam's offspring sinned in his first transgression. But when one abandons Edwards' doctrine of mankind's identity with Adam, said Goodrich, there is no alternative except to agree with Taylor.[12] Therefore Harvey must "either go back to the doctrine of imputation" and accept the "monstrous notion of sinning in the act of another," or else go "forward to the principle of Dr. Taylor." [13]

Goodrich was extremely irked by the notion, advanced by Harvey, that in order to account for the absolute certainty of sin in Adam's posterity from the commencement of moral agency, it is necessary to presuppose a sinful nature in man at birth. This idea, he observed, rested upon the premise "that a

[11] *Ibid.*, p. 348.   [12] *Ibid.*, pp. 371–372.   [13] *Ibid.*, p. 349.

cause must have the same properties as its effect." But he considered this assumption to be "totally erroneous." "Acts of thought, for example, are the certain and exclusive effect of our intellectual nature. Yet that nature is one thing, and acts of thought are entirely different." [14] It was fortunate, he thought, that Harvey's idea was untenable, for its ultimate moral implications were shocking. In the last analysis, one must ask what it implied with respect to God. "Each soul as it enters on existence, receives its nature from Him; and to affirm that this 'nature is *itself* sinful,' and that every cause partakes of the character of its effect, is not only to make God the author of sin, but to make Him *sinful* too!!" [15]

But if one may not presuppose a sinful nature in the child at birth, is there any certainty that the child will sin on becoming a moral agent? In response to this question Goodrich gave an affirmative answer which is not essentially different from that given by John Taylor and Henry Ware. According to him, the child comes into the world "with a variety of appetites and desires" which are "neither sinful nor holy." Being utterly helpless, the child is "the object of unceasing care, watchfulness, and concession, to those around it." Consequently, "the natural passions are first developed; and each advancing month brings them new objects of gratification." "Thus by repetition is the force of constitutional propensities accumulating a bias toward self-gratification, which becomes incredibly strong before a knowledge of duty or a sense of right and wrong, can possibly have entered the mind." [16] When the child arrives at the stage of moral agency he is already so completely under the power of his self-centered propensities that he will certainly yield to temptation. If temptation overcame a mature Adam, said Goodrich, it will all the more certainly overcome the immature child. "Could the uniform certainty of this event be greater, if the

[14] *Ibid.*, p. 365.   [15] *Ibid.*, p. 352.   [16] *Ibid.*, p. 366.

114

hand of Omnipotence were laid upon the child to secure the result?" [17]

In explaining how sin arises in the life of the child, Goodrich acknowledged the environment (the indulgence of parents) to be a potent factor in creating a bias toward sinful conduct. In his opinion both native propensities and environmental forces are active in rendering sin a certainty with the dawn of moral agency. Interestingly, he attributed the same opinion to Nathaniel Taylor.[18] Therefore he maintained that Taylor occupied "the middle ground" between the extremes of Harvey and Arminianism. Whereas Harvey predicated "the certainty [of sin] on the *internal constitution* alone," and Arminianism predicated "the certainty on PECULIAR *circumstances* of an unfavorable kind," Taylor predicated certainty upon the influence of both internal propensities and environmental circumstances. "Notwithstanding Mr. Harvey's cavils," concluded Goodrich, "this middle point is the true ground of Calvinism, when freed from the doctrine of the imputation of Adam's sin." [19]

Now, Goodrich might well enough call Taylor's theory of original sin "the true ground of Calvinism," but he had no success in persuading Harvey to agree with him, for within a few months Harvey published a pamphlet severely criticizing Goodrich, and retracting none of his previous charges against Taylor.[20] Though the pamphlet carried no name of the author and referred to "Harvey" in the third person, everybody knew its identity. Harvey first endeavored to clear up alleged misrepresentations of his views. He denied that his view of native depravity implied or involved the doctrine of imputed sin. There is, he explained, "a station between *imputation* on the one hand, and *entire rejection of all connexion between Adam and his*

---

[17] *Ibid.*, p. 367.   [18] *Ibid.*, p. 377.   [19] *Ibid.*, p. 378.
[20] *An Examination of a Review of Dr. Taylor's Sermon on Human Depravity, and Mr. Harvey's Strictures on that Sermon* (Hartford, 1829).

posterity on the other, which appears to be the true scriptural ground, and which has been occupied by the most respectable divines [in New England] for the last fifty years." [21] Identifying himself with this New Divinity position, he said the doctrine of original sin only meant "that the posterity of Adam are in fact, and in their own personal characters, sinners from their birth." [22] But even though men be sinners from birth, Harvey urged that they are neither guilty of Adam's sin nor liable to be punished for it.[23]

He denied emphatically that his "doctrine of native sin" involved so-called "physical depravity." In declaring man's nature to be sinful he had only intended to signify "that the moral state of man is sinful from his birth." "A moral being, for aught we know," he explained, "may commence his existence in an active, voluntary state of the will, he may be a voluntary agent from his birth, and thus, in fact, to a certain extent sinful, and that without supposing that depravity is seated in any thing but the will." [24]

Having removed these alleged misconceptions of his doctrine of "native sin," Harvey declared that the only issue of the controversy centered in a single question: *"Are men, in consequence of the fall of Adam, sinners from their birth?"* [25] In defending the affirmative of this question he expended thousands of words, but his arguments covered essentially old ground, and therefore need concern us no further. He did, however, take special note of Goodrich's theory of predicating the certainty of sin in Adam's offspring upon the action of over-indulged natural appetites. He argued that this theory attributed depravity "wholly to circumstances, and not to nature"; that it assigned "a limited variable cause for a certain universal effect";

---

[21] *Ibid.*, p. 6.   [22] *Loc. cit.*   [23] *Ibid.*, pp. 6, 8.
[24] *Ibid.*, p. 11.   [25] *Ibid.*, p. 20.

and that "though it may account for some kind of action in men, [it] does not account for sinful action." [26]

Upon the appearance of Harvey's pamphlet, Taylor, professing to see in it a partial surrender, replied to it at once under the pseudonym of Clericus.[27] He asserted (prematurely) that the controversy "must soon terminate in entire harmony," since the two parties now agree on the main point at issue, namely, "that sin, even the sin of men from their first existence, is in deed and in truth, VOLUNTARY ACTION!" [28]

Yet Taylor was not a man to purchase peace at the price of dodging issues, and therefore he pointed out some remaining problems in Harvey's position. For one thing, Harvey believed that a child might begin his existence as a voluntary sinner, and yet not have any knowledge of the moral law. Taylor considered this notion "almost incredible." Yet he expected that Harvey, having taken the first step (that sin is voluntary action), would "ere long certainly take the second." That is to say, he would finally admit that voluntary sin must be attended with some knowledge of duty.[29] In the next place, Taylor accused his opponent of trying to evade the main point at issue by introducing the question, "Are men sinners from their birth?" The original point of debate, he urged, had nothing to do with the question as to how early children begin to sin, but only with the question as to whether human nature was itself sinful. A final criticism of Harvey was that he, in trying to explain why the will yields to the power of motives, had traced the cause "to a previous *corrupt voluntary* state of the

[26] *Ibid.*, pp. 37–38.
[27] *An Inquiry into the Nature of Sin, as Exhibited in Dr. Dwight's Theology, with Remarks on an Examination of Dr. Taylor's and Mr. Harvey's Views of the Same Subject* (New Haven, 1829). The remarks bearing upon the *Examination* are given in the Postscript, pp. 22–43.
[28] *Ibid.*, p. 26.   [29] *Ibid.*, p. 28.

will!" But to take this position, said Taylor, is to fall into the old error of postulating sin before all sin. "Here then we have an act of will as *the cause* of an act of will; a *corrupt* or *sinful* state of *the will,* the *cause* of the existence of sin,—sin, the cause of all sin—*sin* before *all* sin!" [30]

At the outset of his remarks Taylor had optimistically prophesied that the controversy would soon terminate in complete harmony, but his later strictures of Harvey's views were not of the character to hasten that outcome. At any rate, the fires of controversy were destined to spread widely before dying down.

Growing uneasiness among conservative Edwardeans over Taylor's views led some of his friends to endeavor to remove the causes of mistrust. This was true, for example, of Joel Hawes, the highly respected minister of South Church in Hartford, Connecticut. On January 23, 1832, he addressed a short letter to Taylor in which he began by commending him for the sermons he had recently preached in South Church, and especially for what he had said with respect to "the doctrine of man's entire moral depravity, and his consequent dependence on the Holy Spirit for regeneration." "I see not," he continued, "how the orthodox doctrine on this subject could have been stated with more clearness than it was by yourself in parts of several discourses which you delivered here to crowded and deeply solemn assemblies." But although Hawes professed himself to be "fully satisfied" with Taylor's views, he reported that there were "not a few" in Hartford who felt otherwise. Consequently, Hawes advised him to give a full and frank statement of his views, especially on the points under debate.

On February first Taylor complied with his friend's suggestion, submitting to him a careful statement of his personal faith on eleven points. Being "much gratified" with Taylor's

[30] *Ibid.,* p. 39.

"candor and frankness," Hawes released their correspondence for publication in the *Connecticut Observer*.[31]

Although Taylor's "creed" included doctrines ranging all the way from the Trinity to final perseverance, he gave most attention to total depravity, moral agency, and the work of the Holy Spirit. In article three he affirmed that "all mankind in consequence of the fall of Adam, are born destitute of holiness, and are by nature totally depraved; in other words, that all men, from the commencement of moral agency do, without the interposition of divine grace, sin and only sin, in all their moral conduct." [32] In this connection he carefully delineated his position on certain points in debate. For example, he denied that Adam's posterity begin their existence with a sinful nature, or that God punishes them for the nature with which they come into the world. He reiterated his conviction that men become sinners only through their own act.[33]

Taylor closed his letter with the comment that he "could wish" the explanation of his views "might be satisfactory to all our Orthodox brethren." His wish was in vain. The letter, far from satisfying the Edwardean conservatives, only added new coals to the fires of controversy.

II

Among Taylor's most vigorous critics was Bennet Tyler (1783–1858), a highly respected conservative Edwardean. A graduate of Yale College, he served as President of Dartmouth College from 1822 to 1828. From 1828 to 1833 he was pastor of

[31] See *Connecticut Observer*, February 20, 1832, pp. 1–8. Taylor's reply also appeared in *The Quarterly Christian Spectator*, IV (March, 1832), 171–176, and *The Spirit of the Pilgrims*, V (March, 1832), 173–179.
[32] *Connecticut Observer*, February 20, 1832, p. 3.
[33] *Ibid.*, p. 4.

Second Congregational Church in Portland, Maine. The closing period of his ministry was spent as President of the new Theological Institute of Connecticut (1834–1857). Even before the Hawes-Taylor correspondence was printed, Tyler had already accused Taylor of holding unsound views on the "means of regeneration." [34] One of his criticisms was that Taylor had in effect denied total depravity. In reply, Taylor accused Tyler of holding a doctrine of "physical depravity" which denied moral agency and discouraged the use of the means of grace.[35]

When Taylor's letter appeared in the public press, Tyler at once issued strictures against its author's doctrine of original sin.[36] He complained that while Taylor acknowledged all men to be depraved in consequence of the fall, he allowed no real connection between Adam's sin and that of his posterity. Since he allowed no real connection, it was only logical that he should have denied that Adam transmitted to his descendants a morally corrupt and sinful nature. On his premises men come into the world as pure as Adam was before he fell and with a nature as sinless as that with which Jesus was born.[37] "To what purpose then are we told that, in consequence of Adam's fall, all mankind have become sinners,—and that they are sinners by nature—when the whole is virtually denied?" [38] In stating his own position, Tyler maintained that the fall brought upon mankind a morally contaminated nature which, like a mental property, is hereditarily transmitted from parent to child.[39]

Tyler's sweeping indictment called forth from Taylor an ex-

[34] Cf. *Strictures on the Review of Dr. Spring's Dissertation on the Means of Regeneration* (Portland, 1829).
[35] "Review of Dr. Tyler's Strictures on the Christian Spectator," *The Quarterly Christian Spectator*, II (March, 1830), 150–151. For a continuation of this controversy, see Tyler, *A Vindication of the Strictures on the Review of Dr. Spring's Dissertation on the Means of Regeneration, in the Christian Spectator for 1829* (Portland, 1830).
[36] *Remarks on Rev. Dr. Taylor's Letter to Dr. Hawes* (Boston, 1832).
[37] *Ibid.*, pp. 5–6.   [38] *Ibid.*, p. 8.   [39] *Ibid.*, pp. 7–8.

tremely caustic and searching reply.[40] He said that the nature of men differed in degree from that with which Adam was created. In consequence of the fall, present human nature does not seem to resist temptation to the degree that Adam's nature did prior to his first sin. On the other hand, Taylor contended that Adam's original nature and that which we possess at birth are alike in kind. "If Dr. Tyler means the same nature *in kind,* so that in this respect we are as truly *human beings* as Adam was, he rightly understands my belief." [41] Taylor insisted that his theory of depravity predicated a real connection between Adam's fall and the sin of his offspring. "All I now say in reply is, that if *in consequence* of Adam's sin, his posterity uniformly sin . . . I *do* see a connexion between his sin and theirs." [42] But even though Taylor professed to see a connection between Adam's sin and that of his posterity, it must be said that he was never able to specify the exact nature of that connection.

Taylor was not content merely to clarify and defend his own views; he especially determined to show the evil consequences which logically derived from Tyler's notion of original sin. Consequently, he promptly followed up the *Reply* with a second installment, published in the *Christian Spectator,* deducing numerous evils arising from Tyler's theory of natural depravity.[43] In the *Remarks* Tyler had asked, "What inconsistency is there in supposing that there is in man a native propensity to evil propagated from parent to child, like other natural propensities?" In that case, replied Taylor, "the very constitution of the mind itself" is depraved. This theory logically involves the gravest consequences. For example, (1) it makes God "the responsible author of sin"; (2) it "accounts for *all* sin, by assert-

[40] *Dr. Taylor's Reply to Dr. Tyler's Examination* (Boston, 1832). Originally published in *The Spirit of the Pilgrims,* V (August, 1832), 425–448.
[41] *Dr. Taylor's Reply,* etc., p. 4.   [42] *Ibid.,* p. 15.
[43] "Dr. Tyler's Remarks and Dr. Taylor's Reply," *The Quarterly Christian Spectator,* IV (September, 1832), 456–493.

ing a *previous* sin as its cause"; (3) it "is inconsistent with the doctrine of *natural ability,* and of course with the moral agency of man"; and (4) it "subverts the doctrine of *moral inability.*" [44]

Taylor pressed Tyler to recognize that if sin could be accounted for only by postulating a previous sin as its cause, one would ultimately have to explain how Adam and Satan could become sinners. "Whatever expedient Dr. Tyler may devise to account for the first propensity to sin in these creatures of God, one thing is certain, *viz.* that being without father and without mother, they did not become the subjects of such a propensity 'by propagation.'" [45] In effect, Taylor was telling Tyler that he must either follow Nathanael Emmons, and regard God as the efficient cause of sin, or else leave the question of the origin of the first sinful propensity totally unanswered.

Knowing Tyler's admiration for Edwards, Taylor concluded his rejoinder with a most provocative remark: "Such are some of the reasons which have led us, in common with President Edwards, to reject the theory, that there is in man a *specific* propensity to sin, distinct from the natural appetites implanted in our race at the first creation." [46] Nothing could have been more insulting to Tyler, because he fully believed that it was he, not Taylor, who stood on the side of the great Edwards.

Tyler came forward with an extremely heated answer, taking his adversary sharply to task.[47] "I am charged," he lamented, "with having advanced opinions which not only lead to the worst of heresies, but which involve the most horrid blasphemy." [48] He protested that his views had been "entirely misrepresented." He had, indeed, insisted that the fall fundamentally changed human nature, but he had "not undertaken"

[44] *Ibid.,* pp. 458–459.   [45] *Ibid.,* p. 461.   [46] *Ibid.,* p. 463.
[47] *A Letter to the Editor of the Spirit of the Pilgrims, to which are added Remarks on a Recent Letter of Dr. Taylor in the Christian Spectator* (Portland, 1833).
[48] *Ibid.,* p. 3.

to define the nature of that change, much less to say "that it is a change in the physical structure of the mind." He had asserted "that mankind possess a native, hereditary propensity to evil," but he had "not undertaken to tell in what this propensity consists," to say nothing of calling it sinful. To be sure, he had maintained "that all men are *naturally* inclined to evil," but he had also insisted "that they are laid under no natural necessity to sin, but are as free and voluntary in every act of sin, as Adam in his first transgression." [49]

Tyler was extremely furious that Taylor could be so unperceptive and so prejudiced as to place him outside the camp of Edwards. "Have I maintained that mankind come into the world with a propensity to sin?—so did Edwards. Have I maintained that this propensity is hereditary, transmitted in some way or other, from parent to child?—So did Edwards." [50]

Taylor speedily replied to Tyler, but he did so in a form which is most amazing. His purpose, he at once explained, was "not controversy but peace." Why? Because Tyler now "disclaims the opinions, which I had most sincerely and honestly supposed him to maintain," and has thus "removed all ground for further debate." [51] He now denies "that there is in the human mind, a constitutional propensity to sin"; he "disclaims the opinion, that this propensity to sin in the human mind, is itself sinful"; he admits "that all mankind come into the world *with the same nature in* KIND, as that with which Adam was created"; and he maintains "that the *only reason,* that the posterity of Adam do not exhibit the same moral character which Adam exhibited, is,—not that they have a different nature,—but that they are placed *in different circumstances.*" In sum, he now "agrees with me in the views which I have always maintained

---

[49] *Ibid.*, pp. 15–18.   [50] *Ibid.*, p. 19.
[51] "Letter to the Editor from the Rev. Dr. Taylor," *The Quarterly Christian Spectator,* V (September, 1833), 467 [468], 459.

of the doctrine of depravity by nature." [52] In other words, he has at last fallen into line with Edwards and true Calvinism! Taylor added, "Neither the high Hopkinsians, nor the advocates of physical depravity, or the taste scheme, will, in view of Dr. Tyler's last explanations, consider him as any longer on their side of the question." [53]

Whereas Tyler had closed his previous reply "praying" that he and Taylor "may yet see eye to eye," he was thrown into double rage over the latter's astonishing charge that they now saw eye to eye, thanks to his disclaiming his original views. "This allegation," retorted Tyler, "is altogether without foundation." "I have not abandoned one of the positions which I have taken, but have vindicated them all, and have shown that they do not involve the consequences charged upon them." [54]

Tyler had good reason to resent Taylor's claim that, since they both subscribed to the views of Edwards on native depravity, there was no longer any disagreement between them. The fallacy of this reasoning, as Tyler saw, lay in the assumption that they both agreed in their interpretation of Edwards. It was Tyler's firm belief that Taylor had identified Edwards with views which contradicted his basic teaching. [55] Thus, although Tyler preferred peace to strife, he insisted that "peace must not be purchased at the expense of truth. We must even *contend* for the faith once delivered to the saints." [56] Accordingly, he brought this bitter controversy to an indecisive conclusion by stubbornly maintaining that he alone was right and that Taylor "entirely subverts the doctrine of original sin, as generally maintained by Calvinists." [57]

By the time the Taylor-Tyler debate reached its climax, Con-

[52] *Ibid.*, pp. 460, 462, 464, 467.   [53] *Ibid.*, p. 467.
[54] *A Letter to the Editor of the Spirit of the Pilgrims, to which are Added Remarks on a Recent Letter of Dr. Taylor in the Christian Spectator* (Portland, 1833), pp. 24, 26.
[55] *Ibid.*, pp. 35–36.   [56] *Ibid.*, p. 39.   [57] *Ibid.*, p. 38. Cf. p. 40.

necticut Congregationalism was in a state of turmoil. In a series of *Letters,* published in the year 1832, Joseph Harvey wrote: "If our theological affairs go on as they have for ten years past, the time is not far distant when Congregationalism in Connecticut, will be rent in twain, no more to be united." [58] In his opinion, the Yale liberals were entirely to blame for the existing crisis, and he warned that if they persisted in spreading their speculations, "the friends of sound doctrine in the State, will soon seek other Seminaries for their children, and Yale will become, in Connecticut, what Harvard is in Massachusetts." [59]

The conservative Edwardeans made a concerted effort to fulfill Harvey's prophecy. They organized the Doctrinal Tract Society (1831), established *Evangelical Magazine* (1832), formed the Connecticut Pastoral Union (1833), and founded the Theological Institute of Connecticut (1834). Bennet Tyler became the Institute's first President and Professor of Theology, and in this capacity led the attack upon the New Haven doctrines. Fortunately, however, the conservatives were unable to produce schism in Connecticut Congregationalism.

III

The conservative-liberal conflict within Congregationalism had its counterpart in Presbyterianism; and since the New Haven doctrine of original sin was also an important factor in it, we must give attention to intra-Presbyterian developments. As already seen, the editor of the Presbyterian *Christian Advocate,* Ashbel Green, challenged the New Haven conception of original sin, as presented by Eleazar Fitch, as early as the year

[58] *Letters on the Present State and Probable Results of Theological Speculations in Connecticut* (n. p., 1832), p. 41.
[59] *Ibid.,* p. 41.

1826.[60] Nevertheless, the New Haven views penetrated Presbyterian theology. The process was facilitated by the Plan of Union under which Congregationalists and Presbyterians labored from 1801 to 1837. Under the operation of the Plan, ministers of one communion frequently served churches of the other. Also ministerial students of both communions often attended the same theological seminary. These contacts resulted in communicating New Haven notions to the Presbyterian Church. Hence, in the course of time two schools of theological thought emerged: Old School and New School. The former followed older federalist Calvinism and the latter the New Haven version of Calvinism.[61]

About five months after Nathaniel Taylor had delivered his *Concio ad Clerum,* Albert Barnes, Presbyterian minister at Morristown in New Jersey, preached a sermon on "The Way of Salvation" which aroused anxiety within Old School circles.[62] In this sermon, delivered while his church was experiencing a vigorous revival, Barnes enunciated certain Christian doctrines which he considered pertinent to the immediate situation. He gave special attention to the subject of native depravity. "God's plan of saving men," he observed, "is based on the fact that the race is destitute of holiness." According to him, the race was poisoned at its fountain by the "first pair of apostates," in consequence of which "not one of all their descendants would escape the contagion to the end of time." [63] Even though little

---

[60] See *supra,* pp. 100–101.

[61] For accounts of the origin and growth of these two parties, see Zebulon Crocker, *The Catastrophe of the Presbyterian Church, in 1837* (New Haven, 1838), and Samuel J. Baird, *A History of the New School* (Philadelphia, 1868). The former favors the New School, and the latter the Old School.

[62] *The Way of Salvation; A Sermon Delivered at Morristown, New Jersey, February 8, 1829* (2nd edition: Philadelphia, 1830).

[63] *Ibid.,* p. 7.

children may love their parents and manifest many other amiable character traits, these characteristics must not be regarded as evidence that they have any love to God. In fact, "the first act of the child when he becomes a moral agent" is to violate God's moral law; and, indeed, this will be "the continued act of his life, unless he is renewed." [64]

In the general context in which he had charged apostate man with numerous forms of wickedness, Barnes relieved the bleak picture somewhat by remarking incidentally that of course, "Christianity does not charge on men crimes of which they are not guilty." "It [Christianity] does not say, as I suppose, that the sinner is held to be personally answerable for the transgressions of Adam, or of any other man." That would "be most clearly unjust." [65]

In these remarks Barnes challenged the federal doctrine of imputed guilt. This challenge might have received only minor attention, however, had it not been for the fact that in the spring of 1830, the influential and somewhat liberal First Presbyterian Church in Philadelphia sought him as the successor to the Reverend James P. Wilson, then in poor health and wishing to retire. In light of this prospect, an Old School man saw fit to criticize Barnes' sermon in the public press. Wilson publicly defended Barnes. Although Barnes was finally installed in First Church (June 25, 1830), Old School clergymen, led chiefly by Ashbel Green and George Junkin, resorted to every judicatory of the Presbyterian Church to secure his conviction as a heretic. Twice his case was brought before the highest tribunal of the Church, the General Assembly.

In the spring of 1831 the Presbytery of Philadelphia declared Barnes' Morristown sermon to be infected with errors of dangerous tendency, notably with regard to the doctrine of original sin. The case was brought before the General Assembly

[64] *Ibid.*, p. 6.   [65] *Ibid.*, pp. 5. 6.

of 1831. The Assembly acknowledged that the sermon "contains a number of unguarded and objectionable passages," but it expressed the judgment that "the Presbytery of Philadelphia ought to suspend all further proceedings in the case of Mr. Barnes." [66] In the eyes of the Old School men, the New School party had won a signal victory. Nevertheless, the Old School leaders did not relax their efforts to purge the Presbyterian Church of alleged heresy, and they kept an especially alert eye upon Barnes.

Evidently Barnes had not been intimidated by the criticism growing out of his Morristown sermon, for soon thereafter he published a commentary on Paul's Letter to the Romans in which he most vigorously opposed the federal doctrine of original sin.[67] He expressly denied that God entered into a covenant with Adam, constituting him the federal head and representative of his posterity. "There is not one word of it in the Bible," declared Barnes. It "is a mere philosophical theory," designed "to explain what the Bible has left unexplained." But in fact "it explains nothing." [68] On the contrary, it creates a problem that need never have arisen. That is to say, it raises the false idea of the imputation of Adam's sin, a notion which is not only alien to the Scriptures, but which is unquestionably unjust, because it results in taxing the innocent with sins which they did not and could not commit. "How *could* millions be responsible for the one who acted long before they had an existence, and of whose act they had no consciousness, and in which they had no participation?" [69]

But even though Barnes rejected the federal doctrine of imputed sin, he acknowledged that there was a positive connec-

[66] *Minutes of the General Assembly of the Presbyterian Church in the United States of America* (1821–1835), p. 329.
[67] *Notes, Explanatory and Practical, on the Epistle to the Romans* (New York, 1835).
[68] *Ibid.*, p. 128.   [69] *Loc. cit.* Cf. pp. 117–122.

tion between Adam's first sin and that of his offspring. In commenting on Romans 5:12, for example, he explained that Adam's disobedience "was the occasion of the introduction of all sin into all the world." [70] But the Apostle, he added, did not undertake to define the exact manner in which this result was accomplished. Paul meant only to establish "the simple *fact* that Adam sinned, and that this made it certain that all his posterity would be sinners." [71] Yet although it is a fact that, in consequence of Adam's sin, all men will certainly sin, the only sin for which they are guilty is that which they commit personally against known moral law.

Shortly after *Notes* came from the press, the Old School stalwart, George Junkin, served notice that he would prosecute its author for teaching doctrines contrary to the Westminster Confession of Faith. Accordingly, action was instituted against Barnes in the Second Presbytery of Philadelphia on March 23, 1835. The charges were based upon ideas presented in *Notes*. Among other things, Barnes was accused of denying that God entered into a covenant with Adam, constituting him the federal head and representative of his posterity; that the first sin of Adam is imputed to his descendants; and that men are liable to punishment on account of the sin of Adam.[72] After considerable delay, the trial was held and Barnes was overwhelmingly acquitted. Junkin took an appeal to the Synod of Philadelphia. The Synod found Barnes guilty under the doctrinal standards of the Presbyterian Church. He was forthwith suspended from all ministerial functions "until he shall retract the errors hereby condemned, and give satisfactory evidence of repentance." [73]

[70] *Ibid.*, p. 113.　　　　　　　　[71] *Ibid.*, p. 128.
[72] Cf. Baird, *op. cit.*, pp. 476–477.
[73] A. J. Stanbury, *Trial of the Rev. Albert Barnes, Before the Synod of Philadelphia, in Session at York, October, 1835* (New York, 1836), p. 248. The *Appendix* (pp. 1–107) contains Barnes' defense.

Taking exception to the alleged *ex parte* proceedings of the Synod, Barnes appealed to the General Assembly of 1836.[74] After arguing the merits of the case for many days, the Assembly sustained the appeal by a vote of 134 to 96. His suspension from the ministry, imposed by the Synod of Philadelphia, was reversed by a vote of 145 to 78.[75] Immediately following these actions, the Old School party offered a resolution expressing it to be the judgment of the Assembly that Barnes, in his *Notes*, had published opinions "materially at variance with the Confession of Faith," "especially with regard to original sin, the relation of man to Adam, and justification by faith," but this was rejected by a vote of 122 to 109.[76] Thoroughly chagrined, the Old School men next presented two signed protests against the decisions of the Assembly. These, on recommendation of a special committee, resulted in some remarkable findings on the part of the Assembly. For one thing, it held that Barnes nowhere denied that Adam was the covenant and federal head of his posterity!

The Old School men were not unjustifiably shocked, because any careful study of Barnes' *Notes* will show that he not only rejected in so many words the federal doctrine of imputed sin, but that he also emphatically declared there was no biblical authority for the belief that God entered into a covenant with Adam, constituting him the federal head and representative of his posterity.

The Barnes trial made two things clear: first, that a large segment of Presbyterianism had, with respect to the doctrine of original sin, adopted New Haven views; second, that the New School men held decisive power in the Assembly of 1836. In

[74] *Ibid.*, pp. 108–117.
[75] *Minutes of the General Assembly of the Presbyterian Church in the United States of America* (1835–1840), pp. 268–270.
[76] *Ibid.*, pp. 270–271.

combination with the "moderates," they were invincible. The tragic schismatic action of the Assembly of 1837, however, is an indication that the New School men probably used their power in 1836 too inconsiderately. At any rate, an Old School sympathizer later wrote: "Nothing in the whole history so shocked the conscience of the Church, or so prepared it for the action of 1837, as did this attempt to cover the doctrinal derelictions of Mr. Barnes and the party." [77]

No less unpalatable to the Old School party was the final outcome of the Lyman Beecher case. In the fall of 1832 Beecher gave up his Boston Congregational pastorate to assume the presidency of Lane Theological Seminary, located at Cincinnati, Ohio. Soon after his arrival in that city he offered himself for membership in the Presbytery of Cincinnati. He was admitted, but the Old School moderator, Joshua L. Wilson, protested the action of the Presbytery. Wilson continued his agitation against Beecher until finally, in the fall of 1834, he was permitted to file charges against him in the Presbytery. The charges included allegation of error in respect to native depravity, human ability, and the regenerative work of the Holy Spirit. After a delay until June of 1835, the case was prosecuted, resulting in the acquittal of Beecher. Wilson appealed from this decision to the Synod of Cincinnati; but the Synod's action also disappointed him. The Synod saw "nothing in his [Beecher's] views, as explained by himself, to justify any suspicion of unsoundness in the faith." Yet the Synod expressed the opinion that he had "indulged a disposition to philosophize" with respect to total depravity, human ability, and the work of the Holy Spirit in effectual calling, and therefore it admonished him "to be more guarded in the future." [78] It also "requested" him to publish as soon as possible "a concise

[77] Baird, *op. cit.*, pp. 487–488.
[78] Beecher, *Autobiography*, II, 358–359.

statement" of his views on those theological points which had been involved in his trial.

The outcome of the trial gratified Beecher. In 1836, in compliance with the request of the Synod, he published his doctrinal beliefs in a lengthy treatise called *Views in Theology.*[79] Meanwhile Joshua L. Wilson, Beecher's relentless adversary, appealed from the decision of the Synod to the General Assembly of 1836.[80] When the Assembly met, however, he accepted friendly advice and withdrew his appeal.[81] His action was motivated in part at least by the fact that Albert Barnes, a much more outspoken critic of Old School views, was already scheduled for a second trial in that same session.

In his *Views on Theology* Beecher employed every possible semantic device in order to remain loyal to the New School and yet placate his Old School foes. His involved effort is well illustrated in the following summary of his conception of original sin:

1. Original sin is the effect of Adam's sin upon the constitution of his race, in consequence of his being their federal head and representative by a divine appointment or covenant.

2. It does not consist in the sinfulness of matter, according to the Gnostics, or in the sinfulness of the soul's essence, according to the Manichaeans: but

3. It consists in the perversion of those constitutional powers and susceptibilities, which in Adam before the fall eventuated in actual and perfect obedience, and which in their perverted condition by the fall, eventuate in actual and total depravity.

4. It is in its nature involuntary; and yet, though certain and universal in its influence to pervert the will and affections, does neither force the will, nor by an absolute necessity of nature

---

[79] Cincinnati, 1836.
[80] *Minutes of the General Assembly of the Presbyterian Church in the United States of America* (1835–1840), p. 243.
[81] *Ibid.*, p. 257.

determine it to evil, or impair obligation or excuse actual sin. It descends from Adam, by natural generation, through all the race.[82]

Quite obviously that synthetic statement was a puzzle to Old School critics; for they could find scarcely a word in it which could not be given more than one interpretation. Thus both Old School and New School men might find some comfort in it. This may well have been designed. Beecher once boasted, "You see, in my trial [before the Synod], I had taken the New School doctrines, and expounded and proved them under the Confession, and now, if the trial went on [at the General Assembly of 1836], those doctrines would be sustained by the General Assembly." [83] In any case, the 1836 Assembly would have sustained Beecher, because a majority of the commissioners favored the New School party. Yet even if that Assembly had been composed of an Old School majority, the eclectic form in which Beecher had phrased his opinions would have made the outcome of his trial quite unpredictable. This may partly explain why Joshua Wilson withdrew his appeal.

Nevertheless, a critical analysis of the four-point summary quoted above will show that Beecher belonged essentially to the New School party. For one thing, he did not hold to the doctrine of the imputation of Adam's sin, which was a basic element in Old School thought. In the second place, he did not predicate a sinful and corrupt nature in mankind in consequence of the fall (another Old School tenet), even though original sin was said to descend through the race by natural generation. Thus, for him original sin consisted essentially only in hereditarily perverted powers which, with the dawn of moral agency, would serve to occasion voluntary sinful action.

[82] *Views in Theology*, p. 193.
[83] Beecher, *Autobiography*, II, 360.

IV

During this period of turmoil, Gardner Spring, the Old School minister of Brick Presbyterian Church in New York, joined in the attack upon the New School version of original sin. Recognizing its chief theological exponent to be Nathaniel Taylor, Spring assailed the New Haven "error" in an unusually scathing tract.[84] When Taylor and his allies made their "first assault" on native depravity, said Spring, they proceeded in a "covered way." But in more recent times, he continued, they had come out into the open and asserted boldly that men "come into existence in the same state in which Adam was before his fall, and in which the holy child Jesus was when he was born in the manger."[85]

Spring devoted practically his entire ninety-three page "dissertation" to a defense of the doctrine "that INFANTS ARE SINNERS."[86] He scorned the idea that infants are merely defective in holiness. That would be tantamount to viewing the infant mind as a "moral vacuum." "It is as essential to the nature of mind to be positively holy, or positively sinful, as it is to the nature of a line or rod, to be positively straight, or positively crooked. A being invested with the faculties of perception, reason, and conscience, is under law; and he must either positively fulfill or positively violate it. There is no such thing as the failure to fulfill, without positive violation. . . . Sin would be a very harmless thing if it consisted in the mere defect of holiness."[87] Pointing out that all sin involves voluntary exercise or action, he declared: "When we say that men are sinners, we

---

[84] *Dissertation on Native Depravity* (New York, 1833). Along with the New Haven men, Spring criticized Moses Stuart of Andover Theological Seminary (cf. *ibid.*, pp. 20, 35n., 38n., 75–76).

[85] *Ibid.*, pp. 3–5. Spring was here echoing Bennet Tyler's charge against the New Haven theologians.

[86] *Ibid.*, p. 6. [87] *Ibid.*, p. 7.

mean to say, that they are doers and perpetrators of this foul deed." [88] He further observed that the age of the sinner does not alter the essential nature of sin; that what would constitute a person a sinner at sixty would also constitute him a sinner at birth.[89]

How early do children begin to sin? According to Spring, the child is a sinner "from the moment he becomes a child of Adam." That is to say, infants are sinners from the very instant of their creation. "If infants belong to the *children of men;* if they have a *heart* and soul; then from the moment they are human and descendants of Adam, they are sinners." [90] Infants are understood to be sinners at birth, not merely in the sense that they are born with a corrupt nature, but in the sense that they are actual sinners. "There is not a single principle in this discussion," said Spring, "but is intended to recognize the fact, that infants make themselves sinners, as really, as adults." [91] Furthermore, he insisted that "Sin in an infant is as *really* ill-deserving, as it is in an adult." [92]

Smarting under Spring's denunciation of the New Haven doctrine of native depravity, Taylor replied promptly in a caustic article, published in the *Christian Spectator*.[93] He bluntly accused his adversary of propounding "an entirely novel and peculiar dogma" as the only biblical doctrine of native depravity, and then using it to "unchurch the whole orthodox community." [94] Noting that Spring charged "his New Haven brethren" with advancing "novel speculations" on the subject of native depravity, he retorted, "What 'novel speculations'?" Do we speculate as to the nature of sin? But New Haven men "fully agree with Dr. Spring" that sin consists in

[88] *Ibid.,* p. 9.   [89] *Ibid.,* p. 10.
[90] *Ibid.,* p. 23. Cf. pp. 10, 20.   [91] *Ibid.,* p. 75.   [92] *Ibid.,* p. 67.
[93] "Spring on Native Depravity," *The Quarterly Christian Spectator,* V (June, 1833), 314–332.
[94] *Ibid.,* p. 315.

the known transgression of law.[95] "Is it then, that we do *not* affirm, that infants commit known *actual* sin at the very instant of their creation? But no theologian in the land, old school or new school, has ever affirmed this, except Dr. Spring of New York." [96]

Even here, however, Taylor thought the difference had been exaggerated. "Dr. S. maintains, that mankind sin at *the instant* of their creation, while we [New Haven men] maintain that they sin as soon as they *can*. Such is the length and breadth of the difference between Dr. Spring and those whom he denies christian fellowship." [97] "It is possible indeed," said Taylor, "that a new sect of *Purists* may arise among us, who under the pretense of superior illumination on this subject, shall invest this petty speculation with the dignity of a fundamental truth. But until this, or something like this, shall occur, Dr. Spring, so far as New England is concerned, must appropriate to himself the undivided honors of this spirit of exclusion." [98]

At the root of Taylor's pungent rejoinder lay the intense feeling that he had been harshly treated, not merely by Spring but by many other critics in the course of the bitter controversies in which he had been involved. "We are the very object of assault," he exclaimed. "Our voice of remonstrance, therefore, will be likely lost on those who assail us. Some we know, would propose to us to retire from the discussion. This, we think, is not our duty." [99] Taylor's nerves were doubtless wearing thin. And no wonder, for the conservative Calvinists had assailed his views unceasingly for many years. But although his orthodoxy was "loudly and extensively impeached," his sense of duty would not allow him to retire from the discussion.

[95] *Ibid.*, p. 320. [96] *Loc. cit.* [97] *Loc. cit.*
[98] *Ibid.*, p. 321. [99] *Ibid.*, p. 331.

CHAPTER SEVEN

THE "CONDITION
OF UNNATURE":
HORACE BUSHNELL

I

AT the height of Nathaniel Taylor's controversy with the conservative Calvinists, a young man of great promise entered Yale Divinity School: Horace Bushnell (1802–1876). Following his graduation from Yale College in 1827, he had tried his hand successively at school teaching and journalism. Since neither of those activities proved sufficiently satisfying, he had returned to Yale in 1829 to study law. Along with this study he served as tutor in Yale College. He had passed his final examinations and was about ready to embark upon a legal career when his plans were suddenly altered. During the winter of 1831 Yale was the scene of a powerful religious revival. At first Bushnell was unmoved by it. Eventually, however, in spite of "arrant doubts," he underwent a quiet spiritual awakening which issued in a decision to enter the Christian ministry. Abandoning his plans for the bar, he began his ministerial preparation in the fall of 1831.

Bushnell relished the spirit of free inquiry that prevailed in Yale Divinity School, but the most popular teacher on the faculty, Nathaniel Taylor, made little appeal to him. His daughter remarked after his death that "his rebellious intellect soon asserted its independence of methods of thought which appeared to him mechanical, and this fact made him an inconvenient member of so small a school." [1] Apparently he had already imbibed enough of the romantic spirit, as encountered in Coleridge's *Aids to Reflection,* not to enjoy Taylor's theological dialectics. Probably the gospel already appeared to be what he later termed "a gift to the imagination," and therefore he was beginning to rely more upon religious intuition than upon the conventional modes of theological inquiry.[2]

In May of 1833 Bushnell became the pastor of North Church in Hartford, Connecticut, remaining there until 1859, when failing health forced his retirement. When he assumed the leadership of this church he found it torn from within by the same party spirit which was then disturbing many other Congregational churches in Connecticut. In his illuminating twentieth anniversary discourse of 1853 he described his initial delicate position as being that of one who was "daintily inserted between an acid and an alkali," and having as his task "both to keep them apart and save himself from being bitten of one, or devoured by the other." [3] Conservative and liberal Edwardeans were about equally strong, and their relations were strained. Neither party was as interested in what Bushnell was trying to accomplish in his preaching as in which side he would take. He surprised and somewhat bewildered them by actually preaching "both sides." Why both sides? Certainly it was not because he preferred a false peace in his flock; nor was it because he wished to conceal his convictions. As he explained twenty years later, Bushnell preached both sides because he "was just then passing into the vein of comprehensive-

[1] Mary B. Cheney, *Life and Letters of Horace Bushnell* (New York, 1880), p. 62.
[2] Cf. Theodore Munger, *Horace Bushnell: Preacher and Theologian* (Boston, 1899), pp. 28–29, 40–44.
[3] *A Commemorative Discourse, Delivered in the North Church, of Hartford, May 22, 1853* (Hartford, 1853), p. 8.

ness, questioning whether all parties were not in reality stand-
ing for some one side or article of the truth." [4] In the course of
time he became firmly attached to what he called the "comprehensive method" of settling theological differences. In the
year 1848 he published a penetrating essay in which he interpreted and defended this method.[5]

In the comprehensive school [of thought] it will be a first conviction, that all serious, earnest men have something in their
view which makes it truth to them; therefore that all serious,
earnest men, however repugnant in their words, have yet some
radical agreement, and if the place can be found, will somewhere reveal their brotherhood. Therefore they are not only to
tolerate, but to love and respect each other. Nay, they are each
to ask, what has the other, which is necessary to its own com-
pleteness in the truth? [6]

Hence, as Bushnell observed in his anniversary sermon, the
effect of his ministry "never was to overthrow one school and
set up the other"; rather, "it was to comprehend, if possible, the
truth contended for in both." [7]

Bushnell believed that the "comprehensive method" could
be the means of transcending religious sectarianism. He did
not regard the rise of different denominations as necessarily
an evil; indeed, he maintained that each had stood for a truth
which otherwise might not have gained recognition. Still, he
viewed the perpetuation of separate denominations as evidence
that Christianity was still in "a crude state." When, therefore,
the comprehensive method is fully applied to the doctrines and
polities of the rival bodies, "the sects will disappear and die." [8]

[4] *Ibid.*, p. 13. Taylor's intense partisanship may explain in part why
Bushnell was not more closely drawn to him.
[5] "Christian Comprehensiveness," *The New Englander*, VI (January,
1848), 81–111.
[6] *Ibid.*, p. 87.   [7] *A Commemorative Discourse*, p. 14.
[8] "Christian Comprehensiveness," *op. cit.*, pp. 81, 110.

But America was not yet ready for Bushnell's theological catholicity. He might well enough say, for example, "Unite the Arminian and the Calvinist . . . and we have the Christian truth," but the stout partisans of his generation were in no mood to agree with him. Thus paradoxically he who advocated the comprehensive method in achieving Christian fellowship was destined to be still another center of theological conflict within his communion. Bushnell's thought involved him in conflict at several points, notably with regard to the Person of Christ and the Atonement, but we are here concerned only with his conception of original sin.

II

When Bushnell began his ministry at North Church, the question of native depravity had already been continuously debated within Congregational circles for some fifteen years. Doubtless he had no desire to see this question further argued. Yet one of his early concerns drew him into this very question. The question emerged over the issue of revivalism. Ever since the Great Awakening revivalism had been the chief method of Christian evangelism in American Protestantism. At the outset of his ministry he found the churches deeply attached to what he called the "machinery system of revivals." In his *Commemorative Discourse* he gave a vivid description of the situation as it existed in the early 1830's.

Things had come to such a pitch in the churches by the tensity of the revival system, that the permanent was sacrificed to the casual, the ordinary swallowed up and lost in the extraordinary, and Christian piety itself reduced to a kind of campaigning or stage-effect exercise. The spirit of the pastor was broken, and his powers crippled by a lack of expectation; for it was becoming a fixed impression that effect is to be looked for only under instrumentalities that are extraordinary. He was coming to be scarcely more than a church clock for beating time and marking the years, while the effective ministry of the word was to be dispensed by a class of professed revivalists.[9]

From the first Bushnell frankly criticized the revival system to his congregation; but evidently his views were not shared, because he later observed that the result "was painful for a time." In the year 1838 he laid his convictions before the church at large in a searching article, published in *The Quarterly Christian Spectator*.[10] His aim, he said, was "to establish a higher and more solid confidence in revivals, and, at the same time, to secure to the cause of evangelical religion a more natural . . . as well as a more constant movement."[11] It is not true, as some have supposed, that Bushnell intended to abolish revivals altogether. Since he believed God to have "ordained fluctuations and changing types of spiritual exercise," he held that revivals could play a constructive role in the "spiritual economy" of the church.[12] Nevertheless, he viewed the existing revivalist system as extraordinarily debilitating to the church. This was the result, he thought, of mistaken notions concerning revivals. For, in the first place, it was commonly assumed that the church must be in a constant tense state of revival; second, that nothing of spiritual significance could be accomplished unless there was an "artificial firework," a "combined jump and stir"; third, that the chief thing was to convert people, not to nourish them in the Christian life; fourth, that the main business at the close of a revival was to prepare for still another revival. Because of these distorted notions, Bushnell considered revivalism mostly a liability to the church of his time.

[9] *A Commemorative Discourse*, pp. 19–20.
[10] "Spiritual Economy of Revivals of Religion," *The Quarterly Christian Spectator*, X (No. 1, 1838), 131–148.
[11] *Ibid.*, p. 132.   [12] *Ibid.*, pp. 137–139.

Reflecting on this situation, he published a remarkable essay in *The New Englander* in the year 1844: "The Kingdom of Heaven as a Grain of Mustard Seed." [13] The most prophetic section of this essay is that in which he proposed a constructive alternative to a spiritually sterile revivalism. The essence of it is as follows:

We hold that children are, in a sense, included in the faith of their parents, partakers with them in their covenant, and brought into a peculiar relation to God, in virtue of it. On this ground, they receive a common seal of faith with them, in their baptism; and God on his part, contemplates, in the rite, the fact that they are to grow up as Christians, or spiritually renewed persons. As to the precise time or manner in which they are to receive the germ of holy principle, nothing is affirmed. Only it is understood, that God includes their infant age in the womb of parental culture, and pledges himself to them and their parents, in such a way, as to offer the presumption, that they may grow up in love with all goodness, and remember no definite time when they became subjects of Christian principle. Christian education is then to conform to this view, and nothing is to be called Christian education which does not.[14]

This prophetic passage contains three ideas which deserve special attention: (1) that the children of the Christian family participate in the faith of their parents under the household covenant; (2) that infant baptism is the seal of the common faith of parent and child; and (3) that children of the covenant may grow up as spiritually renewed persons.

In proposing the household covenant as the basis for Christian nurture, Bushnell was reminding New Englanders of one of their original Puritan principles. According to the faith of the Founding Fathers, the infant offspring of believers were, in consequence of the divinely established covenant, eligible for baptism, which was regarded as "the seal of the righteous-

[13] *The New Englander,* II (October, 1844), 600–619.
[14] *Ibid.,* p. 610.

ness of faith." Though these children were required later to "own the covenant" and manifest Christian commitment as a condition of being admitted to full membership in the church and to the Lord's Supper, the supposition was that in some essential sense they actually participated in the household faith from the beginning and should "grow up in the Lord." As one of the early ministers, Thomas Shepard, put it, infants of believers "may be in God's account professors of ye Faith parentally, as well as personally." [15]

But this covenant scheme of Christian nurture had come to have very little weight with Edwardean revivalists. Indeed, they were skeptical of its value. It was in this mood that Bushnell's local ministerial Association—Hartford Central Association—requested him to give a further account of the ideas which he had advanced in the 1844 essay. Therefore Bushnell speedily wrote and delivered to his congregation two discourses on Christian nurture, and afterwards laid the substance of his doctrine before the Association. In the ensuing discussion no serious objection was raised to his main thesis, although a few minor verbal emendations were proposed. In the end a "venerable father" offered a motion that the author be requested to publish the discourses, and the motion carried without opposition. So far all went well.

Bushnell then got busy preparing the discourses for the press. In the meantime a member of the Publication Committee of the Massachusetts Sabbath School Society asked to be allowed to submit the manuscript to that Society. Although in some doubt, Bushnell finally gave his consent. The Society, after considering the manuscript for some six months, had it published in a small book of seventy-two pages.[16] But not long

[15] Quoted in Perry Miller, *Orthodoxy in Massachusetts,* 1630–1650 (Cambridge, 1933), p. 201.
[16] *Discourses on Christian Nurture* (Boston, 1847).

after the book came from the press, "panic mongers," as Bushnell styled them, caused the Society to suspend its publication. Regarding this as a spineless action, the author assailed the Society in a caustic pamphlet, in which he argued strenuously for the truth contained in the discourses.[17] He not only answered the objections which his critics had raised, but he cited the views of recognized theologians, both ancient and modern, to show that his position, far from being heretical, actually enjoyed a long and honorable heritage. In particular he stressed the fact that the Fathers of New England Puritanism had been solidly on his side.

Refusing to be silenced by the "censors of orthodoxy," Bushnell took immediate steps to give his discourses "their liberty." Combining with them the *Argument,* an essay each from *The Quarterly Christian Spectator* (1838) and *The New Englander* (1844), and two unpublished sermons, he issued the whole in a work entitled *Views of Christian Nurture, and of Subjects Adjacent Thereto.*[18] Stressing the vital importance of the question at issue, he said, in the Preface, "Let us handle it earnestly, neither fearing to make the decision, nor making it hastily." He added, and truly, that the question involved "all the most abstruse points in theology."

III

Now one of the most basic theological questions raised in Bushnell's theory of Christian nurture was that of native de-

[17] *An Argument for "Discourses on Christian Nurture," Addressed to the Publishing Committee of the Massachusetts Sabbath School Society* (Hartford, 1847).

[18] *Views of Christian Nurture, and of Subjects Adjacent Thereto* (Hartford, 1847). In 1861 Bushnell published a revised and enlarged edition of this work under the short title, *Christian Nurture,* and in this form it is generally known today.

pravity. At first he seemed inclined to skirt this question. In his 1844 essay he had said, "Nor is our view any infringement upon the doctrine of depravity, in whatsoever manner it may be held. It only declares that depravity is best rectified when it is weakest, and before it is stiffened into habit." [19] In his *Discourses* of 1847 he referred to native depravity briefly, but again he tended to view it as only a minor theological point. Still, he presupposed it as a fact. "Assuming the corruption of human nature," said he, "when should we think it wisest to undertake or expect a remedy? When evil is young and pliant to good, or when it is confirmed by years of sinful habit?" [20]

Whether this somewhat casual attitude was prompted by Bushnell's belief that the issue of original sin was relatively remote from the main point that he was then concerned to make, or whether it grew out of his desire to avoid a theme which had already been fervently debated for many years, is a matter of conjecture. Both reasons may have influenced his attitude. In any case, his critics soon made it entirely clear that his doctrine of Christian nurture had to take seriously the question of original sin. One of those who brought out this fact was the irrepressible Bennet Tyler. Ever since Bushnell's settlement at Hartford, Tyler had been a thorn in his side, and the moment the *Discourses* of 1847 came from the press, Tyler assailed them in a severely critical open *Letter.*[21] What was it that made the *Discourses* so unpalatable to Tyler? Beyond all else it was his belief that they did not explicitly teach the doctrine of native depravity. They did not show that the child's

[19] "The Kingdom of Heaven as a Grain of Mustard Seed," *The New Englander,* II, 611.

[20] *Discourses on Christian Nurture,* p. 19.

[21] *A Letter to Dr. Bushnell* (East Windsor Hill, June 7, 1847). It was mainly this *Letter* that had prompted the Publication Committee of the Sabbath School Society to cease printing the *Discourses* (*An Argument,* pp. 27–28).

corrupt heart had to be changed into a "new heart" as a condition of spiritual growth. "It is a fundamental principle of the Christian scheme, that every child born into the world, is by nature totally depraved, and must be born again in order to become a child of God, and an heir of heaven." [22]

Tyler urged that Bushnell's theory of the organic connection of parent and child involved pernicious implications. For one thing, it implied that grace is "hereditary," and consequently that "children born of parents already pious, must be Christians by nature"; and, second, it suggested that the child is already regenerate at baptism.[23] Consequently, morally corrupt children will be falsely led to regard themselves as needing no conversion. But in truth it is the duty of the Christian parent to "lead his child, as soon as possible, to a knowledge of . . . the wickedness of his heart, and the necessity of a new heart to prepare him for heaven." [24]

The formidable controversialist, Charles Hodge, Professor of Theology in Princeton Theological Seminary, also assailed the *Discourses*.[25] He warmly applauded Bushnell for advocating the doctrine that the children of the covenant are uniquely heirs of divine grace and should be expected to "grow up the children of God." [26] In fact, he added, parental nurture "is the great means for the salvation of the children of the church." [27] He also commended Bushnell for pointing out that the modern church had come to rely too exclusively upon revivals to do the whole work of Christian evangelism.[28]

On the other hand, Hodge found Bushnell's doctrine seriously defective in two respects. In the first place, it confined

---

[22] *A Letter to Dr. Bushnell*, p. 3.　　　　[23] *Ibid.*, pp. 9–12.
[24] *Ibid.*, p. 16.
[25] "Bushnell on Christian Nurture," *The Biblical Repertory and Princeton Review*, XIX (October, 1847), 502–539.
[26] *Ibid.*, pp. 504–509.　　　　[27] *Ibid.*, p. 509.
[28] *Ibid.*, pp. 519–520.

the divine action to the natural law; it recognized God as a power within nature, but not as a power over nature. "There is nothing supernatural in this process, nothing out of analogy with nature, nothing which transcends the ordinary efficiency of natural causes as the vehicles of divine power." [29] In the second place, Bushnell based his doctrine of Christian nurture upon a false assumption with regard to man's native state. "It assumes that men are not by nature the children of wrath, that they are not involved in spiritual death." [30] According to Hodge, the second weakness was father to the first. It was because Bushnell had not taken natural depravity seriously that he had developed "a naturalistic doctrine of conversion." [31]

A prominent theologian in the German Reformed Church, John W. Nevin, was requested by Bushnell to comment on the *Discourses*. Nevin complied with the request and devoted a series of four articles to an analysis of Bushnell's doctrine of Christian nurture.[32] He commended Bushnell for his penetrating criticism of the "fanatical individualism" which characterized current evangelical religion. "The whole constitution of the world contradicts the unit or atom theory of religion." [33] On the other hand, he loudly protested that Bushnell's treatise was "seriously defective" in that "it bases its theory of educational piety on the constitution of nature" rather than upon the constitution of grace. "In other words, the argument is rationalistic." This appeared "in the first place, in the view which the tract [*Discourses*] takes of original sin or natural depravity. . . . Dr. Bushnell assents fully to the doctrine of our general natural depravity; but it is certainly made to assume, under his hands, a form that robs it at least to a great extent of its proper

[29] *Ibid.*, p. 530. [30] *Ibid.*, p. 536. [31] *Ibid.*, p. 537.
[32] "Educational Religion," *The Weekly Messenger of the German Reformed Church*, XII (New Series: June 23–July 14, 1847).
[33] *The Weekly Messenger*, June 30, 1847, p. 2.

force. If I have properly apprehended his meaning, he makes it to be a sort of necessary accident merely to our moral probation." [34]

Here, then, we find three outstanding theologians from three different denominations making substantially the same criticism: Bushnell's doctrine of Christian nurture is too naturalistic, and this is the result of his having given up or at least attenuated the doctrine of total depravity. All three of these critics were theological conservatives. Liberal Edwardeans did not, as a rule, find particular objection to Bushnell's doctrine of original human nature. This suggests that Bushnell agreed more nearly with the New Haven liberals on the question of original sin than he did with the rigid Edwardeans. In his anniversary discourse of 1853, Bushnell explained in what respect he preached "both sides" on the subject of native depravity. "I preached inherited, constitutional, physiological depravity; and side by side with this, the responsibility of men only for what is of themselves and a right or wrong use of their possibilities." [35]

The first part of that statement would seem to ally Bushnell with the rigid Edwardeans, but the latter part implies that he stood with the New Haven liberals. Significantly, Bushnell confessed that it was the conservatives who gave him trouble. "I had no difficulty," he reported, "except upon the old school side." [36] Despite his efforts to meet their objections, some of them, prompted by "instigators of suspicion without," actually withdrew from his church. On the other hand, the New Haven liberals remained in his church, and, on his own word, caused him no trouble. Thus, Bushnell seemed to stand theologically

[34] *The Weekly Messenger,* July 7, 1847, p. 2.
[35] *A Commemorative Discourse,* p. 16.
[36] *Ibid.,* p. 18.

nearer to them than he did to their opponents. This impression is deepened when one examines his *Argument* for the *Discourses*. In that tract he asserted that his view of Christian nurture "may be easily set in connexion with" any of the existing theories of original sin. Nevertheless, he acknowledged that his idea would doubtless "fit more awkwardly in some than in others." [37] The implication of that remark is made perfectly clear in a subsequent passage in which he took special note of the fact that all of his critics had condemned his notion of native depravity. All of his opponents, he observed, based their arguments "on a certain theory of depravity and regeneration that was debated, to the complete satisfaction of the public, some fifteen years ago, and, as I believe, forever exploded." [38] That theory, he added, proceeded on the assumption that the human race must instinctively hate, and only hate, God "until after a certain divine stroke or *ictus* reverses the instinct." He would not argue "this worn out question," because he considered it "as distant from me as the supremacy of the Pope, and shortly to be as distant from the world."

Bushnell was undoubtedly describing the view that Tyler and other conservative Edwardeans defended when they challenged the New Haven doctrine of original sin. He was so firmly convinced that their notion had been "forever exploded" that he refused to concern himself with it. Here then we have explicit testimony that Bushnell did not really agree with the rigid Edwardeans on the question of original sin.

IV

What, then, was Bushnell's doctrine of the fall and of original sin? In order to give an answer to that question we must

[37] *An Argument*, p. 23. [38] *Ibid.*, p. 29.

consider not merely his writings on the doctrine of Christian nurture, but also his sermons, and especially his profound treatise, *Nature and the Supernatural.*

Unlike his orthodox contemporaries, Bushnell did not resort to the Scriptures in his argument for the fall and original sin. He deliberately refrained from doing so, not because he himself doubted the authenticity of the Scriptures, but because he desired to establish the fact of the fall and original sin upon grounds that would command attention from those rationalistic theologians, such as Theodore Parker, who denied the historicity of much of the Bible.[39]

We may begin with the question of the fall. Instead of resorting to the Genesis account of the origin of man, Bushnell simply assumed as a fact that Adam and his posterity "began to be." Although supposing Adam to have been created in a state of maturity and with a nature keyed to harmonious response to God, Bushnell held that he and his offspring alike were initially involved in "a condition privative." By that term he signified "a moral state that is only inchoate, or incomplete, lacking something not yet reached, which is necessary to the probable rejection of evil."[40] Adam's privative condition was manifest in three respects. For one thing, he was deficient in empirical knowledge. From the first he possessed as the law of his being certain "necessary ideas" of the true and the good, but precisely what those ideas meant in terms of experiential truth he did not know. The fact that he started life "in the full maturity of his person" did not change this limitation.[41] In the next place, Adam's moral powers were lacking in that kind of "empirical training, or course of government" which would be necessary in order "to get them established in the law of

---

[39] Cf. *Nature and the Supernatural* (3rd edition: New York, 1858), p. 110.
[40] *Ibid.,* p. 109. [41] *Ibid.,* pp. 110–117.

duty." [42] Finally, Adam was deficient in the sort of moral equipment that would result from exposure to and conflict with "bad
spirits" or "malign powers." Since he had had no experience
in detecting and resisting these malign powers, he was necessarily more or less vulnerable to their blandishments.[43] Because
of these limitations, which are "necessary incidents in the begun existence and trial of powers," Bushnell regarded the fall
of Adam and of all mankind as a certainty. Since God created
a realm of powers, "a prior and eternal certainty" confronted
him "of their outbreak in evil." [44] "These conditions privative
are in the nature of perils," Bushnell wrote, "and while they
excuse nothing, for the law of duty is always plain, they are
yet drawn so close to the soul and open their gulfs, on either
hand, so deep, that our expectation of the fall is really as press-
ing as if it were determined by some law that annihilates
liberty. Liberty we know is not annihilated. And yet we say,
looking on the state of man made perilous, in this manner, by
liberty, that we can not expect him to stand." [45]

In saying that the privative condition of the human creature
rendered his lapse a certainty, Bushnell was aware that he exposed his theory to the charge that it destroyed the basis of
sin and guilt. This would be true, he agreed, if the fall were a
physical necessity; but he contended that no such necessity
was involved. The certainty of the fall resulted, not from any
positive cause or ground, but only from that deficiency which
is involved in the "condition privative." Thus, one "is not
obliged to choose wrong, more than a child is obliged to

[42] *Ibid.*, p. 117.
[43] *Ibid.*, pp. 123–127. Bushnell did not believe in Satan, or the Devil,
considered as an individual being, but only in a group of bad spirits and
powers of which Satan was symbolic (*ibid.*, pp. 134–135).
[44] *Ibid.*, p. 134.
[45] *Ibid.*, p. 128. Cf. p. 107. See also *Discourses on Christian Nurture*, pp.
21–22.

thrust his hand into the blaze of a lamp, the experience of which is unknown." [46] Yet Bushnell was not quite satisfied to let the matter rest there; in fact, he conceded that a deficiency in empirical knowledge would mitigate somewhat the guilt of sin, although it would not relieve the agent of substantial guilt. "The right and only true statement is, that the guilt of sin is not as greatly enhanced as it would be, if all the knowledge needful to the strength of virtue were supplied." [47]

V

Assuming then the certain lapse into sin of all human creatures, what are the consequences of the fall? Before answering that question, it is necessary first to describe briefly Bushnell's conception of the structure of reality. In his *Nature and the Supernatural* he declared that "the one system of God" consisted of two orders or realms of being. The first is the realm of nature, which constitutes, so to speak, the thing-order of reality. It is the sphere of natural law. [48] The second is the realm of the supernatural. The term "supernatural," as used by Bushnell, denoted all "that is either not in the chain of natural cause and effect, or which acts on the chain of cause and effect, in nature, from without the chain." [49] This is the realm of free spirits, and includes God the supreme Spirit.

These two orders of being—the natural and the supernatural—are not disjunct from each other; rather, they complement and constantly interact with each other. Together they constitute one organic whole. [50] Still, they constitute two very distinct orders of existence; neither can be equated with or resolved into the other. They are indeed as uninterchangeable as things and

---

[46] *Nature and the Supernatural*, p. 115.   [47] *Loc. cit.*
[48] *Ibid.*, p. 36–37.   [49] *Ibid.*, p. 37.   [50] *Ibid.*, p. 38.

persons.[51] Furthermore, nature is the secondary realm of being. "Nature, in short, is only stage, field, medium, vehicle, for the universe; that is, for God and his powers. These are the real magnitudes; because they contain, at once, the import and final causes, or last ends, of all created substance." [52]

Bushnell's effort to prove the superior power of persons over nature was prompted by his fear that a naturalistic tendency in religious thought was already threatening to leave God out of the universe altogether, or at least to restrict his actions to the operations of natural law. "Thus far the tendency is visible, on every side, to believe in nature simply, and in Christianity only so far as it conforms to nature and finds its shelter under her laws. And the mind of the christian world is becoming every day, more and more saturated with this propensity to naturalism." [53] To the extent that naturalism prevails, said Bushnell, Christianity will lose its redemptive power over fallen mankind. It was with this danger in mind that, following lines already marked out by Samuel Taylor Coleridge, he declared that powers are supernatural and can therefore apply their wills to nature in either creative or destructive ways. The very idea of human personality, he explained, is that of a being not confined within the chain of natural cause and effect. Man, to be sure, is rooted in nature, and is certainly conditioned by nature. Even so, at the point of self-determination man is essentially sovereign over nature. Being thus a sovereign volitional agent, he is able to act upon the chain of cause and effect in nature from outside the chain and produce results which, by mere nature, could never come to pass. In producing these results, man does not suspend any of nature's laws; he only applies them in new combinations which would otherwise never take place.[54] If man can

[51] *Ibid.*, pp. 84–86.   [52] *Ibid.*, p. 90.   [53] *Ibid.*, p. 21.
[54] *Ibid.*, pp. 43, 51. Cf. Coleridge, "Aids to Reflection," *Works* (edited by W. G. T. Shedd: New York, 1868), I, 263, 272.

thus act supernaturally upon natural events, how much more can God, the supremely supernatural Power. As in the case of human agents, he achieves changes by new combinations of nature's elements and forces, never by the suspension or disruption of any of nature's laws.[55]

In light of this background, let us now note Bushnell's conception of the effects of the fall. Those effects, according to him, are radical and far-reaching. Though human sin does not annul or discontinue any one of the laws of nature, it can, and inevitably does, institute a wrong conjunction of causes which forces nature to act "as it was not made to act." From this false conjunction of causes springs a train of woe which ultimately involves every form of existence. It all begins in a revolting human will. In vivid imagery Bushnell compared the effect of sin in the soul to that of a grain of sand inserted in the eye. Though all the laws remain intact and operative, "the soul has become a weeping organ, not an organ simply of sight." The ferment that is created in the soul by a rebellious will Bushnell elaborated in great detail. For example, the motions of sins discolor the perceptions, excite the passions, warp the conscience, and distort the imagination. "No one that looks in upon the ferment of its [the soul's] morbid, contesting, rasping, restive, uncontrollable action can imagine, for a moment, that he looks upon the sweet, primal order of life and nature. No name sufficiently describes it, unless we coin a name and call it a condition of unnature." [56]

Since soul and body are intimately related, the effects of the disorder of the soul, said Bushnell, cannot be confined to itself. Whatever "unnatures" the soul must also unnature the body. "Nor is any thing better understood than that whatever vice of the mind—wounded pride, unregulated ambition, hatred, covetousness, fear, inordinate care—throws the mind

[55] *Nature and the Supernatural*, p. 59.   [56] *Ibid.*, p. 173.

out of rest, throws the body out of rest also. Thus it is that sin, in all its forms, becomes a power of bodily disturbance, shattering the nerves, inflaming the tissues, distempering the secretions, and brewing a general ferment of disease." [57]

Nor can the effects of sin be shut up within the individual self. This results from the fact that the race is "an organic whole." Therefore when Adam fell, he originated sinful effects that inevitably resulted in disordering the natures of his offspring. This raises at once the question of original sin. Interestingly, Bushnell's thought on this question has received practically no consideration by modern theologians. For example, Theodore Munger, in his study of Bushnell's thought, gave no serious concern to it.[58] Noting the tendency to minimize the idea of original sin, Bushnell wrote: "Under the old doctrines of original sin, federal headship and the like, cast away by many, ridiculed by not a few, there yet lies a great and momentous truth, announced by reason as clearly as by scripture —that in Adam all die, that by one man's disobedience many were made sinners, that death hath passed upon all men for that all have sinned." [59]

What, then, did Bushnell hold to be the "momentous truth" about original sin? This truth did not include the doctrine of imputed sin. "The sin of no person can be transmitted, as a sin, or charged to the account of another." [60] Nevertheless, he firmly contended that there has been "an organic depravation of humanity" in consequence of the fall. Mankind being "an organic whole," the effects of sin are necessarily propagated from generation to generation under the laws of heredity. "It is not even supposable that organic natures, injured and disordered,

[57] *Ibid.*, p. 175.
[58] Cf. Munger, *Horace Bushnell: Preacher and Theologian* (Boston, 1899), pp. 82, 216–224. Munger thought Bushnell went much too far in emphasizing the bondage of the will under sin (*ibid.*, pp. 215, 219).
[59] *Views of Christian Nurture*, p. 192.　　　　　[60] *Loc. cit.*

as we have seen that human bodies are by sin, should propagate their life in a progeny unmarred and perfect. If we speak of sin as action, their children may be innocent, and so far may reveal the loveliness of innocence;—still the crystalline order is broken; the passions, tempers, appetites, are not in the proportions of harmony and reason; the balance of original health is gone by anticipation; and a distempered action is begun, whose affinities sort with evil rather than with good." [61] Moreover, when evil once begins, it "inevitably becomes organic, and constructs a kind of principate or kingdom opposite to God." [62]

Bushnell's theory of hereditary depravity becomes all the more significant in view of the fact that he believed acquired traits could be inherited. According to him, character traits which get deeply ingrained in a culture tend to become an integral element of the human stock and may ultimately be transmitted by natural descent. Evidence of this fact, he thought, might be seen on the animal level. The domesticated dog, said he, was originally not a hunting animal. The hunting trait was at first an "artificial quality," but it eventually became so firmly rooted in the canine nature as to pass by natural descent. The same thing was observable, Bushnell thought, on the human plane. The Jew of biblical times, said he, was not characterized by the miserly and usurious propensity which now distinguishes the Jewish race. What caused the change? It was due, he argued, to the extremely harsh treatment which had been accorded the Jew by Christian governments. The latter confined him to narrow, foul precincts of the city and denied him every possession except money. He was thus edu-

[61] *Nature and the Surpernatural,* pp. 177–178.
[62] *Ibid.,* p. 135. Bushnell here anticipated Walter Rauschenbusch's conception of the "Kingdom of Evil" (*A Theology for the Social Gospel* [New York, 1917], Chapter IX).

cated into a miserly habit, which, after many generations, became a part of his native endowment.[63]

This theory, first advanced in 1847, was no passing fancy with Bushnell, for when he published the definitive edition of his treatise on Christian nurture in the year 1861, he maintained the same doctrine with even greater emphasis.[64] This theory may explain why Bushnell attached so much importance to that period in infancy which he termed "the age of impressions," the age which is prior to language. During this age the child is especially responsive to the forces that play upon him from within the family; indeed, he absorbs all the moods and dispositions of the household as inevitably as a sponge absorbs water. Hence, sinful parents "propagate their own evil in the child, not by design, but under the law of moral infection." [65] Furthermore, the evil which is propagated in the child under the law of moral infection may eventually be propagated in the race under the law of heredity.

Thus far we have been concerned with Bushnell's doctrine of original sin as it related to man. But his doctrine included the idea that sin produces disorder throughout the physical world. This far-reaching impact of sin is a revelation of the amazing power of the deranged human will. "The immense power of the human will over the physical substances of the world and the conjunctions of its causes is seldom adequately conceived. Almost every thing, up to the moon, is capable of being somehow varied or affected by it." [66] Hence, according to Bushnell, all of nature's disharmonies, abortions, and monstrosities have arisen as consequences of the "supernatural" action of individual and collective wills which have come under

[63] *Views of Christian Nurture,* pp. 189–190.

[64] *Christian Nurture* (Centenary edition: New York, 1910), pp. 98–99, 202–207.

[65] *Views of Christian Nurture,* p. 191.

[66] *Nature and the Supernatural,* p. 186.

the power of sin.[67] One might contend that since these natural distortions preceded the advent of man, they could not be the consequence of human sin. Bushnell anticipated this objection, and his answer is novel if not convincing. There are, he said, two kinds of consequences: (1) those that follow upon the sin of man and (2) those that anticipate the sin of man.[68] The second kind of consequence is the result of the action of a sovereign Cosmic Mind that has eternally in view the certain fact of sin. "As certainly as sin is to be encountered in his [God's] plan," contended Bushnell, "its marks and consequences will appear anticipatively, and all the grand arrangements and cycles of time will be somehow preluding its approach, and the dire encounter to be maintained with it." [69]

The foregoing analysis shows, then, that Bushnell viewed the consequences of sin as encompassing the whole of reality. "The whole solidarity of being in the creation, physical and spiritual," he summarized, "is necessarily penetrated by it [sin] and configured to it." [70] Thus it is not surprising that he should call sin "that central fact, about which the whole creation of God and the ordering of his providential and moral government, revolves." [71]

VI

Since Bushnell held that the fall introduced a state of "unnature" throughout all forms of existence, we may ask what it means for man to be in a state of unnature. Quite specifically, did Bushnell hold to the doctrine of total depravity?

Light may be thrown on this question by comparing Bushnell's view with the views of his influential contemporaries. Considering our previous discussion, it is unnecessary to argue

[67] *Ibid.*, pp. 186–188, 190–193. [68] *Ibid.*, pp. 195–196.
[69] *Ibid.*, p. 201.   [70] *Ibid.*, p. 215.   [71] *Ibid.*, p. 214.

further that Nathaniel Taylor believed in total depravity. He said repeatedly that, unless saving grace be interposed, every son of Adam "will sin and only sin" as soon as he can.[72] Bennet Tyler, as already observed, was a relentless champion of total depravity, denying that any descendant of Adam could escape being born in that condition. Directly challenging Bushnell, he wrote: "Every child, whatever be the character of his parents, is born totally depraved, and spiritually dead, and will continue so, till spiritual life be imparted from on high." [73] Furthermore, he insisted that until the heart of the child "has been gained by [sudden] conquest," "we are to expect" that the child "will grow only in rebellion." [74] Thus it is clear that even though Taylor and Tyler represented two different parties in New England Calvinism, they agreed that man comes into the world in a state of total depravity. Only after a certain divine stroke or "ictus" has reversed the bad legacy entailed upon man by the fall can he choose the good.

Bushnell could not support any such notion. "There could not be a worse or more baleful implication given to a child, than that he is to reject God and all holy principle, till he has come to a mature age." [75] He based his doctrine of Christian nurture upon an opposite assumption. "That there is a susceptibility to good, in every mind, fallen though it be, is to me beyond a reasonable question. The soul has that within it, which may be appealed to by what is right and holy." [76] Rea-

---

[72] *Concio ad Clerum*, pp. 13, 23. Cf. his *Essays, Lectures, Etc. upon Select Topics in Revealed Theology*, edited by Noah Porter, *et al.* (New York, 1859), p. 192.

[73] *Letters to the Rev. Horace Bushnell, D. D., Containing Strictures on His Book, entitled "Views of Christian Nurture, and Subjects Adjacent Thereto"* (Hartford, 1848), p. 38.

[74] *Ibid.*, p. 54.   [75] *Discourses on Christian Nurture*, p. 12.

[76] *An Argument*, p. 26. Cf. Bushnell, *Sermons for the New Life* (New York, 1858), p. 63.

soning on this assumption, he declared that there was no reason why the first moral act of the child must be wrong rather than right. According to him, a child born into a Christian family "ought to grow up as a Christian." To be sure, he acknowledged that the child will have to struggle with sinful tendencies from the first, and that, like older Christians, he will always lead a "mixed" life. In other words, the process of Christian growth involves a conflict with good and evil impulses from birth to death. Nevertheless, the good is a positive force from the opening of life. "The good in him [the child] goes into combat with the evil, and holds a qualified sovereignty." [77]

Bushnell's belief in the child's initial capacity for Christian growth led many Edwardeans to accuse him of being Unitarian in his doctrine of human nature. Even some Unitarians considered him to agree substantially with them at this point. But as a matter of fact he did not agree with the Unitarian view of human nature. His conflict with the Unitarian conception is evident in his thought at two points. In the first place, as against the Unitarians, he maintained that Adam's fall necessarily had a disordering effect upon the physical and mental characteristics of his offspring.[78] He even appeared to think at times that the fall involved the loss of the very principle of good. In a letter dated January 23, 1850, he wrote to his intimate Unitarian friend, Cyrus A. Bartol of Boston, as follows:

Your scheme of virtue [as set forth in your sermon on "Human Nature"] . . . I must quarrel with. It does not recognize the great Scripture law, that he who is guilty in one point is guilty of all; that is, that when a creature descends into evil, it is not by casual dip or slip, but that the great *one* principle of good has to go out as a principle. We do not sin by homeopathic doses or quantities; no one sin is done under the principle of

[77] *Discourses on Christian Nurture,* p. 14.
[78] *Christ and His Salvation* (3rd edition: New York, 1866), p. 275. *Nature and the Supernatural,* pp. 224–225.

obedience; the principle itself must go, and that is a fall, a disability, a state of unnature and bondage.[79]

In ignoring Bushnell's emphasis upon the loss of the principle of good in the fall, some have misunderstood his doctrine of original nature. Yet he tried to guard against misunderstanding. In his *Argument* of 1847, for example, he observed that it is one thing to believe the child susceptible to good, and quite another to believe the child morally good on this account. "There is not and really can be no proper goodness in a soul till it practically embraces, as its final end and law, and thus becomes united to *the right,* or what is the same to *God and the principles of God.* Previously to this the power we have to feel the right and be attracted by the good are only the more conclusive proofs of depravity, inasmuch as we are found to reject what we practically approve, and to mortify the noblest wants of our being." [80]

Since Bushnell disagreed with the Unitarian doctrine of original nature, he also disagreed with the Unitarian view of regeneration. For him, Christian regeneration was no mere process of eliciting the good within man. In a penetrating discourse on "Regeneration," he urged that Christianity "is not any doctrine of development, or self-culture; no scheme of ethical practice, or social re-organization; but it is a salvation; a power moving on fallen humanity from above its level, to regenerate and so to save." [81]

For these reasons the orthodox should not have confused Bushnell's doctrine of man with that of Unitarianism. Doubtless this confusion is traceable mainly to certain principles that he advanced or implied in his advocacy of Christian nurture. In his revulsion against a revivalistic theory that generally treated

[79] Cheney, *op. cit.*, p. 231.   [80] *An Argument*, p. 26.
[81] *Sermons for the New Life,* p. 109. Cf. *Nature and the Supernatural,* Chapter VIII.

young children as mere candidates for future conversion, he went so far as to suggest that, under the right sort of antenatal nurture by Christian parents, the infant might even be "regenerated from the womb." [82] He also took the position that by this sort of "propagated piety" Christianity could out-populate the un-Christian stock. [83] This belief rested upon a twofold assumption: (1) that antenatal nurture could predispose the nature of the infant while still within the womb; (2) "that what gets power in any race, by a habit or a process of culture, tends by a fixed law of nature to become a propagated quality, and pass by descent as a property inbred in the stock." [84]

In the view of Edwardeans, those highly unconventional notions smacked of naturalism and romanticism. And, in truth, their apprehensions were not entirely groundless. For Bushnell's idea that a grace-filled family could be the means through which to predispose the foetus to a regenerate state logically implied that the state of "unnature" could be transformed prior to the infant's exercise of moral choice. Even though Bushnell insisted that the transaction was supernaturally wrought, the suspicion persisted that the process was largely biological. Thus the only grace which seemed to be involved was that which could be mediated through the laws of nature. In this respect, as John W. Nevin saw, Bushnell's theory of nurture did bear a certain cast of naturalism. Moreover, Bushnell's faith in the out-populating power of the Christian stock, as a result of Christian nurture, especially during the "age of impressions," bore a romantic tinge. All the more weight was given to romanticism by reason of Bushnell's assumption that qualities acquired by culture could be inbred in the stock and passed by descent to subsequent generations. Although he observed that a depravated quality could be transmitted as well as a good

[82] *Christian Nurture*, p. 232.   [83] *Ibid.*, pp. 195–207.
[84] *Ibid.*, p. 204.

one, this fact did not keep his critics from believing that he had, albeit subtly, espoused a doctrine that softened the effects of the fall.

Yet even when full weight is given to these unrealistic aspects of Bushnell's anthropology, it remains clear that he cannot be aligned with the Unitarians in their doctrine of man. Indeed, he stands much closer to Edwardean Calvinism at this point than to Unitarianism. On the other hand, his view of native depravity cannot be equated with that of either the conservative or the liberal wing of Edwardeanism. Here he is in tension with both Tyler and Taylor, although less so with the latter. In reality, then, his basic principle of "comprehensiveness," to which he was devoted, led him to formulate a position that was uniquely his own.

CHAPTER EIGHT

THE IDEA OF
ORIGINAL SIN OUTMODED:
THE NEW THEOLOGY

WHEN Horace Bushnell left the earthly scene (1876), the Edwardean version of the fall and original sin was already being confronted with its greatest challenge: the Darwinian theory of evolution. While he himself held a developmental view of the world, he was inhospitable to Darwinism. Should the Darwinian theory of the mutability of the species ever be conclusively proved, he observed in the year 1868, "we may well enough agree to live without religion." [1]

But although Bushnell could not accept the theory of organic evolution, his theological successors found a way to do so and still maintain their religious faith. They therefore became leaders in a movement of religious thought which they sometimes styled "progressive orthodoxy," but which they more often called "the new theology." All the leading advocates of the new theology emerged from within the Edwardean school of Calvinism. Hence, when they compared the new theology with the old, they usually identified the old theology with the Calvinistic tradition as interpreted by the later Edwardeans. By the time the new theology arose, Edwardean Calvinism was generally known as "The New England Theology."

[1] "Science and Religion," *Putnam's Magazine*, I (New Series: March, 1868), 271.

The creators of the new theology, it is important to note, were by no means religious radicals. They were avowed evangelical Protestants and believed they maintained essential continuity with historic Christianity. "The New Theology does not part with the historic faith of the church," said one of the earlier members of this school of thought, "but rather seeks to put itself in its line while recognizing a process of development." [2] This attitude was shared by all the participants in the new theological movement. They had no intention of breaking with the old faith; they only insisted upon reinterpreting it in the light of modern thought. As a group they took seriously (though not uncritically) the Darwinian theory of evolution, and they endeavored to harmonize their theological conceptions with that theory as fully as possible consistent with maintaining the essential elements of the Christian faith. They did not sanction Darwin's theory of the survival of the fittest, nor did they accept his doctrine of evolution save on theistic premises. But they saw in the doctrine of evolution, as thus qualified, an important truth which had to be taken into account by modern theology. One result of their acceptance of the idea of evolution was belief in a progressive philosophy of history. Intellectual and moral progress became a basic presupposition of their social and religious thought. Moreover, they labored earnestly to achieve progress in all aspects of life. As one of their sympathizers, William Jewett Tucker, put it, "the desire and struggle for progress became the unifying purpose of the generation." [3] Since they regarded religious progress as a fact, the new theologians urged the necessity of continually revising theological thought so as to keep it relevant to changing spiritual needs. A dynamic society demanded a dy-

[2] Theodore T. Munger, "The New Theology," *The Freedom of Faith* (Boston, 1883), p. 8.
[3] *My Generation: An Autobiographical Interpretation* (Boston, 1919), p. 2.

namic theology. An unfolding revelation required a progressive reconstruction of theological categories.

In accepting the doctrine of evolution, the new theology necessarily became involved in revising the traditional view of the fall and original sin. The points of conflict were sharp and not easily reconciled. On the whole, the new theology made a sincere effort to safeguard the essential truth contained in the traditional forms of thought. The conclusions reached did not satisfy their contemporary opponents, nor do they satisfy the realistic theologians of the present day. It is important, nevertheless, to understand how the new theology attempted to deal with the questions which they confronted. Our survey will seek to indicate the solutions that were offered by considering briefly the anthropological views of nine representatives of the new theology. Five of these were parish clergymen and the other four were teachers of theology in theological seminaries.

I

We may begin with Theodore Thornton Munger (1830–1910), a gifted minister-theologian who from 1885 to 1901 brought national renown to the pulpit of the United Church (Congregational) in New Haven, Connecticut. For many years he served as a valued Fellow of the Corporation of Yale University. A bronze tablet in Yale's Memorial Hall hails him as the "Prophet of the Freedom of Faith." [4]

Although Munger had been thoroughly instructed in the New Haven version of Calvinism by Nathaniel W. Taylor, he finally revolted against it. Under the stimulus of the thought of Frederick W. Robertson, Frederick D. Maurice, and Horace

[4] For a general account of his life and thought, see Benjamin W. Bacon, *Theodore Thornton Munger: New England Minister* (New Haven, 1910).

Bushnell, he slowly achieved a new perspective which definitely identified him with the new theology. His two best works, *The Freedom of Faith* (1883) and *The Appeal to Life* (1887), exercised great influence among more reflective Christians. Since they consist mostly of sermons, they are by no means systematic treatises. Nevertheless, they contain several excellent essays which clearly demonstrate his advocacy of the new theology.[5]

Munger prefaced *The Freedom of Faith* with an especially illuminating essay entitled "The New Theology," that won instant recognition. Like much of the new theology of this period, it is tantalizingly vague at basic points; nevertheless, it enunciated certain central principles to which the new theology was committed. Primarily, the new theology attached high value to reason and would believe in revelation only in so far as reason was not contradicted; it accepted evolution as the method of creation; it regarded the Scriptures as presenting an unfolding revelation and as reflecting moral evolution; and it emphasized the social solidarity of the human race.[6]

Unlike the older Edwardean Calvinists, Munger had very little to say with regard to man's original or native state. To the extent that he did express himself, he revealed a definite divergence from traditional conceptions. Since he assumed man to have emerged from an animal ancestry, he gave no attention to the idea of original righteousness. He viewed primitive existence as a mixture of brute and human tendencies, and as having the capacity either to rise or to fall.[7] The failure to answer the call of the higher life might, according to Munger, repre-

[5] See especially "The New Theology," and "On the Reception of New Truth," in *The Freedom of Faith* (6th edition: Boston, 1883), pp. 3–69; "Evolution and the Faith," and "Man the Final Form of Creation," in *The Appeal to Life* (Boston, 1887), pp. 209–243, 283–306.
[6] *The Freedom of Faith,* pp. 11–12, 19, 22–23, 26–27.
[7] *The Appeal to Life,* p. 301.

sent the fall. Presumably there would be many such falls in the course of the moral ascent of mankind. Munger said the new theology was "not disposed wholly to part company with the old in respect to the 'fall of Adam,'" although it regarded the older notions as "crude and harsh." [8] On the other hand, he thought the essential truth of the old view could be preserved in the modern conception of physical heredity.

In speaking of regeneration, Munger gave a clue to his view of man's native state. "We must be born again," he wrote, "not merely because we are wicked, not because of a lapse, but because we are flesh, and need to be carried forward and lifted up into the realm of the spirit." [9] There is little evidence to show that Munger held a serious view of the human predicament. He was much more impressed with man's capacity to conquer the fleshly impulses and grow up in the divine life.

II

A more capable proponent of the new theology was Munger's contemporary, Newman Smyth (1843–1925), whose most distinguished pastorate was that at Center Church (Congregational) in New Haven, Connecticut, where he served for twenty-five years.

Upon the close of the Civil War, in which he participated, Smyth entered Andover Theological Seminary. There he came in contact with the powerful Abbot Professor of Theology, Edwards A. Park, then in the prime of his power and influence. But from the outset Smyth felt a distinct distaste for his teacher's "orthodox rationalism." [10] Although he reluctantly re-

[8] *The Freedom of Faith*, pp. 23, 62.   [9] *Ibid.*, p. 62.
[10] Newman Smyth, *Recollections and Reflections* (New York, 1926), pp. 79–80. For a critical analysis of Park's brand of speculative rationalism, see Smyth, "Orthodox Rationalism," *Princeton Review*, May, 1882, pp. 294–312.

mained to graduate (1867), he left Andover feeling himself scantily equipped to meet the new theological problems of a scientific age.

After preaching for a year in a mission chapel, he went to Germany for first-hand study of the newer currents in theological thought. The lectures and writings of I. A. Dorner, of the University of Berlin, were "epoch-making" in his theological conversion.[11] His first book, *The Religious Feeling* (1877), revealed that his reorientation in religious thought had been accomplished under the theological influence of Schleiermacher as mediated through Dorner. "Whoever goes down with Schleiermacher to that sense of dependence in which he found the lowly source of religion," said Smyth, "goes beneath all rationalism." [12] While Smyth never abandoned this anti-rationalist emphasis, his later writings were largely concerned with the problems involved in adjusting theology to historical biblical criticism and especially to the doctrine of evolution. First in this series of studies was *Old Faiths in New Light,* published in 1879. This work is significant not only for its appropriation of the findings of biblical criticism, but also for its adoption of a progressive philosophy of history. This "new light" was destined to be of great influence in shaping his later theological thought.

Beginning with his New Haven pastorate, Smyth became deeply absorbed in natural science, and he made some first-hand investigations of his own in the Yale biological laboratory. Numerous treatises grew out of this phase of his study and research, including *The Place of Death in Evolution* (1897), *Through Science to Faith* (1902), *Constructive Natural Theology* (1913), and *The Meaning of Personal Life* (1916). By the opening of the twentieth century he had become convinced

[11] Smyth, *Recollections and Reflections,* p. 87.
[12] *The Religious Feeling* (New York, 1877), p. 33.

that "only a theology fairly won from nature and experience can command the modern mind." [13] Thus Smyth's mature new theology grew out of a synthesis of insights which derived from Schleiermacher on the one hand and from modern evolutionary thought on the other.

His new theology made a sharp break with the old theology's doctrine of the fall and original sin. To begin with, the idea of a fall in any sense seemed of little importance to him; what most impressed him was the benevolent character of the evolutionary process and the "unmistakable evidence of progress" in the history of mankind.[14] In so far as Smyth incorporated the doctrine of the fall in his theology, he reinterpreted it in terms of his general evolutionary presuppositions. Specifically, he regarded the fall as a "retrogression in evolution." He admitted that there had been times in nature's progress when "some slipping backwards" had occurred. The human being, he thought, was very liable to slip; that is to say, to "fall away from his type." [15] Yet the fact that man may now and then lapse from his type is not something to despair of, because it "is never a fall *out of* the evolution; it is included in the vast benevolence of the whole process of life." When viewed in the perspective of the ages, the fall is but an incident to a higher development. Evolution "moves on through the fall and beyond it, as was determined even from the foundation of the world." This divinely determined evolutionary movement is in fact "infrustrable" and "carries man's fall on to its triumph of creative and redeeming love." [16]

Whereas the old theology viewed native depravity in serious terms, one looks in vain for any corresponding emphasis in

[13] *Constructive Natural Theology* (New York, 1913), p. 5.
[14] *Through Science to Faith* (New York, 1902), pp. 116–117, 120, 130–132.
[15] *Ibid.*, p. 202.   [16] *Ibid.*, pp. 202–203. Cf. pp. 217–219.

Smyth's writings. It was man's moral progress, not man's basic estrangement from God, which was central in his religious thought. Thus it is not surprising that he practically ignored the whole question of original sin.

III

In George Angier Gordon (1853–1929) the new theology had one of its most eloquent exponents. Born on a farm in Scotland, he migrated to Boston in the summer of 1871, where, during the next three years, he was in succession safe-builder, stonemason, and painter.[17] Meanwhile he attended the Fourth Presbyterian Church, of which Luther H. Angier was the minister. Owing chiefly to the influence of the Angiers, he entered Bangor Theological Seminary in the fall of 1874 with a view to preparing for the ministry. Although he had only a common school background, he completed creditably the three-year course in divinity. The ruling theology at Bangor at this time was, as he later remarked, "a good version . . . of the old New England Calvinism." [18]

Ordained in June of 1877, he became pastor of a home missionary church at Temple, Maine. After only one year, however, he entered Harvard College as a special student. Three years later, in 1881, he received the degree of A. B. *magna cum laude*, with honors in Philosophy. President Eliot invited him to go abroad on a fellowship to prepare himself for a professorship in ecclesiastical history at Harvard. Only the necessity of caring for his widowed mother prompted him to decline this invitation. He therefore accepted a call to the Second Congregational Church in Greenwich, Connecticut. In the spring of 1884, however, owing largely to the recommendation

[17] Gordon, *My Education and Religion* (Boston, 1925), p. 142.
[18] *Ibid.*, p. 177.

of President Eliot, he was invited to become the minister of historic Old South Church in Boston. There he labored until his death in 1929. He and his intimate friend, Phillips Brooks, minister at Trinity Church (Episcopal), gave Boston a national reputation for eminent preaching.

But Gordon was more than a distinguished preacher; he was also an accomplished theologian, whose writings explored the basic questions of contemporary religious thought. His *Ultimate Conceptions of Faith* (1903), for example, was regarded as one of the most persuasive interpretations of the new theology.

Gordon's departure from the old theology was due in no small measure to his study of German idealistic philosophy at Harvard. He rated Hegel as "the greatest of modern philosophical scholars." [19] Along with his study of German Idealism, he mastered Plato and Aristotle in the original Greek, in which he was highly proficient. He became so steeped in Greek modes of thought that the late John W. Buckham, a warm admirer of Gordon, called him "the Origen of our age." [20] Hence, by the time he graduated from Harvard he had been "shorn of all faith in the New England theology." [21] The Hopkinsian type of Calvinism was especially obnoxious to him, and he lost no opportunity to ridicule it. In one of his earliest essays, for example, he charged that Hopkinsianism was "atheism." [22]

Like Newman Smyth, he firmly championed the theory of evolution and interpreted the origin and destiny of man in light of it. The New England Theology, he argued, finally collapsed because it insisted on holding to a pre-evolutionary view of man. "In spite of the new vista introduced by evolution," he wrote, "the New England divines continued to build their doc-

[19] *Ibid.*, p. 259.
[20] *Progressive Religious Thought in America* (Boston, 1919), p. 133.
[21] *My Education and Religion*, p. 214.
[22] "The Contrast and Agreement Between the New Orthodoxy and the Old," *The Andover Review*, XIX (January, 1893), 5.

trine of man upon a Hebrew myth." [23] He frankly declared that the old theology's ideas of the fall and original sin were outmoded. "It is past belief that two human beings created in moral integrity could by one act of disobedience dissolve themselves and their descendants into a universal sea of depravity. The notion of the fall can no longer serve as an account of the source of moral disorder." [24]

But to what, then, is moral disorder attributable? According to Gordon, the cause of man's moral disorder is threefold. First, it is produced partly by the downward pull of the instinct of the brute, which, despite moral evolution, still persists in human nature. In this respect the "new doctrine of original sin goes deeper than the old; it passes below the first man," descending finally into the arena of the untamed beast.[25] Second, moral disorder is due in a measure to "the weakness of reason." Man's reason is relatively feeble as compared with the force of primeval tendencies and impulses. Besides, just plain ignorance is a factor in causing moral disorder.[26] But these two causes, influential though they be, will not fully account for the existence of moral disorder. It "is impossible," said Gordon, "to crowd back into these [two] sources of animalism and ignorance all the streams that run through the consciousness of moral insolvency." Therefore he affirmed that a third, and basic, factor in creating moral disorder was perversity of will. "The personal will is the center of conduct, and the doings and misdoings of men obstinately refuse every reference as a finality other than this." [27]

On the whole, however, Gordon's doctrine of human nature assumed an optimistic cast. This optimism derived from two

[23] "The Collapse of the New England Theology," *Harvard Theological Review*, I (April, 1908), 152.
[24] *The New Epoch for Faith* (Boston, 1901), p. 35.
[25] *Ibid.*, p. 37.
[26] *Immortality and the New Theodicy* (Boston, 1897), p. 102.
[27] *The New Epoch for Faith*, p. 40.

firm convictions. The first was his conviction that man is divine in his essential nature. In numerous instances he severely criticized the traditional doctrine of total depravity. He argued repeatedly that to William E. Channing must go the credit for rediscovering the Christian doctrine of man. The idea of man's "likeness to God" was as fundamental with Gordon as it was with Channing.[28] Gordon contended for man's likeness to God on the basis of Christ's likeness to God. "The doctrine of man depends upon the doctrine of Christ; if Christ is only similar to God, then man is only similar. If Christ is consubstantial with the Father, so are all his children in time." [29] Because Gordon predicated Christ's consubstantiality with the Father, he held mankind to be consubstantial with the Father.

The other conviction that gave his theory of human nature an optimistic color was his strong faith in moral progress. At the dawn of the twentieth century he confidently declared that "the historic movement is slowly but surely away from the brute." "Under the august pressure of the universe inhumanity is dying; the campaign of the Infinite in history is slow, but it is finally fatal to lies, lust, and all brutality." [30] Gordon was no historical perfectionist. Nevertheless, he believed that such evil as might still persist in mankind at the end of history would be overcome in the after life, so that God finally would be "all in all." [31]

[28] Cf. *Ultimate Conceptions of Faith* (Boston, 1903), pp. 33–34; "The Collapse of the New England Theology," *Harvard Theological Review*, I (April, 1908), 149.

[29] "Some Things Worth While in Theology," *Harvard Theological Review*, III (October, 1910), 391; cf. "The Contrast," *op. cit.*, XIX, 13; Gordon, *The Christ of To-day* (Boston, 1895), pp. 234–235.

[30] *The New Epoch for Faith* (Boston, 1901), pp. 18, 362. Cf. *Ultimate Conceptions of Faith*, pp. 237–249.

[31] *Immortality and the New Theodicy*, pp. 76–80, 85–89; *Ultimate Conceptions of Faith*, pp. 135–136; Gordon, *Through Man to God* (Boston, 1906), pp. 389–394.

IV

An equally enthusiastic advocate of the new theology was Washington Gladden (1836–1918), who is best known perhaps for his great hymn, "O Master, Let Me Walk with Thee." A native of Pennsylvania, he was educated at Williams College during the Presidency of the celebrated Mark Hopkins. Although he held successful pastorates in New England, his greatest ministry was at the First Congregational Church in Columbus, Ohio, where he served from 1882 to 1918. During his Columbus ministry he was known as one of American Protestantism's most outstanding liberal spokesmen.

Although Gladden seems to have been started on the road to a liberal faith by his favorite teacher at Williams College, John Bascom, it was Horace Bushnell who did most to emancipate him from the old theology.[32] Two strong currents, however, carried Gladden well beyond the frontier of Bushnell's theological thought: the new industrialism and Darwinian evolution. In response to the former, he became a pioneer in the "social gospel" movement, and under the impact of the latter he adopted a progressive philosophy of history which turned him into a vigorous advocate of the new theology. Numerous books sprang out of these two concerns. Among those dealing directly with the new theology, two are of particular significance in relation to our present problem: *How Much Is Left of the Old Doctrines?* (1900), and *Present Day Theology* (1913).

From the days of his earliest writing, Gladden manifested impatience with the notion of the imputation of Adam's sin. Edwardean thought had, of course, abandoned this idea during the latter part of the eighteenth century, but federalist Calvinists still gave at least lip-service to it. In the year 1873, while serving as religious editor of *The Independent*, he wrote

[32] Gladden, *Recollections* (Boston, 1909), p. 119.

a pungent editorial on "immoral theology," in which he charged it to be blasphemous to believe God might justly punish a person for the sins of his ancestors. To claim scriptural authority for this notion "is to say that the Bible clearly teaches a monstrous lie." [33] In his treatise of 1900 he recurred to this theme with even sharper strictures. One's moral sense, he urged, "must be imperfectly developed" if one fails to see "that guilt cannot be inherited." "My child can no more be guilty or deserving of punishment for my sin than he can see with my eyes or feel with my nerves." [34]

In his *Present Day Theology*, published in 1913, Gladden observed that "the new theology does not believe in" "what the theologians call original sin." [35] By this remark he apparently meant that the new theology did not accept the doctrine of imputed sin. As already shown, the new theology believed in what may be called hereditary depravity; that is, it considered the effects of sin to be transmissible under the laws of natural descent. Gladden himself, at least until 1900, held to a kind of hereditary depravity. "Disease, disorder, infirmity, both of body and mind, may be transmitted to offspring, and thus children may be born with predispositions to vice and wrongdoing." [36] He was convinced "that the children of drunkards do inherit from their parents a neurotic diathesis which predisposes them to intemperance." He even thought pauperism and crime could cause disorders which would eventually reproduce themselves in the life of the race.[37]

Gladden was strikingly optimistic in his view of man's original nature and historical possibilities. His optimism was rooted in two convictions. One of these was the belief that man's

[33] Gladden, *Recollections*, p. 224.
[34] *How Much Is Left of the Old Doctrines?* (Boston, 1900), p. 116.
[35] *Present Day Theology* (3rd edition: Columbus, Ohio), p. 69.
[36] *How Much Is Left of the Old Doctrines?*, p. 121.
[37] *Ibid.*, pp. 123–124.

freedom is of such a nature that he can progressively eradicate his inherited evil tendencies.[38] The other conviction was that man's good tendencies would prove more enduring in the long run than his evil tendencies. "Can any sane man believe that he [God] is on the side of evil tendency? No; the evil is in its very nature temporary; it cancels itself; the good has in it the life of eternity. . . . The evil entail dies out after a few generations, the grace of God lives and grows for a thousand years. And thus in this very law of heredity is lodged the power that is yet to redeem the race." [39] In view of his romantic faith in moral progress, Gladden had no reason to take a serious view of the human situation. It is no wonder that his new theology was highly moralistic.

V

A great popularizer of the new theology was Lyman Abbott (1835–1922), an influential preacher, lecturer, and journalist. After graduating from New York University (1853), he served for six years as a member of the Abbott law firm in New York. Owing mainly to the influence of Henry Ward Beecher, whose Plymouth Church in Brooklyn he attended, Abbott abandoned the bar for the ministry.[40] His first important step toward a national reputation was taken when, in the fall of 1876, he joined Beecher in the editorship of *The Christian Union,* a non-sectarian weekly. Although Beecher held temporarily the title of editor-in-chief, the full direction of the journal fell to his junior partner. The notorious Beecher-Tilton scandal

[38] *Ibid.,* pp. 125–127.
[39] *Ibid.,* p. 130. Cf. Gladden, *Ruling Ideas of the Present Age* (Boston, 1895), pp. 23–24, 290–291.
[40] Lyman Abbott, *Reminiscences* (2nd edition: Boston, 1923), pp. 125–137. Two other "prophetic spirits" who influenced Abbott's decision were Charles G. Finney and Horace Bushnell (*ibid.,* p. xxx).

had brought the *Union* into disrepute, greatly reducing the subscription list, but within a few years Abbott restored its prestige. Renamed *The Outlook* in 1893, it achieved a nation-wide recognition as an unexcelled molder of liberal social and religious thought.

Beecher's death in 1887 left Plymouth Church without a minister. Abbott was asked to serve as pulpit supply until a permanent pastor could be found. Although not a Beecher, he tided the church over the crisis so well that he was chosen as regular minister. Thus until his health gave way, eleven years later, he carried the double task of preacher and editor. Meanwhile he also lectured widely in colleges and universities. His greatest medium of public influence, however, was the magnificent *Outlook*.[41]

Up through at least 1875 Abbott seems to have adhered basically to the "new school" version of Calvinism. Neither biblical criticism nor liberal theological doctrines had yet taken root in his mind.[42] By the early 1880's, however, he had undergone a theological change not unlike that of Gladden and other liberals. It was chiefly the theory of evolution that transformed his theological outlook. In his *Reminiscences* he declared, "I have been an evolutionist, but not a Darwinian." [43] That statement is true in the sense that he could not agree with Darwin's doctrine of the struggle for existence and the survival of the fittest. Nevertheless, he certainly was essentially a Darwinian; that is to say, he accepted Darwin's fundamental principle of the derivation of higher from lower forms of life.

That Abbott's new theology was framed upon the premise of modern evolution is clearly demonstrated in two of his most popular theological works: *The Evolution of Christianity*

---

[41] For an excellent study of Abbott's life and contributions to American culture, see Ira V. Brown's *Lyman Abbott* (Cambridge, 1953).
[42] *Ibid.*, pp. 54–56.   [43] *Reminiscences,* p. xxxi.

(1892), and *The Theology of an Evolutionist* (1897). Here he firmly accepted the Darwinian idea that life has ascended progressively through a series of organic changes extending from the lowly amoeba to man. From this hypothesis he drew the conclusion that human history is dynamic and progressive. In particular, he emphasized the fact that the Bible is a record of the growth of the moral and religious consciousness.[44] Believing Christianity itself to be progressively evolving, Abbott urged that theology should undergo continuous change in order to remain relevant to religious experience. A living theology would thus necessarily be an ever-growing theology.

As between the old theology and the new, Abbott saw a basic and unavoidable conflict; and nowhere did this conflict seem to him more sharply drawn than with regard to the old doctrine of the fall and original sin. To begin with, the old theology predicated a state of original righteousness or perfection. On Abbott's hypothesis, however, man had gradually emerged from animal forebears, having in the beginning only the most primitive mental and moral powers. But if man began existence on this basis, could the old idea of the fall be maintained? According to Abbott, it could not.[45] On the other hand, he sought to salvage a fragment of truth from the old theology's idea of the fall. The child, he explained, begins existence on the plane of "a little animal" and in a state of innocence. In the course of growth a rudimentary moral consciousness dawns, resulting in a conflict between the child's higher (human) and lower (animal) nature. At this point or moment it is theoretically conceivable that the higher impulse might be responded to without any deviation. "But in fact," said Abbott, "man never thus progresses. He deliberately, and again and

[44] *The Evolution of Christianity* (Boston, 1892), p. 66.
[45] *Ibid.*, pp. 122, 204–206.

179

again, turns his back upon the higher life, and goes down into the lower life from which he has emerged." [46] It is this refusal to obey the impulse of one's higher nature which Abbott would call the fall. "Every man falls when, by yielding to the entice-ments of his lower, animal nature, he descends from his van-tage-ground of moral consciousness to the earthiness out of which he had begun to emerge." [47]

Since he acknowledged man to have repeatedly turned his back upon the higher good, one might suppose that Abbott would have emphasized the tenacity of sin in the human self. Actually he did not. The explanation lies in the fact that he was captivated by the idea of moral progress. "The individual man," he remarked, "is partly the animal from which he has come, and partly the God who is coming into him; but God is steadily displacing the animal." [48] Not even the hurricane of the First World War could topple Abbott from his romantic pedestal. Musing upon the raging savagery in the year 1915, he could blandly say, "The human race falls down occasionally, bruises itself, and weeps some bitter tears; but picks itself up and goes on walking, and persistently in the right direction." [49]

VI

The preceding pages have been concerned with the doctrine of man's native state as expressed in the new theology of par-ish clergymen. The remainder of this chapter will consider this same doctrine as it was developed by professional teachers of the new theology.

Let us begin with Lewis French Stearns (1847–1892), a sig-nificant thinker who stood largely within the circle of the new

[46] *Ibid.*, p. 226.   [47] *Ibid.*, p. 227.   [48] *Ibid.*, p. 255.
[49] Quoted from Ira V. Brown, "Lyman Abbott: Christian Evolutionist," *The New England Quarterly*, XXIII (June, 1950), 229.

theology and yet who preserved in his thought important elements of the old. He represents a transitional stage between the old and the new. A New Englander by birth, he graduated from Princeton in 1867. When well along in Columbia Law School, he decided to enter the ministry. From 1869 to 1872 he engaged in theological study successively at Princeton Theological Seminary, the Universities of Berlin and Leipzig, and Union Seminary in New York. Then followed some three years each in the pastorate and in teaching at Albion College (Michigan). From 1880 until his death in 1892, he taught theology at Bangor Theological Seminary.

Stearns was projected into the theological spotlight by a brilliant book, entitled *The Evidence of Christian Experience* (1891), which was originally delivered as a series of Ely Lectures at Union Theological Seminary. Shortly thereafter Union invited him to become Roosevelt Professor of Systematic Theology. Although greatly drawn to that strategic post, he declined it after much thought because "he could not take the seminary pledge" to the Westminster Confession of Faith.[50]

When Stearns began his work at Bangor he was already thinking within the broad framework of the new theology. This is clearly reflected in his challenging inaugural address, "Reconstruction in Theology," delivered in June, 1881.[51] Two aspects of that address are especially worth emphasizing. For one thing, he explicitly asserted that the doctrine of evolution could "render the richest service to religion." [52] One of its services was already "a grander conception of God, a pro-

[50] George L. Prentiss, "Biographical Sketch," in L. F. Stearns, *Present Day Theology* (New York, 1893), p. xv. "I am not an Arminian," Stearns explained in a letter, "but I am not a Calvinist in the sense in which I have supposed the Westminster Confession to be Calvinistic" (*ibid.*, p. xv).
[51] Stearns, "Reconstruction in Theology," *The New Englander*, V (New Series: January, 1882), 82–102.
[52] *Ibid.*, p. 85.

founder sense of his power, a broader view of his activity in the universe." Thus, whereas the old theology laid its main emphasis upon the transcendence of God, the new theology was viewing God as immanent within nature, and as progressively achieving important ends by the slow processes of natural law.[53] Stearns saw the direct bearing of the doctrine of evolution upon theological reconstruction. A static, unchanging theology he perceived to be outmoded. "Each period," said he, "must draw the material of its theology out of its own profound convictions, mold it by its own intellect, and utter it in its own words." [54]

The other significant aspect of Stearns' Bangor inaugural was his explicit rejection of the old theology's principle of external authority. Said he, "The infallible authority to which the believer must bow is not the Church, as the Romanist says; it is not human reason, as the rationalist says; it is not the Scripture, as the reformation theology said; it is God speaking in Christ to the soul, speaking to conscience and through conscience." [55] The authority of the Christian consciousness, of the experience of the new life in Jesus Christ, was made the central theme of his Ely Lectures.[56] It was Stearns' emphasis upon the authority of the Christian consciousness which made him insist that the new theology should be Christocentric. "About him [Christ] all the truths and doctrines must group themselves." [57]

How, then, did Stearns revise the traditional doctrine of original sin? Fortunately for our inquiry, he gave careful atten-

---

[53] *Ibid.*, pp. 86–87.   [54] *Ibid.*, p. 82.   [55] *Ibid.*, p. 91.
[56] *The Evidence of Christian Experience* (New York, 1891), pp. 28–29. Stearns acknowledged his indebtedness in this respect to I. A. Dorner and F. H. R. Frank of Germany (*ibid.*, p. 401).
[57] "Reconstruction in Theology," *op. cit.*, p. 90. Cf. Stearns, "The Present Direction of Theological Thought in the Congregational Churches of the United States," *Present Day Theology*, pp. 540–542.

tion to this doctrine in a systematic treatise, published post-humously under the title of *Present Day Theology* (1893). Despite his belief that evolution contained much truth, he could not agree with the Darwinian theory that man had emerged from an animal order. "There is a gap," he declared, "between the highest animal and the lowest man which the theory of evolution is utterly incapable of bridging over." [58] He conceded that man's lower nature might well be allied to the animal, indeed might even be derived by descent from the animal, but he contended that man as a living spirit came into being only by a special creative act of God.[59] In contrast to the typical adherent of the new theology, Stearns believed the Genesis story of the origin of Adam and Eve to represent a "historical reality." Thus Adam, he observed, "came from the divine hand a perfect being. The divine image shone forth from him in its untarnished brightness. All his faculties and powers were complete and in perfect working-order." Intellectually he was "a man in capacity though still a child in acquisition." In moral capacity also he was perfect. "Above all, he had free-will and the power to attain the chief end of his being without slip or fall." [60]

Yet when exposed to probationary trial, Adam fell and thereby brought upon himself not only temporal death, but also estrangement from the kingdom of God. "The natural bias toward God and His kingdom became transformed into a bias toward sin." [61] The disorder which sin introduced into Adam's moral and physical nature could not be confined to himself. Owing to the fact of racial solidarity, a corrupt nature "was transmitted by Adam to his descendants, who in turn passed it on to theirs, with such increments of evil habit as

[58] *Present Day Theology* (New York, 1893), p. 297.
[59] *Ibid.*, pp. 297–298. Cf. pp. 255–256.   [60] *Ibid.*, p. 325.
[61] *Ibid.*, p. 327.

their own sin produced." [62] What the exact nature of the connection was between Adam's first sin and that of his descendants Stearns confessed his inability to fathom; nevertheless, like the Edwardeans of former generations, he insisted that there was some kind of positive relationship whereby universal sin had been rendered unavoidable. Hence, he formulated his doctrine of original sin in these words: "As a result of Adam's sin, all men come into the world with a corrupt or disordered nature, inherited from their ancestors, which, in connection with the sinful influences of their surroundings, leads them all into sin." [63]

In order to place his view of original sin in its true perspective, certain qualifications are necessary. For one thing, the disordered nature that one inherits is not itself sinful. In the second place, the inherited disordered nature is only the occasion of sin, not its cause. The true cause is a misuse of freedom. Lastly, although man inherits a fundamentally disordered nature, he is not totally depraved. The image of God in the natural man is seriously marred by sin, but it is not destroyed.[64]

In estimating man's historical possibilities, Stearns reflected a mixture of realism and optimism. He had no confidence in the romantic notion that evolutionary progress would eventually eliminate man's sinful tendencies. According to him, sin has its source not in brute instinct but in a perverted will, in the abuse of human freedom. It is man's true end to love God supremely, but in fact he "makes himself the center around which his moral life revolves." [65] Consequently, the "natural man becomes no holier in the progress of evolution." [66] Still, there is an unmistakable strain of evolutionary optimism in Stearns' new theology. It reveals itself, first of all, in his faith in the possibilities of Christian nurture. He held that if children be from birth

[62] *Ibid.*, p. 337. Cf. pp. 334–335.   [63] *Ibid.*, p. 341.
[64] *Ibid.*, pp. 291, 337, 341.   [65] *Ibid.*, p. 305.   [66] *Ibid.*, p. 308.

nurtured in the Christian faith of their parents, "their growing freedom may be so guided from stage to stage that they will never wander from the fold of the Good Shepherd." [67] This is the ideal, he said, "toward which we are rapidly moving. In the last days it will doubtless be universal." [68] At this point Stearns is a convinced Bushnellian.

Stearns' evolutionary optimism is further reflected in his idea of the progressive coming of the kingdom of God. Jesus, he said, brought the kingdom of God in absolute fulness in his person, but that kingdom must work itself out gradually in history. It begins in the individual will, but it works itself outward until it penetrates and regenerates all the social institutions of mankind, including the family, the state, commerce, the trades and professions. We must never forget, he urged, "that the kingdom of God is to be established here in this earth." [69] Stearns stressed the historical progress of the kingdom of God. Since apostolic times, he declared, the direction of the kingdom "has been steadily forward." "There have been, indeed, periods of apparent retrogression, but they have been like the recession of the waves upon the beach as the tide comes in, a gathering of strength for a new advance." [70] To be sure, perfection would not result merely from the progressive growth of the kingdom; for, in the Last Day, God must usher in the kingdom through the Second Coming of Christ.[71] Nevertheless, Stearns did not regard the two events as opposed to each other. He held that the kingdom would "go steadily on its way . . . with unhindered progress, until he come whose right the kingdom is." [72]

In thus uniting the idea of progress with the idea of the

[67] *Ibid.*, p. 353.   [68] *The Evidence of Christian Experience*, p. 417.
[69] *Present Day Theology*, p. 125.
[70] *Ibid.*, p. 119. Cf. Stearns, *The Evidence of Christian Experience*, pp. 364–368.
[71] *Present Day Theology*, p. 126.   [72] *Ibid.*, pp. 515–516.

Parousia Stearns definitely reflected the optimistic spirit of the new theology.

VII

Stearns had a more liberal theological contemporary in George Harris (1844–1922), who played a prominent role in helping Andover Theological Seminary to make its transition from the old to the new theology. Born in Maine, he graduated from Amherst College (1866) and Andover Seminary (1869). After serving two New England pastorates, he held the influential Abbot Professorship of Theology at Andover Seminary from 1883 to 1899.

His predecessor at Andover, Edwards Amasa Park (1808–1900), who occupied the Abbot Chair from 1847 to 1881, remained to his death a devoted Hopkinsian. Frank Hugh Foster, his favorite pupil, said that Park "never perceived that the positions of the New England Theology had been shaken by the newer thought." [73] Park's doctrine of man, for example, remained completely unmodified by the advent of the theory of evolution. With respect to original sin, he argued to the very last that because of a divinely established "connection" between Adam and his offspring, the fall determined that all men would be born in a state of total depravity. [74]

Harris, on the other hand, taught from the perspective of the new theology, a fact which greatly disappointed Park and his followers. In 1884 he disclosed the germ elements of his theology in an illuminating essay, "The Function of the Christian Consciousness," published in *The Andover Review*. [75] He

[73] Foster, *The Life of Edwards Amasa Park* (New York, 1936), p. 261.
[74] Cf. F. H. Foster, *A Genetic History of the New England Theology* (Chicago, 1907), pp. 506–508.
[75] "The Function of the Christian Consciousness," *The Andover Review*, II (October, 1884), 338–352.

revealed considerable affinity with Stearns' Bangor inaugural address of 1881. For example, he appealed to the Christian consciousness, rather than to the church or the Bible, as the primary source of authority. "One cannot go beneath his consciousness," he wrote. Furthermore, one "cannot dispute nor doubt the deliverances of his consciousness." [76] He espoused an evolutionary philosophy of history and showed its implications for theological revision. Believing as he did in "the progressive development of theology," he insisted that "theologizing must always go on." [77] In 1896 Harris published *Moral Evolution*, his most influential book. It became a favorite work in colleges and universities, and had a large sale. Although it is addressed mainly to the question of moral evolution, it contains the broad framework of the author's religious thought. Being strongly influenced by Ritschlian thought, he emphasized the ethical character of Christianity. According to him, "Jesus was a moral teacher" whose essential message was the fatherhood of God and the brotherhood of men.[78] His new theology, therefore, was developed as an integral part of Christian ethics.

Far more sharply than Stearns, Harris broke with the Edwardean doctrine of the fall. His new theology made no place whatever for the Adam of traditional thought. Though he considered it probable that the human race descended from one man or a single pair, he urged that the knowledge of primitive men and of the progress of the race from lowly beginnings had basically modified the older conception of man's original state.[79] Man began, according to him, not in a state of moral righteousness, but only with such primitive naked powers as would in the course of experience result in moral character.

[76] *Ibid.*, p. 341. [77] *Ibid.*, p. 348.
[78] *Moral Evolution* (2nd edition: Boston, 1896), p. 392.
[79] *Ibid.*, p. 405.

Thus, though one might start out in a state of innocency, character as such would have to be grown under conditions of experimental trial and error. Presumably, on Harris' theory, man could have climbed steadily up the long ladder of moral evolution. But in the course of the upward climb there had been what Harris called "reversion and degeneration." To such reversion he applied the term sin. It signified a departure from the true type of humanity.[80] In his departure from type, man has separated himself from God. "Degeneration, or sin, in the last analysis and the deepest consciousness is alienation from God." [81]

Is it possible to explain why man departs from moral type? No complete explanation is possible, said Harris, because "sin is irrational." "It is against reason because it is against nature. . . . There is no *reason why* a man should sin, for sin is transgression of the laws of his own constitution." [82] He saw only a partial truth in the claim that degeneration could be explained as the downward pull of man's animal instincts. Many sins, he conceded, do spring out of these subhuman urges and desires. Yet, as he pointed out, the more subtle sins, such as envy, revenge, pride, and ambition, occur only because man is superior to the brute. The most comprehensive explanation of man's degeneration or departure from type is to attribute it to selfishness, or to a sense of self-sufficiency.[83]

Harris observed that the term "original sin" had been banished from the newer modes of theological thought. The element of truth left in the old doctrine could be preserved in the theory of racial heredity. The new theology "recognizes and emphasizes heredity as transmitting moral disease, and so is in complete accord with modern science." [84] But even though

[80] *Ibid.*, pp. 274–275, 418. [81] *Ibid.*, p. 284.
[82] *Ibid.*, pp. 282–283. [83] *Ibid.*, pp. 280–281, 284.
[84] *Ibid.*, p. 419. Cf. p. 405.

Harris tacitly agreed that moral disorder could be transmitted through hereditary channels, his theological thought reflected no deep insight into man's native predicament. This is probably due to two factors. One of these was his firm faith in the divine immanence, in virtue of which he accented man's native capacity for God-consciousness. In the second place, he was strongly committed to the doctrine of moral progress. It was with this optimistic note that he climaxed his *Moral Evolution*. While by no means an unqualified perfectionist, he held that mankind was, on the whole, morally progressing. He conceded that the human climb had been slow, somewhat fitful, and at times even retrogressive. Nevertheless, he urged that the moral gain was unmistakable. "Man has grown to be of a larger stature. Society has improved. By distant contrast, the moderns are better than the ancients. The retrospect which sobers also animates. At a slow rate indeed mankind advances, but it does advance. And so optimism is more than a hope for the future." [85]

VIII

By the last decade of the nineteenth century the new theology had reached the point where a systematic exposition of its leading conceptions was possible. And there was at hand a thinker who was strikingly qualified to undertake this service: William Newton Clarke (1840–1912). Receiving the A. B. degree from Madison University in 1861, he graduated from the Seminary of that institution two years later. In 1890, after serving several Baptist pastorates, he became Joslin Professor of Christian Theology at Colgate University, occupying that chair until his retirement in 1908.

[85] *Ibid.*, p. 445. Cf. Harris, *A Century's Change in Religion* (New York, 1914), pp. 181–182, 187–188.

Clarke's chief contribution to the new theology was his book, *An Outline of Christian Theology*. After its use in a privately printed form for some four years, it was published by Charles Scribner's Sons in 1898. By 1914 it had passed through twenty-one editions. Clarke published several other able works, including *The Use of the Scriptures in Theology* (1905), *The Christian Doctrine of God* (1909), and *Sixty Years with the Bible* (1909), but none of them received the acclaim of the *Outline*. Unquestionably, it played a major role in the liberalization of American Protestant thought.

Clarke's new theology, like that of Lewis French Stearns, was avowedly Christocentric in its principle of authority. Whereas the old theology was Bible-centered, Clarke pointed to Christ as the one who "gives us the Bible." [86] "We must transfer our faith from the book that reveals God in Christ," said Clarke in his Nathaniel Taylor Lectures of 1905, "to God in Christ whom the book reveals,—from the telescope to the sun." [87] Furthermore, he developed his new theology from the perspective of modern evolution. Accordingly, he viewed the physical world and man in terms of growth. Likewise he regarded the Scriptures as progressively revealing God, culminating in Jesus Christ.[88] It might be expected, then, that Clarke would take the view that theology must be continually revising itself in terms of changing experience. "Theology can never stand still while the divine life of the Church is moving forward." [89]

What the evolutionary principle involved with respect to a doctrine of man Clarke clearly recognized. His new theology, unlike the old, did not turn to Genesis for an historical account

[86] *An Outline of Christian Theology* (4th edition, New York, 1899), p. 21.
[87] *The Use of the Scriptures in Theology* (New York, 1905), p. 170.
[88] *An Outline*, pp. 31–32. Cf. *The Use of the Scriptures*, pp. 128–132.
[89] *An Outline*, p. 20.

of man's origin; instead it appealed to the verdict of modern scientific thought.[90] Since it regarded man as emerging gradually from an animal ancestry, it openly abandoned the traditional notion that the race had originated in a special Adamic creation. "It has long been believed," wrote Clarke, "that God created a single pair, unconnected with other living creatures, to be parents of the coming race. But it is now accepted on sufficient evidence that he brought mankind into existence by long and gradual process, so ordering his world that animal life and experience should develop those powers of intelligence and will by possession of which man came at length to bear God's likeness." [91]

Clarke fully recognized the bearing of this evolutionary theory of human origin upon the entrance of sin into the life of the race, and at this point his new theology parted company with the old. Whereas the old theology predicated the origin of sin upon the fall of man from a state of original perfection, he urged that sin made its entrance into the race through man's failure to rise into the higher life of the spirit. The human being emerged, he observed, in a mixture of animal and divine impulses, a condition which resulted in conflict. Sin originated in consequence of man's refusal to respond to his higher nature.[92]

Obviously, Clarke's new theology had no place for Adam as the first sinner. Nevertheless, he considered it important to preserve an essential truth contained in the old doctrine of original sin. By natural propagation, said he, the qualities of human nature, whether good or bad, are transmitted from parent to child. Clarke was a traducianist, and therefore he insisted

[90] *Ibid.*, pp. 222–223.
[91] *The Christian Doctrine of God* (New York, 1909), p. 139.
[92] *An Outline*, pp. 240–242; *The Christian Doctrine of God*, pp. 177–178, 183–184.

that the "entire being of the individual, body and soul together, is derived by natural process from the previous being of the parents." [93] If evil once enters the racial stream, said he, evil is perpetuated indefinitely in the life of mankind. Sin and guilt are personal and nontransferable, and therefore they cannot be propagated in the race. Nevertheless, a depraved stock is transmitted from parent to child. Thus "children are not born either wholly good or neutral between good and evil, but with evil tendencies which grow into sin when responsible life begins." [94]

The idea that children are born with sinful tendencies must be seen in relation to Clarke's belief that children are also born with good tendencies. He held to what he called the "double flow" of good and evil in the human stream. Because of this double flow children at birth cannot be regarded as totally depraved. But even though Clarke recognized the double flow of good and evil in the human race, he inclined toward an optimistic view of human destiny. "When a high degree of goodness has prevailed for generations," said he, "children will be born with better tendencies than they could inherit in an inferior age. Humanity certainly is by nature a slowly rising race, with a native tendency to outgrow faults." [95] If that statement were taken by itself, one could suppose Clarke to be about as optimistic in his doctrine of man as Lyman Abbott. But that would be untrue. He did not hold to the complete perfection of mankind within history. [96] Yet, when all allowances are made, it remains a fact that his faith in man's historical possibilities was relatively optimistic.

IX

The outstanding systematist of the new theology was the late William Adams Brown (1865–1943). His academic equipment

---

[93] *An Outline*, p. 217.   [94] *Ibid.*, p. 244.   [95] *Ibid.*, p. 245.
[96] *Ibid.*, pp. 414–417.

for this task was far superior to that of William Newton Clarke. At Yale he completed studies leading to three degrees: A. B. (1886), M. A. (1888), and Ph. D. (1901). He received the B. D. degree from Union Theological Seminary in 1890. Then followed two years of advanced study in church history at the University of Berlin under the world-famous Adolf Harnack. In 1892 Brown became a member of the faculty at Union, serving at first in the department of Church History. A year later he was transferred to the department of Systematic Theology. Promoted to the Roosevelt Professorship of Systematic Theology in 1898, he held that influential position for thirty-two years. Meanwhile he not only wrote many books, but he took an active part in numerous practical enterprises of the church, including missions, education, and social service. He also exercised great influence in the growing ecumenical movement of the churches.[97]

Of all Brown's writings, his *Christian Theology in Outline* (1906) was by far the most influential. Like Clarke's *Outline*, it was used as a textbook in the leading Protestant denominations of this and other countries. It was superior to Clarke's in its grasp of the history of Christian thought and in its employment of historical method. Recently Walter Horton called Brown's *Outline* a "revised version" of Clarke's *Outline*.[98] So far as basic presuppositions are concerned, this seems especially true. For example, Brown's new theology is as avowedly Christocentric in its normative principle as that of Clarke.[99] Also it is written in the light of scientific thought. "By the new theology," he wrote in 1911, "we mean the type of theology

[97] For a fascinating story of Brown's life and activities, see his autobiography, *A Teacher and His Times* (New York, 1940).
[98] Horton, "Systematic Theology," *Protestant Thought in the Twentieth Century*, edited by Arnold Nash (New York, 1951), p. 108.
[99] Cf. Brown, *Christ the Vitalizing Principle in Christian Theology* (New York, 1898); *Christian Theology in Outline* (New York, 1906), pp. 39–41.

whose method is determined by the modern scientific movement and which is hospitable to its results." [100] Explaining his theological creed in 1933, he said, "I am a Modernist, and as such I am committed to follow the scientific method wherever it shall take me." [101]

Brown's commitment to modern science had a decisive influence upon his theory of the origin and native character of man. Since he predicated "a ceaseless evolution from the simpler to the more complex" forms of life, he found it impossible to regard Genesis as an historical explanation of creation. In other words, he rejected the idea of a sudden, special creation of a full grown "first man." [102] Along with this he also repudiated the idea of a state of moral perfection, from which the first man fell. Moral goodness, he urged, could not be suddenly imparted to mankind; it could only be achieved through a gradual process of growth and development. Nor did he think that sin, any more than goodness, could be suddenly introduced into the human race. "Sin is not a foreign intruder making its appearance in the universe suddenly at a moment of time, and bringing about an abrupt transformation in human nature as a whole." [103]

How then may one explain the entrance of sin into the universe? To this question Brown gave a typically synoptic answer, ascribing a measure of validity to all the leading explanations. For example, he thought the evolutionist was partly right in explaining the origin of sin in the downward pull of the animal in man's nature. The Arminian idea that sin begins in the exercise of free will seemed to him not entirely wrong.

[100] Brown, "The Old Theology and the New," *The Harvard Theological Review,* IV (January, 1911), 1.
[101] Brown, "Seeking Beliefs That Matter," *Contemporary American Theology,* edited by Vergilius Ferm (Second Series: New York, 1933), p. 98.
[102] Brown, *Christian Theology in Outline,* pp. 213–214, 218–219, 239–240.
[103] Brown, "The Old Theology and the New," *op. cit.,* p. 15. Cf. *Christian Theology in Outline,* p. 275.

Nor, finally, did he believe the dualist was completely in error in attributing the origin of sin to the influence of malign powers. Yet, in the end, Brown found all these explanations less than fully convincing. He had no unique solution of his own, and therefore he concluded, "We have here a mystery which we cannot explain, yet may not deny." [104]

Brown's *Outline* gives only the most incidental attention to the doctrine of original sin. His later systematic treatise, *Beliefs That Matter* (1928), is even more indifferent toward this doctrine. On the whole, he seems to agree substantially with Clarke. He assumed that when sin once gets into the human race, the laws of heredity will guarantee the propagation of its effects to subsequent generations. "Both through direct inheritance and through the environment which it [sin] creates, its consequences extend beyond the individual and affect those who come after." [105] But although Brown believed the effects of sin to be inheritable, there is no evidence to show that he subscribed to the doctrine of total native depravity. Indeed, since he believed the principle of kinship between God and man to be basic to Christian theology, he could not accept that doctrine. [106]

Yet although Brown rejected total depravity, he did not rebound to the opposite idea of unqualified human goodness. While he predicated man's essential kinship to God, he recognized that sin is also deeply rooted in human nature. To be sure, he believed man could achieve a progressive victory over sin, but he also held that sin would persist in the life of the believer to the end of his historical journey. He observed that it was the truly good Christian who knew himself to be far from perfect. [107] Nor did he hold to a perfectionist view of the

[104] *Christian Theology in Outline*, pp. 271–276.
[105] Brown, "Seeking Beliefs That Matter," *op. cit.*, p. 69.
[106] *Christian Theology in Outline*, p. 239. [107] *Ibid.*, p. 415.

social order. Though he did, to be sure, urge that the kingdom of God could be significantly realized on the historical plane, he also warned "that every victory of the Christian principle seems to call forth new and subtler manifestations of the forces of selfishness and oppression." [108]

It must be admitted, however, that the measured realism revealed in the *Outline* was considerably toned down in Brown's wartime treatise, *Is Christianity Practicable?* He now saw "no reason to doubt" that a Christian social order could be brought about if the church would only appeal to the "better man in men" and apply "a virile gospel." [109] But this ebullient hope was a quickly passing phase of Brown's thought; his more truly representative view is to be found in the *Outline*.

X

It is manifest from our survey that the new theology definitely modified the Edwardean doctrine of original sin. For one thing, it did not continue the idea that sin was introduced into the world by the fall of a morally perfect "first man." As an alternative, it viewed man as emerging from lower forms of life and as becoming aware at some indeterminate moment of a conflict between his higher and lower nature. In so far as the new theology made any attempt to maintain the idea of the fall, it usually interpreted the fall as man's failure to answer the call of his higher nature, or as man's departure from his true spiritual type. Again, whereas Edwardean theology predicated the entrance of sin into the world through the fall of the "first man," Adam, the new theology ceased to think in terms of either a first man or a first sin. Precisely how or when sin first found its way into the human race was regarded as a

[108] *Ibid.*, p. 417.
[109] *Is Christianity Practicable?* (New York, 1916), pp. 133–138, 141.

matter of minor importance. The new theology did, however, hold that when sin once entered the life of mankind, its effects could be perpetuated through biological reproduction. Such inherited disabilities, although not themselves sinful, were believed to be an occasion of actual sin. The old term "original sin" was viewed as misleading and it was rarely used. Finally, the new theology rejected the Edwardean doctrine of total depravity. It replaced that doctrine with the idea that human nature, at birth, consists of a mixture of tendencies toward both good and evil. But because of its faith in moral progress, it tended to magnify the growing goodness of man and to obscure the fundamental roots of human sinfulness.

CHAPTER NINE

THE REVIVAL OF
THE IDEA OF THE FALL
AND ORIGINAL SIN

WRITING in *Beliefs That Matter*, in the year 1928, William Adams Brown observed that one of the prominent marks of contemporary religion "is a loss of the sense of sin." "You will hear ministers preaching about almost everything else except the forgiveness of sins." [1] This was no unique observation; what Brown said could be duplicated in substance in the writings of many of the more thoughtful Christians of this period. If Professor Mary Frances Thelen is correct, some responsibility for this situation lies at the doors of the theological seminaries in America. In an excellent analysis of contemporary realistic theology, she said, "Teachers of the philosophy of religion and systematic theology in the major liberal seminaries during the first third of the twentieth century have little in their writings on the subject of sin." [2]

I

While Professor Thelen's claim is, on the whole, true, there is at least one important exception: Walter Rauschenbusch

[1] *Beliefs That Matter* (New York, 1928), p. 126.
[2] *Man as Sinner in Contemporary American Realistic Theology* (New York, 1946), p. 13.

(1861–1918). To be sure, he was not a teacher of systematic theology, but of church history; still, he was perhaps the foremost molder of American Christian thought in his generation. It is not too much to say that, in his final phase of thought, he foreshadowed a realistic view of sin which found fulfillment in Reinhold Niebuhr.

Stemming from generations of German ministerial stock, Rauschenbusch was born at Rochester, New York, where his father was then a professor in the "German Department" of Rochester Theological Seminary.[3] For his undergraduate study, he was sent to the Gymnasium of Gütersloh in Westphalia. Later he received degrees from the University of Rochester (1884) and Rochester Theological Seminary (1886). After serving eleven years (1886–1897) as pastor of the Second German Baptist Church in New York City, he accepted a call to Rochester Theological Seminary, where he spent the remainder of his life. Beginning in the German Department, he was transferred, in 1902, to the chair of Church History.[4]

Somewhat to his amazement, he was projected into the national spotlight by his *Christianity and the Social Crisis* (1907), a work that attained a circulation of over fifty thousand copies. The outgrowth of his New York ministry, it was decisive in shaping Rauschenbusch's future leadership and in determining the focus of his later research and writing. Of his later books, *Christianizing the Social Order* (1912), *Social Principles of Jesus* (1916), and *A Theology for the Social Gospel* (1917) were notable contributions. He was undoubtedly the major architect of American Protestant social thought.

His religious thought was most at home in the new theology,

[3] The purpose of the so-called German Department was to qualify German-speaking immigrants for ministerial service among their people on the Western Frontier.

[4] For an inspiring story of his life and contributions, see Dores R. Sharpe, *Walter Rauschenbusch* (New York, 1942).

already characterized in the previous chapter. That is to say, he based his theology upon an evolutionary view of the universe, a progressive philosophy of history, an immanental conception of God's relation to man and nature, and a Christocentric interpretation of the kingdom of God. Yet there is an element of realism in his conception of human nature that cannot be found in the thought of any other new theologian. Much in his earlier thought about the human situation is, of course, similar to that of a Gladden or a Harris. For example, in his *Christianity and the Social Crisis* he remarked, "With all our faults and our slothfulness we modern men in many ways are more on a level with the real mind of Jesus than any generation that has gone before." [5] While he conceded that "there is no perfection for man in this life," he was deeply stirred by recent progress toward perfection. He admitted that "the hope surges up that perhaps the long and slow climb may be ending." Ever since the Reformation, he thought, "there has been a perceptible increase of speed." "Humanity is gaining in elasticity and capacity for change." "The swiftness of evolution in our own country proves the immense latent perfectibility in human nature." [6]

This optimistic American mood was even more manifest in his *Christianizing the Social Order,* which appeared on the brink of the War of 1914–1918. "The largest and hardest part of the work of Christianizing the social order has been done," he wrote.[7] He appealed to his fellow Americans to heed Christ's summons "to complete the task of redemption." Urging the importance of speeding up the process of social salvation, he said, "If any one thinks it cannot be done, let the unbeliever stand aside and give place to those who have faith. This thing

[5] *Christianity and the Social Crisis* (New York, 1907), p. 416.
[6] *Ibid.,* pp. 420–422.
[7] *Christianizing the Social Order* (New York, 1912), p. 124.

is destiny. God wills it. What is morally necessary, must be possible. Else where is God?" [8]

Those confident words had hardly dried in print when the War broke upon the world with sudden, devastating fury. From 1914 until his death four years later Rauschenbusch experienced what he described as a "deep depression" of spirit.[9] During this dark night of his soul he agonizingly reappraised the human situation, and the result of his reflections may be found in his challenging Taylor Lectures, delivered before Yale Divinity School in April of 1917 and published in the following fall as *A Theology for the Social Gospel*. The treatise is loosely organized; at some points it juxtaposes ideas that seem incompatible, as in his treatment of Eschatology. This may reflect in part a struggle to incorporate new insights into older categories drawn from the new theology. At times the fresh wine of his thought comes near to bursting the older ideological wineskins. The over-all temper of the book is that of a deeply chastened soul groping for larger perspectives and searching for a more fundamental solution to the problems of a war-torn society. True enough, he still talked hopefully of the future of the "social gospel," saying, "After the War the social gospel will 'come back' with pent-up energy and clearer knowledge." [10] But note the words "clearer knowledge." When he said "social gospel," he intended nothing novel; he meant the one and only gospel of the kingdom of God in Jesus Christ. Thus he could say, "The social gospel is, in fact, the oldest gospel of all." [11] When therefore he referred to "clearer knowledge" he was expressing his conviction that the catastrophe of war and its concomitants would reveal afresh the depth of human sin and the world's need of salvation. Hence Rauschenbusch, in his Taylor Lec-

---

[8] *Ibid.*, p. 331.   [9] Sharpe, *op. cit.*, p. 449.
[10] *A Theology for the Social Gospel* (New York, 1917), p. 4.
[11] *Ibid.*, p. 24.

tures, was seeking to anticipate the post-war situation. His new theology, though retaining its earlier basic framework, now became suffused with a realism concerning human nature which cannot be duplicated in the writings of any other American theologian of this period.

Rauschenbusch's Taylor Lectures concentrated upon the theme of sin and salvation. According to him, "the doctrines of sin and salvation are the starting-point and goal of Christian theology." [12] He considered it "a symptom of moral immaturity or of an effort to keep the shutters down and the light out" not to be conscious of sin. He viewed sin not merely as man's inhumanity to man, but as supremely man's rebellion against the kingdom of God. Therefore he maintained that a radical consciousness of sin could only be recovered by restoring the kingdom of God as the object of man's highest devotion. "Our duty to the Kingdom of God," he wrote, "is on a higher level than all other duties. To aid it is the supreme joy. To have failed it by our weakness, to have hampered it by our ignorance, to have resisted its prophets, to have contradicted its truths, to have denied it in time of danger, to have betrayed it for thirty pieces of silver,—this is the most poignant consciousness of sin." [13]

When man rebels against God, explained Rauschenbusch, he does not carry on a "solitary duel," for sin "is not a private transaction between the sinner and God." God transcends human existence, but he is also the vitalizing presence in every life and "the mystic bond that unites us all." Consequently, "our sins against the least of our fellow-men in the last resort concern God." [14] In socializing the conception of sin, Rauschenbusch had no intention of obscuring the radical nature of sin as supremely a revolt against God; he only sought to show that every such individual revolt inevitably includes interpersonal

[12] *Ibid.*, p. 167.　　　[13] *Ibid.*, p. 37.　　　[14] *Ibid.*, pp. 47–49.

involvements and consequences. It was precisely these social involvements which the old theology, in its individualistic conception of sin, had largely ignored. It was to recover an important aspect of the gospel that Rauschenbusch argued that "we rebel against God and repudiate his will when we set our profit and ambition above the welfare of our fellows and above the Kingdom of God which binds them together." [15]

It is of particular relevance to our present theme to note that Rauschenbusch gave direct thought to the question of the biological and social transmission of evil. Recognizing that many modern theologians had rejected the idea of original sin, which was concerned with this problem, he expressly opposed the trend, saying, "I take pleasure . . . in defending it." [16] The old doctrine did not, to be sure, suit him in all respects. Believing as he did in organic evolution, he rejected the historicity of Adam. In his opinion theology had so stressed the first entrance of sin into the race that it had ignored later racial accretions to sin. Yet Rauschenbusch believed that the traditional doctrine contained an important kernel of truth. For example, it "was right in emphasizing the biological transmission of evil on the basis of race solidarity." [17] "Depravity of will and corruption of nature are transmitted wherever life itself is transmitted. . . . Evil does flow down the generations through the channels of biological coherence. Idiocy and feeble-mindedness, neurotic disturbances, weakness of inhibition, perverse desires, stubbornness and anti-social impulses in children must have had their adequate biological causes somewhere back on the line, even if we lack the records." [18]

But although Rauschenbusch would preserve this aspect of

[15] *Ibid.*, p. 48.　　　　[16] *Ibid.*, p. 57.　　　　[17] *Ibid.*, p. 59.
[18] *Ibid.*, p. 58. Much of this same emphasis may be found in other proponents of the new theology. On the other hand, Rauschenbusch's accent upon "depravity of will and corruption of nature" represents a more realistic interpretation of original sin than is characteristic of the new theology.

the doctrine of original sin, his main interest did not lie here; he was chiefly concerned to show that evil is transmitted through social channels. Hence, like Bushnell, he urged that the term "original sin" should be broadened so as to include social as well as biological modes of communicating evil. "It [original sin] runs down the generations not only by biological propagation but also by social assimilation." [19] "Just as syphilitic corruption is forced on the helpless foetus in its mother's womb," said he, "so these hereditary social evils are forced on the individual embedded in the womb of society and drawing his ideas, moral standards, and spiritual ideals from the general life of the social body." [20]

As that last statement shows, Rauschenbusch was especially impressed with the power of the group to influence the moral standards of the individual. "Beyond the feeble and short-lived individual towers the social group as a super-personal entity, dominating the individual, assimilating him to its moral standards, and enforcing them by the social sanctions of approval or disapproval." [21] When, therefore, the social group becomes deeply infected with evil, it is almost unlimited in its capacity to corrupt the individual self. Hence, Rauschenbusch culminated his social theory of original sin with a strong emphasis upon what he called the "Kingdom of Evil." [22] Like all other advocates of the new theology, he had long since abandoned the idea of mankind's complicity in Adam's guilt.[23] On the other

[19] *Ibid.*, p. 61.   [20] *Ibid.*, p. 60.   [21] *Ibid.*, p. 110.

[22] Rauschenbusch was doubtless influenced in this emphasis by Albrecht Ritschl's doctrine of the "kingdom of sin" (cf. *The Christian Doctrine of Justification and Reconciliation* [English translation: Edinburgh, 1902], pp. 338–339).

[23] It may be of interest to note that Rauschenbusch's theological instructor at Rochester Theological Seminary, Augustus H. Strong, advocated the Augustinian doctrine of original sin (cf. Strong, *Systematic Theology* [Rochester, 1886], pp. 330–331).

hand, he believed profoundly in collective guilt based on the social solidarity of mankind. "The sin of all is in each of us, and every one of us has scattered seeds of evil, the final multiplied harvest of which no man knows. . . . By solidarity of action and spirit we enter into solidarity of guilt." [24]

Rauschenbusch's increased realism with respect to the human predicament manifested itself in his eschatology. As in his earlier writings, he still believed in the gradualistic coming of the Kingdom, but he now asserted that its coming would "not be by peaceful development only, but by conflict with the Kingdom of Evil. We should estimate the power of sin too lightly if we forecast a smooth road." [25] Furthermore, he did not now speak of a speedy completion of the work of social redemption; instead, he laid greater emphasis upon the fact that the Kingdom "has no final consummation" on the plane of temporal existence. "The Kingdom of God is always coming, but we can never say, 'Lo here.'" [26] What is more, he acknowledged that even the hope for a higher life for the race would "not solve the problem of the individual." "This planet may end at any time and it is sure to die by collision or old age some time. What then will be the net product of all our labors? Plainly a man has a larger and completer hope if he looks forward to eternal life for himself as well as to a better destiny for the race." [27]

Clearly, then, the Rauschenbusch of 1917 was not the Rauschenbusch of 1907, so far as his doctrine of sin is concerned. The fires of international war had burned into his consciousness an unprecedented sense of individual and social perversity. Had he been spared another decade, he might very well have revised his new theology so as to provide a sounder foun-

[24] *A Theology for the Social Gospel*, pp. 91–92.
[25] *Ibid.*, p. 226. [26] *Ibid.*, p. 227. [27] *Ibid.*, p. 229.

dation for his more realistic perception of the human predicament.

II

But what Walter Rauschenbusch did not live to accomplish, or to see accomplished, has been achieved by his most authentic successor, Reinhold Niebuhr.[28] A native of the Middle West, he received his graduate education at Yale University. From 1915 to 1928 he was the pastor of Bethel Evangelical Church, located in the highly industrialized city of Detroit, Michigan. When he assumed the leadership of Bethel its membership consisted of only eighteen families, but under his vigorous preaching it soon grew into one of the more influential churches of the city. Meanwhile, the new industrial Detroit was as much of an eye-opener to him as had been West Side New York ("Hell's Kitchen") to Rauschenbusch. The experience derived from observing the capital-labor struggle in the automotive industry of Detroit speedily dispelled whatever romantic notions of human nature he may have entertained when he began his ministry.

But his sensitive and candid diary of those Detroit years, *Leaves from the Notebook of a Tamed Cynic*, gives the impression that his romanticism was never much more than a superficial covering of a deep deposit of realism. For instance, he did not capitulate to the wave of pacifism until 1923, long after the conversion of most other prominent liberals; and, fur-

---

[28] In the Preface to his Rauschenbusch Lectures of 1934 (published as *An Interpretation of Christian Ethics* [New York, 1935]) Niebuhr wrote: "I venture to hope . . . that they are an extension and application to our own day of both the social realism and the loyalty to the Christian faith which characterized the thought and life of one who was not only the real founder of social Christianity in this country but also its most brilliant and generally satisfying exponent to the present day."

thermore, he quickly returned to his earlier anti-pacifist perspective. Already he fully perceived the imperialistic impulses of human nature. As early as 1925 he pointed out that the "modern pulpit" was "not really preaching repentance." "Its estimate of human nature," he urged, "is too romantic to give people any appreciation of the brutalities of life." [29] This theme is repeated in various forms and connections in his first book, *Does Civilization Need Religion?* (1927). For example, he wrote: "Modern liberalism is steeped in a religious optimism which is true to the facts of neither the world of nature nor the world of history." [30] What is of especial interest in this book is that Niebuhr had already advanced one of the most characteristic doctrines of his later years, namely, that the group is more immoral and harder to bring under Christian discipline than is the individual member of the group. "All human groups," said he, "tend to be more predatory than the individuals which compose them." [31]

Thus it seems quite clear that by the year 1928, when Niebuhr joined the faculty of Union Theological Seminary, he was already well along on the road to a searchingly realistic conception of human nature. His famous polemic, *Moral Man and Immoral Society* (1932), should therefore be regarded, not as the beginning of his realistic thought, but as a fuller expression of nascent tendencies. Its central thesis, which is not new, is that the egoism of the individual is exceeded by the imperialism of the group. Citing a great wealth of pertinent data, he argued that "group relations can never be as ethical as those which characterize individual relations." [32] Hence, "every effort

[29] *Leaves from the Notebook of a Tamed Cynic* (Chicago, 1929), pp. 90–91.
[30] *Does Civilization Need Religion?* (New York, 1927), pp. 9–10. Cf. pp. 165, 192, 205–208.
[31] *Ibid.*, p. 129. See also pp. 131–134, 156–157, 161.
[32] *Moral Man and Immoral Society* (New York, 1932), p. 83.

to transfer a pure morality of disinterestedness to group relations has resulted in failure." [33]

A careful study of *Moral Man and Immoral Society* gives the
impression that Niebuhr, like Rauschenbusch, was forced into
a realistic view of sin and evil as a result of his reflections upon
intergroup relations and attitudes, especially those manifested
between nations. Perceiving how will-to-power, pride, and
other forms of ego-centrism characterized every type of existing group, large or small, he was impelled to conclude that
modern liberal culture's optimistic estimate of human nature
was fatuous.

In the earlier stages of his realistic thought, Niebuhr interpreted the human predicament predominantly from an ethical
perspective; but he soon moved beyond it to a theological perspective. As *Moral Man and Immoral Society* is characteristic
of the first, so his brilliant Gifford Lectures, *The Nature and
Destiny of Man*, are a forceful demonstration of the latter. He
came to see that while sin always involves social injustice, the
final gravity of sin lies in the fact that it is a revolt against the
sovereignty of God.

As he grappled with the problem of human sin, Niebuhr also
came to the conviction that individual acts of sin are rooted in
a fundamental bias to sin which can be fully explained only in
terms of the doctrine of original sin. Thus, in his Gifford Lectures he declared, "The utopian illusions and sentimental aber-
rations of modern liberal culture are really all derived from
the basic error of negating the fact of original sin." [34] Whereas
the new theology generally viewed the idea of original sin as
outmoded, Niebuhr has revived it as indispensable to an adequate understanding of the human situation. Therefore, Nie-

[33] *Ibid.*, p. 268. Cf. p. 262.
[34] *The Nature and Destiny of Man* (2 volumes: New York, 1941–1943),
I, 273, n. 4.

buhr's idea of the fall and its corollary, original sin, must be given careful study. To understand his doctrine of original sin is to get a central clue to the character of his Christian thought. For example, his basic idea of "grace as power and grace as pardon" is predicated upon the truth of original sin. "The Christian doctrine of grace," says he, "stands in juxtaposition to the Christian doctrine of original sin and has meaning only if the latter is an accurate description of the actual facts of human experience." [35] Probably his doctrine of sin has done more to shake American theology loose from its liberal premises than any other aspect of his thought.

It is manifest that Niebuhr, in his later theological thought, takes the doctrine of the fall of man with profound seriousness. He does so, however, only on the basis of interpreting the fall as myth rather than as literal fact. Thus it is necessary at the outset to understand the sense in which Niebuhr employs the term "myth." According to him, there are mythical elements "irrevocably enshrined" in the canons of all religions. Furthermore, every great mythical heritage contains "a permanent as well as a primitive myth." Permanent myth "deals with aspects of reality which are suprascientific rather than pre-scientific." "That part of mythology which is derived from pre-scientific thought, which does not understand the causal relations in the natural and historical world, must naturally be sacrificed in a scientific age." But "modernistic religion," says Niebuhr, made the serious mistake of disavowing permanent as well as primitive myth, and therefore sacrificed an essential truth of the Christian faith.[36]

Niebuhr, therefore, seeks to recover the truth of the perma-

---

[35] *Ibid.*, II, 108.
[36] "The Truth in Myths," *The Nature of Religious Experience*, edited by J. S. Bixler, R. L. Calhoun, and H. R. Niebuhr (New York, 1937), pp. 118–119.

nent myth of the fall. He joins the new theology in discarding the literalistic notions connected with the garden, the apple, and the serpent as the fruit of a primitive or pre-scientific culture. Likewise he (as well as the new theology) treats as a part of the primitive myth the idea that the fall is historical. "The fall is not historical. It does not take place in any concrete human act. It is the presupposition of such acts." [37] Having freed the doctrine of the fall from these literalistic connotations, Niebuhr finds that the myth of the fall profoundly illuminates the psychological situation in which man encounters temptation and becomes the victim of sin. What is that situation? In a word, it is the situation which arises from the fact that man, who "stands at the juncture of nature and spirit," is the subject of both freedom and necessity. On the one hand, he is involved in the order of nature and is therefore bound. On the other hand, as spirit he transcends nature and himself and is therefore free. Being both bound and free, both limited and unlimited, he inevitably experiences anxiety.[38] In his anxiety man is tempted either to deny the contingent character of his existence (in pride and self-love) or to escape his freedom (in sensuality). Conceivably he might so rely upon God's love and care as to be purged of the tendency toward sinful self-assertion. But, as human experience proves, this ideal possibility does not become an actuality. "When anxiety has conceived," says Niebuhr, "it brings forth both pride and sensuality. Man falls into pride, when he seeks to raise his contingent existence to unconditioned significance; he falls into sensuality, when he seeks to escape from his unlimited possibilities of freedom . . . by losing himself in some natural vitality." [39]

[37] *Beyond Tragedy* (New York, 1937), p. 11. In his Gifford Lectures Niebuhr refers to the fall as "a symbol of an aspect of every historical moment in the life of man" (*The Nature and Destiny of Man*, I, 269).
[38] *The Nature and Destiny of Man*, I, 182.
[39] *Ibid.*, p. 186.

According to Niebuhr, the sin of pride is more basic than that of sensuality. He distinguishes three closely related types of pride: pride of power, pride of knowledge, and pride of virtue. When the sin of moral pride has conceived, it brings forth the worst form of pride—spiritual pride. In his acute analysis of these forms of pride he rises to the height of Augustine and Jonathan Edwards.[40] He completes his realistic study with the familiar claim that the prideful pretensions and ambitions of social groups exceed those of the individual ego. "The group is more arrogant, hypocritical, self-centered and more ruthless in the pursuit of its ends than the individual. An inevitable moral tension between individual and group morality is therefore created." [41]

In his effort to account for the inevitability of sin in the human self, Niebuhr has been driven to revive the idea of original sin. But again he finds it necessary to strip away from the traditional doctrine what he calls its "literalistic errors." These errors, he thinks, were all connected with the effort of orthodoxy to treat original sin as though it had a history, or as a taint or corruption which was transmissible by natural descent. Original sin, he declares, "is true in every moment of existence, but it has no history." [42] The idea of an inherited corruption is as intolerable to him as it was to Nathaniel Taylor. "If original sin is an inherited corruption, its inheritance destroys the freedom and therefore the responsibility which is basic to the conception of sin." [43]

After discarding these "literalistic illusions" of the doctrine of original sin, Niebuhr proceeds to elucidate what he calls "the paradox of inevitability and responsibility," a paradox which he thinks conveys the essential truth to be found in the Pauline-Augustinian tradition. In the first place, he shows how

[40] *Ibid.*, pp. 186–203.   [41] *Ibid.*, pp. 208–209.
[42] *An Interpretation of Christian Ethics*, p. 90.   [43] *Loc. cit.*

temptation is related to inevitability. The temptation to sin, as already pointed out, is inevitably involved in the anxiety which attends man's dialectical situation of finiteness and freedom. "Since he [man] is involved in the contingencies and necessities of the natural process on the one hand and since, on the other, he stands outside of them and foresees their caprices and perils, he is anxious. In his anxiety he seeks to transmute his finiteness into infinity, his weakness into strength, his dependence into independence." [44] But it is especially important to note that, according to Niebuhr, the temptation of anxiety is not strong enough of itself to make sin inevitable. "Sin can never be traced merely to the temptation arising from a particular situation or condition in which man as man finds himself or in which particular men find themselves." [45] Thus the temptation produced by man's situation of finiteness and freedom must be supplemented or reinforced by the presence of some other factor. But what can be the other factor? Niebuhr answers that it is an extra-human principle or force of evil which is introduced into the human situation. The devil,[46] a fallen angel, "insinuates temptation into human life." In other words, Niebuhr concurs in Kierkegaard's notion "that sin presupposes itself." [47] "The sin of each individual is preceded by Adam's sin: but even this first sin of history is not the first sin. One may, in other words, go farther back than human history and still not escape the paradoxical conclusion that the situation of finiteness and freedom would not lead to sin if sin were not already introduced into the situation. This is, in the words of Kierkegaard,

[44] *The Nature and Destiny of Man*, I, 251.
[45] *Ibid.*, p. 254.
[46] "To believe that there is a devil," says Niebuhr, "is to believe that there is a principle or force of evil antecedent to any human action" (*The Nature and Destiny of Man*, I, 180).
[47] Cf. Sören Kierkegaard, *The Concept of Dread* (Tr. Walter Lowrie: Princeton University Press, 1946), p. 100.

the 'qualitative leap' of sin and reveals the paradoxical relation of inevitability and responsibility." [48]

So far we have dealt only with the element of the inevitability of sin in the paradox. But of no less importance to Niebuhr is the element of the responsibility for sin. As already observed, he objects to the traditional notion of "an inherited second nature" because he thinks it is destructive of the idea of man's accountability for sin. But even after he abandons all false notions of a literalistic sort, he admits that the doctrine of original sin still "remains absurd from the standpoint of a pure rationalism, for it expresses a relation between fate and freedom which cannot be fully rationalized." [49] For this reason he treats the relation between inevitability and responsibility as paradoxical. He argues that man is responsible for his sin, despite its inevitability. The feeling of remorse or repentance which accompanies sinful action is, he thinks, an attestation of responsibility. A merely "exterior view" may suggest that a given sin is the necessary result of previous temptations. All purely social interpretations of human actions tend to be deterministic. But an "internal view" serves as a corrective of this deterministic interpretation. Niebuhr writes:

The self, which is privy to the rationalizations and processes of self-deception which accompanied and must accompany the sinful act, cannot accept and does not accept the simple determinism of the exterior view. Its contemplation of its acts involves both the discovery and the reassertion of its freedom. It discovers that some degree of conscious dishonesty accompanied the act, which means that the self was not deterministically and blindly involved in it.[50]

Now all this is impressive, and doubtless is true, but it does not deal with the particular question as to why man should be

[48] Niebuhr, *The Nature and Destiny of Man*, I, 254. Cf. Kierkegaard, *op. cit.*, pp. 43, 100.
[49] *The Nature and Destiny of Man*, I, 262.   [50] *Ibid.*, p. 255.

held responsible for a sin which, in the first instance, is rendered inevitable by the insinuation of evil into the human situation by an extra-human satanic agent. Hence, the Kierkegaardian speculation that "sin presupposes itself" seems more confusing than enlightening.

A final question with which Niebuhr deals illuminatingly concerns the relation of man's essential nature to his sinful state. This relationship, he urges, has been confused by the same literalism that interpreted the fall as an historical event. Perfection was erroneously identified with a paradisical period before the fall. "The relation of man's essential nature to his sinful state," Niebuhr writes, "cannot be solved within terms of the chronological version of the perfection before the Fall. It is, as it were, a vertical rather than horizontal relation." [51] That is to say, man's essential nature is dialectically involved in every moment and act of his life.

A fundamental presupposition with Niebuhr is that nothing can change man's essential nature and structure. But since man is a structure of finite freedom, it is possible for him to employ his freedom in defiance of the requirements of his essential nature. Because of this possibility Niebuhr finds it necessary to distinguish between man's essential nature, and the virtue of conformity to that nature. His reasoning at this point is intricate and must be followed closely. Man's essential nature, he explains, contains two elements; and correspondingly, man's original perfection contains two elements. To essential nature belong, first, all the natural endowments which characterize man "as a creature imbedded in the natural order"; and, second, the freedom of man's spirit, his transcendence over nature and himself.[52] Corresponding to the first element of essential nature is the perfection which "is usually designated as the natural law." It is the law which defines man's normal func-

[51] *Ibid.*, p. 269.　　　　　　[52] *Ibid.*, p. 270.

tions, personal and social, "within the limitations of the natural order." Corresponding to the second element of essential nature are the three virtues which are analogous to the "theological virtues" of Catholic thought: faith, hope, and love.[53] These virtues are not of the sort which, as in Catholic thought, merely complete otherwise incomplete natural virtues. Rather, they "are basic requirements of freedom." Apart from faith in the providence of God, the anxiety of freedom prompts man to inordinate self-reliance and self-assertion. Hope concerns the future, and unless one can hope in God's continuing providence, the unknown future elicits intolerable anxiety. Love is necessary, because otherwise the community into which men are drawn by their social nature is precarious.[54]

From this analysis Niebuhr reaches the conclusion "that sin neither destroys the structure by virtue of which man is man nor yet eliminates the sense of obligation toward the essential nature of man, which is the remnant of his perfection." [55] His view, therefore, qualifies both Protestant and Catholic thought. As against Protestant thought, he maintains that the image of God is preserved despite man's sinful state. As against Catholic thought, he urges that the distinction between a completely lost original justice and an uncorrupted natural justice is unwarranted. Both have been corrupted by sin, yet they are both still with man as requirements.[56]

When the chronological error is corrected and original perfection is no longer identified with a period "before the fall," two questions arise. The first concerns the locus of the original righteousness as requirement upon man. The second relates to the content of original righteousness. In answer to the first, Niebuhr holds that the locus of original righteousness is to be found in that moment of consciousness in which the self tran-

[53] *Ibid.*, pp. 270–271.   [54] *Ibid.*, p. 271.   [55] *Ibid.*, p. 272.
[56] *Ibid.*, p. 276.

scends itself. "The self in the moment of transcending itself exercises the self's capacity for infinite regression and makes the previous concretion of will its object. It is in this moment of self-transcendence that the consciousness and memory of original perfection arise. For in this moment the self knows itself as merely a finite creature among many others and realizes that the undue claims which the anxious self in action makes, result in injustices to its fellows." [57] The fact that the self-as-transcendent is conscious of an original perfection does not mean that the self is in possession of that perfection. In reality, when the self acts "it always uses the previous transcendent perspective partly as a 'rationalization' and 'false front' for its interested action." [58] Hence, the action is always sinful to some degree. "Perfection before the Fall is, in other words, perfection before the act." The term "act" must not be limited to overt action. "Every thought, mood or action which proceeds from the self as anxious, finite, and insecure has some taint of sin upon it." [59]

The second question relates to the content of original righteousness. As already noted, Niebuhr employs the term "natural law" to cover the requirements of man as creature. Likewise it was observed that he regards the virtues of faith, hope, and love as the requirements of man's freedom and as representing the original righteousness. In his analysis of the content of the law of original righteousness, he treats this distinction between the two kinds of "law" as only tentative and provisional. Neither the law of nature nor the law of original perfection is exempt from the corruptions of sin. On the other hand, the image of God remains in man despite sinful corruptions. The content of the *justitia originalis* as law may be found in the three virtues of faith, hope, and love. These are the law of man's freedom. Niebuhr writes: "this character of the theo-

[57] *Ibid.*, p. 277.　　　[58] *Ibid.*, pp. 277–278.　　　[59] *Ibid.*, p. 278.

logical virtues as 'law' to sinful man is perfectly revealed in the 'thou shalt' of the law of love." [60]

This law of love states the ultimate condition of complete harmony between the soul and God, and between neighbor and neighbor. If it were fulfilled, the commandment would be meaningless. On the other hand, if man could not sense the ultimate perfection while in a state of sin, the commandment would be irrelevant. From this reasoning Niebuhr comes to an important conclusion with respect to human nature. Pessimistic theories of human nature, he says, are wrong in asserting the total depravity of man. "If man is totally corrupt he is not sinful at all." [61] But he is no less convinced that all forms of utopianism are wrong in assuming that the law of love is a simple possibility in historical existence. "Love is the law of freedom; but man is not completely free; and such freedom as he has is corrupted by sin . . . . There is, therefore, no historic structure of justice which can either fulfill the law of love or rest content in its inability to do so." [62] At best, then, "the law of love stands on the edge of history and not in history." [63]

III

Next to Reinhold Niebuhr, the theologian in America who has done most to revive the idea of the fall and original sin is Paul Tillich. Although not, technically speaking, an "American" theologian, he has contributed so richly to recent developments in our theological thought that he must be regarded as an integral part of the American scene. When, in 1933, Hitler became Chancellor of Germany, Tillich was Professor of Philosophy at

[60] *Ibid.*, p. 286.   [61] *Interpretation of Christian Ethics*, p. 91.
[62] *The Nature and Destiny of Man*, I, 296. Cf. *Faith and History*, pp. 214, 235.
[63] *The Nature and Destiny of Man*, I, 298.

the University of Frankfurt. He was immediately dismissed from this position. Coming to America in the fall of 1933, at the age of forty-seven, he was appointed lecturer in Philosophical Theology at Union Theological Seminary (New York). Becoming full professor in 1940, he remained with Union until his retirement in 1955. He was recently appointed University Professor in Harvard University.

A prolific writer, Tillich has published many of his most influential books and essays since coming to America. He testifies that the American situation, including American theology and philosophy, has modified not only his forms of expression but to some extent the content of his thinking.[64] "The New World grasped me," he recently remarked, "with its irresistible power of assimilation and creative courage." [65] Not until Tillich published the first volume of his monumental *Systematic Theology* (1951) did many American theologians realize the intricate and massive character of his system of religious thought. As Reinhold Niebuhr has recently remarked, this work "will undoubtedly become a landmark in the history of modern theology." [66]

Unfortunately for the present study, the second volume of his *Systematic Theology*, which will treat his doctrine of the fall and original sin, has not yet been published. Nevertheless, the basic *Propositions* on which this volume will be based have been privately issued by Tillich. Furthermore, one of his former graduate students and assistants, Mr. Peter H. John, has recorded a series of Tillich's class lectures, given at Union Theological Seminary, which covered most of the material to

[64] Tillich, *The Protestant Era* (Chicago, 1948), p. x.
[65] Tillich, "Autobiographical Reflections," *The Theology of Paul Tillich*, edited by Charles W. Kegley and Robert W. Bretall (New York, 1952), p. 20.
[66] "Biblical Thought and Ontological Speculation in Tillich's Theology," *The Theology of Paul Tillich*, p. 217.

be discussed in the second volume.[67] Professor Tillich has graciously permitted our use of these privately issued materials. When these sources are supplemented by certain published essays and articles, the main ideas of his doctrine of the human predicament may be discovered.

Before examining Tillich's doctrine of the fall, it is necessary to indicate briefly his conception of the function and method of theology. According to him, theology is obligated to perform a twofold task: (1) to state the truth of the Christian message, and (2) to interpret that truth for every new generation. Theology therefore moves back and forth between the pole of the Christian message and the pole of the situation in which that message must be received. The term "situation" refers not primarily to the psychological or sociological state of man but to "the totality of man's creative self-interpretation in a special period." More specifically, the term refers to the cultural forms through which the people of a particular period interpret the meaning of existence.

As Tillich observes, theology has found it difficult to preserve a proper balance between message and situation; it has tended either to sacrifice elements of the Christian message or to eschew the cultural forms through which the new generation interpreted its existence, and neither attitude has been healthy.[68] Tillich maintains that if liberalism has been guilty of the first tendency, orthodoxy has been guilty of the second. In the latter category he places Barth's "kerygmatic" theology.

---

[67] *Advanced Problems in Systematic Theology* (Lectures given at Union Theological Seminary in the Spring Semester, 1952, and privately recorded by Peter H. John). It should be said, in fairness to Dr. Tillich, that quotations taken from his class lectures are subject to clerical error in recording. The recorder, Mr. John, reported that his transcriptions were "not corrected by the lecturer."

[68] *Systematic Theology,* I (Chicago, University of Chicago Press, copyright 1951 by the University of Chicago), 3–4.

He thinks that on Barth's premises the message "must be thrown at those in the situation—thrown like a stone." In contrast to Barth, Tillich argues persuasively that an adequate theology must relate itself constructively to the situation. Hence, he seeks to redress the imbalance of kerygmatic theology with "apologetic" theology, without sacrificing the essential content of the *kerygma*.[69]

In his unique scheme of apologetic theology Tillich undertakes so to relate message and situation to each other as to avoid the obliteration of either. To this end he has devised what he calls the "method of correlation." This method "tries to correlate the questions implied in the situation with the answers implied in the message. It does not derive the answers from the questions as a self-defying apologetic theology does. Nor does it elaborate answers without relating them to the questions as a self-defying kerygmatic theology does." [70] Thus Tillich's apologetic theology undertakes to unite message and situation on terms which will safeguard the essential truth contained in both kerygmatic theology and liberal theology and which will eliminate the mistakes of both.

Tillich's correlational method directly determines the structural form of his theological system. His system consists of five major parts, classified as follows: (1) Reason and Revelation, (2) Being and God, (3) Existence and the Christ, (4) Life and the Spirit, (5) History and the Kingdom of God. In order to apply the method of correlation, each of these five parts must be treated in two parallel subdivisions, the first of which develops the question implied in the situation and the second provides the Christian answer to it. By this schematic arrangement the existential questions and the theological answers can be developed in mutual interdependence. This structural pattern "is

[69] *Ibid.*, pp. 5–6.   [70] *Ibid.*, p. 8. Cf. pp. 60–62.

the backbone" of Tillich's system, and indeed is indispensable to the use of his correlational method.

Tillich's correlational method requires him to be especially concerned with the doctrine of man. Since his is a scheme of "answering theology," he must continually have questions to answer or the theologizing process would obviously stop. But the questions can be found only by scrutinizing the human situation. This means that Tillich is required to explore the human situation not merely in part three of his system (Existence and the Christ), but to a greater or less degree in every one of the five parts. Consequently his doctrine of man is pivotal in his theological system.

This means that his interpretation of the human situation will be decisive in determining the character of his theology. It is therefore profoundly significant that Tillich views man as radically estranged from his essential being. This basic estrangement or cleavage is, he thinks, actually coincident with history itself. It "underlies all human history and makes history what it is." [71]

In his effort to disclose the fundamental nature of man's self-estrangement, Tillich revives the idea of the fall. His interpretation of the fall, however, differs significantly from that of orthodoxy. Summarily, he characterizes the fall as "the transition from essence to existence." That condensed, shorthand phrase requires most careful analysis, for it is invested with extremely important meanings. As employed in this particular context, the terms "essence" and "existence" express the basic contrast in man and nature between their "created" (original) character and their disrupted or "fallen" state. The word "contrast" if taken in its absolute import, would mean that essence and existence are totally severed in human life. But in fact this

[71] *The Protestant Era,* p. 166.

is not the case, for actual concrete life, according to Tillich, involves the intermingling of essential and existential elements. It is just this intermingling of both elements which produces ambiguity in life, and which lends life both creativity and destructiveness, totality and fragmentariness, greatness and tragedy, holiness and demonization.[72] The third basic term in Tillich's doctrine of the fall is "transition." Like the term "fall," the term "transition" is used mythologically to describe what in reality is trans-temporal rather than temporal. The transition must be expressed as a temporal event because there is no other way in which to describe existence in distinction from essence.[73]

According to Tillich, the fall is a possibility for man only because he is, in his essential nature, the structure of "finite freedom." That is to say, man partakes of both finiteness and freedom. In common with all creatures, he is finite; but, in contrast to other creatures, he also has the quality of freedom. It is this combination of finiteness and freedom that makes it possible for man to fall into self-contradiction. Self-contradiction would not be a possibility for a tree, for example, because a tree belongs to the structure of finite necessity. Nor, on the other hand, would self-contradiction be a possibility for God, since he is beyond essence and existence and may be symbolically characterized as a structure of infinite freedom. The fall, then, becomes a possibility for man only because he is a structure of finite freedom.[74]

Perhaps further light may be shed on that which renders the fall a possibility if we attend to Tillich's idea of the ontological structure in which man, as finite freedom, is rooted. The self-world structure, he observes, is the basic ontological

---

[72] Tillich, *Advanced Theological Problems in Systematic Theology*, pp. 17, 186–187, 207.
[73] *Ibid.*, p. 24.   [74] *Ibid.*, p. 25.

structure of being. "The self having a world to which it belongs —this highly dialectical structure—logically and experientially precedes all other structures." [75] Self and world are interdependent and constitute a polarity. "Both sides of the polarity are lost if either side is lost. The self without a world is empty; the world without a self is dead." [76] This basic ontological structure of being embraces what Tillich calls "ontological elements" which themselves constitute polarities. He names three such polarities: individuality and universality, dynamics and form, freedom and destiny. "In these three polarities," he explains, "the first element expresses the self-relatedness of being, its power of being something for itself, while the second element expresses the belongingness of being, its character of being a part of a universe of being." [77] As in the case of the basic polarity (self-world), these constituent polarities involve interdependent polar elements. That is to say, one element is incomplete without the other. For example, man has freedom only in polar interdependence with destiny (or necessity), or he has individuality only in polar interdependence with participation or community. But although man's essential nature, as the structure of finite freedom, unites these polar elements, they can be disrupted and become contradictory. As a matter of fact, according to Tillich, the elements of a polar unit are always involved in more or less tension under the impact of finitude, and tend to move in opposite directions. This ontological tension results in anxiety of losing one or the other polar element. "It is anxiety about disintegrating and falling into nonbeing through existential disruption." [78]

If these be the conditions under which the fall is a possibility, it is in order to inquire whether the fall may be regarded as a probability. The fall, in Tillich's thought, is not merely

---

[75] *Systematic Theology,* I, 164.   [76] *Ibid.,* p. 171.
[77] *Ibid.,* p. 165.   [78] *Ibid.,* p. 199.

probable but unavoidable, although not a necessity. Man's original state he describes as that of "dreaming innocence," or of unactualized and uncontested freedom. Original goodness is therefore potentiality, not actuality. "The goodness of man's created nature is that he is given the possibility and necessity of actualizing himself and of becoming independent by his actualization, in spite of the estrangement unavoidably connected with it." [79] Yet man's essential structure as finite freedom gives to his original state of dreaming innocence an ambiguity which produces within him basic anxiety. A double anxiety manifests itself. "Man is anxious to use his freedom, to actualize his potentialities. He is afraid of losing their realization. On the other hand, he is inhibited against using his freedom by the dread of losing himself in this use." [80] Being thus involved in the double anxiety of acting and of not acting, man "is in the state of aroused freedom or temptation." This aroused freedom "drives innocence beyond itself." That is to say, when man's potentialities come before him as possibilities, he trespasses upon his creaturely limits and sacrifices his innocence. When the serpent disclosed to Eve her potentialities by assuring her that, if she ate of the forbidden fruit, she would "be like God, knowing good and evil," her aroused freedom drove her to disregard her contingency and to sacrifice her innocence. Thus "in trespassing on his mere potentiality, he [man] separates himself from his original and immediate unity with the infinite. . . . He tries to reach infinity, not in subjection to the infinite, but by drawing the infinity into his own finite being. He ceases to accept his finitude, contingency, transitoriness, and with them his anxiety, solitude, and mortality. Thus, the dreaming inno-

---

[79] *Ibid.*, p. 259.
[80] Tillich, "Psychotherapy and a Christian Interpretation of Human Nature," *The Review of Religion*, XIII (March, 1949), 265. Cf. *Advanced Problems in Systematic Theology*, pp. 29–30.

cence is lost, man contradicts his own created goodness, he falls under compulsions, self-destructive trends, and despair." [81]

The foregoing psychological description of the transition from essence to existence constitutes what Tillich calls the myth of the "immanent fall." It emphasizes (though not exclusively) the aspect of individuality and freedom in the transition. But the transition, he urges, involves also the aspect of universality and necessity, and in order to describe that aspect he resorts to the myth of the "transcendent fall." [82] Tillich interprets the myth of the transcendent fall in close connection with his doctrine of creation. According to him, there is a point in the actualization of creation where the fall and creation "coincide." At the point where creation ends and the fall begins there is "a break between essence and existence," and this break marks the point where the creation and the fall are simultaneous. This "is the most difficult and the most dialectical point in the doctrine of creation." [83] Tillich describes the myth of the transcendent fall succinctly, saying:

Fully developed creatureliness is fallen creatureliness. The creature has actualized its freedom in so far as it is outside the creative ground of the divine life . . . . To be outside the divine life means to stand in actualized freedom, in an existence which is no longer united with essence. Seen from one side, this is the end of creation. Seen from the other side, it is the beginning of the fall. Freedom and destiny are correlates. The point at which creation and fall coincide is as much a matter of destiny as it is a matter of freedom. The fact that it is a universal situation proves that it is not a matter of individual contingency, either in "Adam" or in anyone else. The fact that it separates existence from its unity with essence indicates that it is not a matter of structural necessity.[84]

[81] Tillich, "Psychotherapy and a Christian Interpretation of Human Nature," *op. cit.,* pp. 265–266.
[82] *Propositions* (Systematic Theology), Part III, pp. 3–4.
[83] *Systematic Theology,* I, 255.   [84] *Ibid.,* pp. 255–256.

Tillich's myth of the transcendent fall has aroused more misgiving than any other aspect of his doctrine of man. Reinhold Niebuhr, for example, refers to it as "ontological speculation," and he declares flatly that there "is no myth of the 'transcendent fall' in the Bible but only the myth of a historical fall." [85] He further asserts that the idea of a transcendent fall has always emerged in Christian thought whenever ontological speculation has led to the conclusion "that evil is involved in finiteness as such." The implication is that Tillich's myth of the transcendent fall tends to identify finitude and evil. The late David E. Roberts apparently shared Niebuhr's misgivings.[86] Another analyst, R. H. Daubney, expressly charges Tillich with equating finitude and evil.[87]

Tillich, in his reply to these men, expresses surprise that they should levy upon him this criticism. He rejoins, "I do not identify finitude and evil, explicitly or implicitly." [88] He reveals sensitivity over what Niebuhr disparages as "ontological speculation." "The universality and consequently the unavoidability of the fall is not derived from 'ontological speculation,' but from a realistic observation of man, his heart, and his history." [89] Even the Bible, he continues, is not without symbols of a transcendent fall. The Bible observes that cosmic powers (the serpent, the beast of chaos, Satan) and even irrational forces of nature "are partly responsible for the human predicament." [90] Does not this imply that, given the conditions of existence, evil is an unavoidable consequence of finitude? "Finite life is

[85] "Biblical Thought and Ontological Speculation in Tillich's Theology," *op. cit.*, p. 220.
[86] "Tillich's Doctrine of Man," *The Theology of Paul Tillich*, p. 126.
[87] "Some Structural Concepts in Tillich's Thought and the Pattern of the Liturgy," *The Theology of Paul Tillich*, pp. 276–277.
[88] "Reply to Interpretation and Criticism," *The Theology of Paul Tillich*, p. 344.
[89] *Ibid.*, p. 343.
[90] *Propositions* (Systematic Theology), Part III, p. 6.

actualized finite freedom. And actualized finite freedom is always estranged finite freedom." [91] This statement could be regarded as merely a description of empirical fact, but it seems to imply that actualized finite freedom necessarily involves estrangement or a fallen state. Thus Tillich's critics have some ground for their concern. It is possible that the next volume of his *Systematic Theology* will remove the cause for these criticisms. In any case, a more dependable judgment must await its appearance.

The radical nature of Tillich's conception of man's self-estrangement under the conditions of finitude becomes evident in his interpretation of history. According to him, the fall coincides with the beginning of history, and the resulting self-contradiction between essence and existence persists throughout the entire period of history. The kingdom of God and the anti-divine or demonic forces will continue in conflict as long as history lasts. Although the kingdom of God will realize fragmentary and preliminary victories within history, the demonic force itself will never be eliminated from the social structures of history. "The struggle of the Kingdom of God in history does not result in its progressive victory since every manifestation of the Kingdom of God stimulates the anti-divine forces at the same time." [92] Then is there no final solution within history to man's self-estrangement? For Tillich, the answer is unequivocally no. "The only unconditional prospect," he affirms, "is the promise and expectation of the supra-historical fulfillment of history, of the Kingdom of God, in which that which has not been decided within history will be decided and that which has not been fulfilled within history will be fulfilled." [93] In other

[91] *Advanced Problems in Systematic Theology*, p. 186.
[92] *Propositions* (Systematic Theology), Part V, p. 15. Cf. Tillich, "The Kingdom of God and History," *The Kingdom of God and History* (Oxford Conference Book: Chicago, 1938), pp. 126–127.
[93] "The Kingdom of God and History," *op. cit.*, p. 140.

words, the final victory over man's historical self-estrangement awaits the *parousia* of Christ.

IV

As between Niebuhr and Tillich, there are two points of divergence that should be noted as we close the discussion of this chapter. The first concerns the scope of the fall. Niebuhr limits the fall to the world of spirits, human or superhuman. Tillich, on the other hand, regards the fall as universal in extent. The transition from essence to existence involves nature as well as personal beings. "Nature is subjected to the same Existential situation as man, as mythologically expressed in the divine curse over the land." [94] How can nature undergo transition if it is a structure of finite necessity? But for Tillich nature is apparently something more than purely finite necessity. "The presupposition of the doctrine of the 'fallen world' is the belief that in nature is imperfectly developed what in man is perfectly developed: Finite freedom." [95] The finite freedom which is characteristic of nature is the result of what Tillich calls "participation." Because of the universal unity of being, nature necessarily participates in the self-world structure, and in doing so, nature participates in both essence and existence.[96]

The second point of contrast between Niebuhr and Tillich is a difference in emphasis rather than an absolute difference. As already implied in our previous discussion, Tillich gives much more attention to the ontological aspect of the fall and original sin than does Niebuhr. In following Tillich's reasoning with regard to a "fallen world," one gets the impression that man's destiny is inescapably bound up with the destiny of

[94] *Propositions* (Systematic Theology), Part III, p. 4.
[95] *Loc. cit.*
[96] *Advanced Problems in Systematic Theology*, pp. 27–28.

the whole cosmic order. The power of the individual to change the course of events seems exceedingly limited. Niebuhr, on the other hand, prefers to analyze the fall in empirical terms. He is especially concerned to maintain human freedom, even while conceding the inevitability of sin. We have already mentioned the fact that he is suspicious of Tillich's "ontological speculations." His suspicions arise from the belief that Tillich, in his theory of the paradoxical relation of fate and freedom, drifts too far in the direction of the fatefulness of sin. "In Tillich's thought the emphasis upon the ontological basis of this paradox [of fate and freedom] seems subtly to shift the meaning of the fate, contained in the idea of 'original sin,' from a historical to an ontological one. With this shift the emphasis falls upon the fatefulness of sin rather than upon our responsibility." [97]

In his argument against Tillich, Niebuhr urges that the Bible contains no myth of a transcendent fall, but only the myth of a historical fall. Yet, interestingly, Niebuhr as well as Tillich denies that the fall is historical. This in itself shows that he too indulges in ontological speculation. Furthermore, as already demonstrated, his own doctrine of original sin is based on a paradox of inevitability and responsibility in which he speculates venturesomely. When, for example, he takes the position that there was sin before Adam's first sin, he engages in a remarkable flight of ontological speculation. It may well be that Tillich's myth of the transcendent fall is causing Niebuhr to rescrutinize the ontological implications involved in his own paradox of inevitability and responsibility.

[97] "Biblical Thought and Ontological Speculation in Tillich's Thought," *op. cit.*, p. 219. Cf. Niebuhr, *The Self and the Dramas of History* (New York, 1955), p. 99.

INDEX

Date Due